CHALLENGING THE POLITICS OF EARLY INTERVENTION

Who's 'saving' children and why

Val Gillies, Rosalind Edwards and Nicola Horsley

First published in Great Britain in 2017 by

Policy Press
University of Bristol
1-9 Old Park Hill
Bristol
BS2 8BB
UK
t: +44 (0)117 954 5940
pp-info@bristol.ac.uk
www.policypress.co.uk

North America office:
Policy Press
c/o The University of Chicago Press
1427 East 60th Street
Chicago, IL 60637, USA
t: +1 773 702 7700
f: +1 773-702-9756
sales@press.uchicago.edu
www.press.uchicago.edu

British Library Cataloguing in Publication Data
A catalogue record for this book is available from the British Library

Library of Congress Cataloging-in-Publication Data
A catalog record for this book has been requested

ISBN 978-1-4473-2410-2 paperback
ISBN 978-1-4473-2409-6 hardcover
ISBN 978-1-4473-2413-3 ePub
ISBN 978-1-4473-2414-0 Mobi
ISBN 978-1-4473-2412-6 ePdf

Cover design by Policy Press
Front cover image: Getty images
Printed and bound in Great Britain by CMP Poole
Policy Press uses environmentally responsible print partners

Contents

Acknowledgements

This book draws on material from two research projects. The 'Brain Science and Early Intervention: Tracing the New Biologisation of Parenting and Childcare' project was funded by the Faraday Institute under its 'Uses and Abuses of Biology' programme. The project received ethical approval from the Faculty of Social and Human Sciences Ethics Committee, University of Southampton. We are grateful to all the policy makers and practitioners who participated in the research, and to the expert group of neuroscientists who gave us the benefit of their knowledge. The '"Troubled Families" and Inter-Agency Collaboration: Lessons from Historical Comparative Analysis' project was funded by the ESRC under its Secondary Data Analysis Initiative, grant number ES/L01453X/1. This project received ethical approval from the Goldsmiths College University of London and the University of Southampton.

ONE

The politics of early intervention and evidence

Introduction

In 2002 a cross-sectional picture of two brains placed side by side was published in an article by Bruce Perry, founder of the ChildTrauma Academy in Houston Texas, an independent agency promoting a 'Neurosequential Model' for working with 'at-risk' children (see Figure 1.1). The image purported to show MRI (magnetic resonance imaging) scans of the structure of the brains of two 3-year-old children. One was the brain of a child who had what was referred to as a 'normal' development, and the other was a rather smaller, shrivelled brain with worrying 'black holes' (Allen, 2011a: 16) indicating enlarged ventricles or cortical atrophy from a child labelled as subject to 'extreme neglect'.

Figure 1.1: Perry brain image

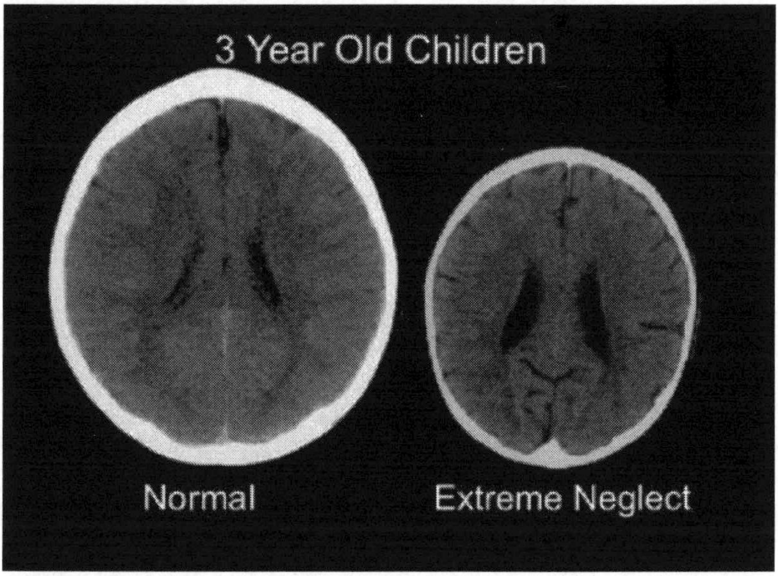

Source: Perry B.D. (2002) 'Childhood experience and the expression of genetic potential: What childhood neglect tells us about nature and nurture', *Brain and Mind*, 3: 79–100.

This brain scans picture has become iconic, a key motif in political and thinktank reports concerning children's upbringing and outcomes from across the spectrum. It provides a graphic visual image for assertions that poor parenting causes lasting damage to babies' and young children's brain development. In two influential policy reports we read that:

> A key finding is that babies are born with 25 per cent of their brains developed, and then there is a rapid period of development so that by the age of 3 their brains are 80 per cent developed. In that period, neglect, the wrong type of parenting and other adverse experiences can have a profound effect on how children are emotionally 'wired'. This will deeply influence their future responses to events and their ability to empathise with other people. (Allen, 2011a: xiii)
>
> From birth to age 18 months, connections in the brain are created at a rate of one million per second! The earliest experiences shape a baby's brain development and have a lifelong impact on that baby's mental and emotional health. (Leadsom et al, 2013: 5)

The Perry image feels like solid, objective evidence of the formative importance of attentive mothering for babies' brain development and the need to intervene early to ensure that children's brains are not damaged by substandard parenting. A Children's Centre supervisor told us during one of the research interviews that we conducted for the project that underpins this book, that the picture of the brains justifies robust interventions: 'But I think just brain science, that photograph shows to me so much, and it gives me so much passion in what I'm doing … and give more definite "this is the right thing to be doing"' (Children's Centre interview 2).

The 'evidence' captured in the MRI scans image thus provides a potent moral call for intervention to take place in the early window of opportunity in a child's life, before it is too late and their brains are hard-wired for failure through deficient parenting (variously, up to the age of 3 or the age of 18 months depending on the report). This is a message that has become an internationally accepted policy and practice truth. Child development reports by the World Health Organization (Irwin et al, 2007) and UNICEF (Bellamy, 2000; Lake and Chan, 2014), and early years policy and service provision in the UK and internationally (Macvarish et al, 2014; see also Bruer, 1999; Wilson, 2002; Wall, 2010; Ramaekers and Suissa, 2012) are now characterised by an emphasis on early intervention in the belief that pregnancy and the earliest years of life are most important for development. It has become the orthodoxy in a whole range of professional practice fields; a professional association review helpfully provides a list of many of the relevant services: family support, parenting support, health visiting, nurseries, early education, day and child care, the interface between early years and health and housing.[1]

The idea is to pre-empt instead of reacting to social, educational and behaviour 'problems' using evidence-based interventions. Rather than the spotlight alighting on the unequal material and social conditions in which children live and doing something about them, it is focused on parents and how they rear their children. These are ideas that blame poor mothers for making their own and their children's deprived bed and lying in it. In the process, it presents them as not quite the human beings that 'we' are, biologically and culturally. In an address to a conference on early intervention attended by practitioners, Graham Allen MP (Labour), then Chair of the Early Intervention Foundation, invoked the notion that disadvantaged mothers, and indeed generations of families, are somehow 'not like us':

> for me early intervention is about giving every baby, child and young person social and emotional capability, you've all got that, you take it for granted, you got it from your parents, you hand it on to your kids, you don't even think about it … we come across those people, you come across those people … a lot of people to whom standard parenting skills are unusual. (Westminster Social Policy Forum, 2013: 16)[2]

In this book we take a critical look at assumptions that 'the wrong type of parenting' has biological and cultural effects, stunting children's brain development and passing detrimental social values and behaviour down the generations. We draw out assertions about foundational, determinist brain development and attachment in the early years as the basis and rationale for interventions to 'save' children from poor parenting, and we subject them to critique. Our aim is to trouble the widespread consensus that has built up around the relationship between brain science and early intervention, and the endeavour of early years intervention itself, through an interrogation of the evidence and the politics of intervention. We explore the history of understandings of children, family and parenting, and the implications for society, and we look at contemporary understanding that poor parenting results in substandard future citizens who are not fit for the economy of today's world. We identify some of the key interests that are in play in early years intervention – who is invoking brain science to argue for such initiatives and to promote particular types of parenting interventions, and why. We consider the ways that decidedly unprogressive assumptions and quite essentialist ideas become embedded in early intervention policies and programmes informed by a version of child brain development that has become detached from actual neuroscientific knowledge and taken on a life of its own.

Policy and the linking of early intervention, brain science and social investment

How mothers and fathers bring up their children has long been an issue of social and political concern, thought to be both a symptom and a cause of the state of the nation – although an explicit family policy was not always evident (Rose, 1987). In the late 1990s, however, parenting practice was pushed to the centre of social policy developments as an overt focus. The New Labour government's *Supporting families* green paper (Ministerial Group on the Family, 1998) marks the emergence into policy of assertions about the determining role of parental behaviour in children's future and a closing down of more structural explanations for life chances (Gillies, 2011), and of a centralised and top-down agenda. There has been a steady intensification of this focus since that time (Edwards and Gillies, 2004), with what started out as parenting support being developed into early intervention (Macvarish et al, 2015). Initially all 'parents' – in actuality mothers – were said to need the help of experts to support them in carrying out the vital work of fostering and transmitting crucial values to their children, so as to protect and reproduce the common good (Ministerial Group on the Family, 1998: 7). Bringing up children came to be seen as the driver of meritocracy, and of a competitive and successful society. The family was regarded as the formative site through which well-parented children would grow up better able to navigate and capitalise on the post-industrial economic landscape (Gillies, 2014). Later, as we discuss, the focus narrowed down to particular sorts of mothers and mothering practices in particular sorts of families. For example, in arguing that a modern definition of poverty must take into account children whose parents are disengaged from their responsibilities, the government-commissioned Field report, *The foundation years: Preventing poor children becoming poor adults* (Field, 2010), identified the rupture of what was said to be a once-strong British parenting tradition as causal in creating poverty and disadvantage. It also made reference to the importance of parenting for young children's brain development.

The explicit linking of brain science claims and early years policy and practice came to the fore in the USA in the late 1990s (Bruer, 1999; Thornton, 2011a). In the UK, the first direct reference to babies' brain development came in the Department for Education and Skills' 2003 *Birth to three matters* review report (see Macvarish et al , 2015), but the major boost to the influence of such claims was provided by the 2008 joint 'thinktank' report, *Early intervention: Good parents, great kids, better citizens* (Allen and Duncan Smith, 2008). This report heralded several of the recurring features of subsequent policy documents arguing for early intervention: its proponents are from across the political spectrum; it asserts the formative importance of attentive parenting ('mothering responsiveness') for babies' brain development and the narrow window available for preventive intervention; it relies on an eclectic mix of sources, most of which do not relate to neuroscience; and it reproduces the Perry (2002) brain images.

The 2008 *Early intervention* joint report was followed by two independent reviews commissioned by the government from one of the authors of the 2008 report: *Early intervention: The next steps* and *early intervention: smart investment, massive savings* (Allen, 2011a, 2011b). The ubiquitous brain images adorned the cover of each report. The first Allen report set up the case for early intervention because of the damage done to a baby's brain architecture by sub-optimal parenting during the first three years of intensive development, while the second emphasised the potential extensive savings to the public purse on the costs of social problems such as teenage pregnancy, low attainment, substance abuse and violent crime through investment in targeted, early intervention parenting programmes. In addition to exhibiting the recurrent features instituted by the 2008 report, the Allen reports display the tendency within such policy-focused outputs towards a cumulative referencing of previous reports as evidence for the arguments being made. To back up their contentions, the reports cite the 2008 Allen and Duncan Smith publication. Such cross-referencing to assertions about the imperative to intervene early to ensure that babies' and children's brains are not damaged by poor parenting, and thus prevent poverty and disadvantage, are found in the Field report, and also in other government-commissioned reports that appeared in the same year as the Allen reports (2011 – the year of the English riots). These include the Munro review of the child protection system, with its stress on a 'now or never' early intervention imperative (Munro, 2011), which cited the neurodevelopment arguments in the Allen report (2011a) in evidence, and the Tickell review of the Early Years Foundation Stage curriculum promoting early intervention for young children in deprived families to promote school readiness, which makes reference to the importance of the 0–3 years period, brain development and parental attachment (Tickell, 2011). These publications were followed swiftly by the Department for Education and Family Justice Council commissioned report *Decisionmaking within a child's timeframe* (Brown and Ward, 2012), which puts forward 'developmental timeframes' that supposedly are informed by neuroscience with the aim of guiding court decision making in care proceedings; and the cross-party 'manifesto' *1001 critical days*, which stresses the importance of the period from conception to age 2 for children's life chances, and emphasises the dangers of a lack of attachment between baby and caregiver (Leadsom et al, 2013). We look at some of these reports in further detail in Chapter Three.

In their quest to make families and children, and through them Britain, fit for the global, competitive environment, successive governments have pursued a social investment approach. The Foresight Report, *Mental capital and wellbeing: Making the most of ourselves in the 21st century*, published in the same year as the Allen and Duncan Smith *Early intervention* (2008), captures the tone, with its assertions that the quality of nurturing 'programmes' the brain. Social investment policies treat public services as investment opportunities that have both beneficial social outcomes and financial returns (for example, HM Government, 2016). A social investment approach positions children primarily as citizen-workers of the future (Lister, 2003) and thus as human capital that requires investment. Over the past decade or so the spotlight of social investment has fallen more and more on those families who are not doing so well educationally and economically (Edwards and Gillies, 2016). The causal features of poverty were identified as 'low achievement, aspirations and opportunity across generations ... worklessness and educational failure and ... family and relationship breakdown' (DWP and DfE, 2011: 8). So poverty and disadvantage for families and children were to be ended through investment in them as human capital, notably using targeted parenting intervention programmes, rather than redistributive policies. This investment was presented as being to the social and economic benefit of the nation. The aim was to pre-empt rather than react to social, educational and behaviour deficiencies, with intervention in families in the early years promoted as an evidenced and efficient policy approach. The front cover of an influential report on early intervention for the government exemplified this 'social investment = social and economic returns' model with its promise of 'smart investment, massive savings' and gold bars image (Allen, 2011b) (see Figure 1.2). We explore this social investment model in some depth in subsequent chapters. Disadvantaged new mothers in particular were targeted for intervention. The intention was to disrupt the transmission of the dysfunctional parenting practices that they had learnt at their own mother's knee, and which was the cause of their marginalised predicament. The minutiae of everyday interactions between mothers and their children were held up as deeply significant and capable of overcoming structurally ingrained disadvantages.

Figure 1.2: Allen Report 2011b

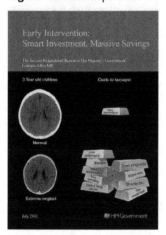

The early years intervention field in Britain is characterised by normative and standardised parenting education packages, with an extensive and elaborate architecture of services inculcating expert-approved parenting practices (Boddy et al, 2011; Lewis, 2011; Daly, 2013). They feature relatively fixed ideas about what constitutes good parental practice, regardless of context, and a number of them are heavily infused with brain science ideas. For example, the Family Nurse Partnership (FNP) is a home-visiting programme in which family nurses deliver intensive interventions with teenagers who are pregnant and first-time mothers, working to a strictly defined programme structure and carefully scripted weekly visits until the child's second birthday. We will return to the commissioning and practices of the FNP at various points in this book. The FNP website quotes a young mother endorsing the intervention: 'When the family nurse came to see me and told me more about the programme and the baby's brain I decided to give it a go.'[3] The Solihull Approach is a systematic psychotherapeutic and behavioural approach for practitioners working with children and families[4] that asserts in its *Facilitators manual*: 'when adults pick [babies] up, talk to them and cuddle them this sends messages to their brain that helps particular parts of their brain to develop' (p. 80). Parent Infant Partnerships (PIPs) offers specialist psychotherapeutic attachment intervention. Its founder argues for the importance of early intervention via PIPs because:

> When a baby is in a 'positive' relationship with its key carer, this part of the baby's brain [the pre-frontal cortex] puts on a huge growth spurt from about 6 months old, until the baby is about 18 months old. If a baby has a negative or inconsistent relationship with the carer, then this part of the brain literally does not grow, and in fact may never grow.[5]

Practitioners working with these and other early years parenting programmes are obliged to undergo extensive and recurrent training in the methods and delivery of the interventions. The programmes also require practitioners to carry out constant measurement of children's development and gather evidence to prove that the interventions work.

Intervening to support mothers and fathers to ensure better material, social and behavioural outcomes for children seems both progressive and morally authoritative. But it is also morally judgemental and constructed around a deficit model of parenting that requires correction, such that the programmes come very close to a takeover of parental agency (Daly, 2013). The intervention literature uses the language of encouraging mothers to talk about how they would like to bring up their baby, but there is only a narrowly acceptable way for them to express their wishes. For example, the FNP material refers to FNP nurses using a 'respectful agenda matching to align clients' aspirations with programme goals'.[6] In other words, the young mothers' values need to be reformed to fit with those of the programme. Further, as we will show in this book, the interventions embed social divisions and inequalities in the underpinning ideas about biological deficits and damaging intergenerational cultures contained in policy reports detailing the apparent physical damage that inadequate parenting inflicts on infant brains (for example, Allen, 2011a, 2011b; Leadsom et al, 2013).

Evidence and early intervention

Rather like the 'black holes' in the neglected infant's brain image (Perry, 2002), there are in fact large holes in our knowledge about what these MRI scans represent. Indeed, there are rather shaky underpinnings to evidence generally that – like the brain images – is used to provide the justification for early intervention in the way that mothers bring up their children. This is in a context where there is a general mantra of evidence-based policy making, exemplified in the early years field by the 'What Works' Centre based at the Early Intervention Foundation (EIF).[7] The foundation seeks to provide research evidence comparing the effectiveness of interventions. This sounds like indisputable common sense, but there are a number of problems with this approach. Not least is that, as we noted above, the early intervention field is characterised by standardised parenting support programmes, most of which are commercial enterprises. For example, the FNP programme is licensed to deliver the USA-based David Olds Nurse Family Program (NFP). Commercial interests make it difficult to make any strong claims questioning their efficacy. Thus the overview review of evidence for the EIF concludes equivocally with a call for more evaluation (Dartington Social Research Unit et al, 2015).

This EIF report conclusion indicates another issue, which is the contradictory logic of the state of evidence about early intervention in the early years field. On the one hand, in order to secure funding, proponents need to assert that there is indisputable evidence that the early years are formative and that early intervention works; on the other, they need to implement further research and evaluation in order to convince service funders that the investment they have made in intervention is working (Edwards et al, 2015b). In other words, research evidence is subject to the politics of interest groups when it comes to policy making, funding of services and service provision, but this becomes hidden behind assertions of 'evidence-based policy making'. It is the assertions and policy objectives of political interest groups that come first and research evidence is then generated to justify interventions (Davies, 2003; Gregg, 2010). Those objectives enable politicians and policy makers to endorse and pursue some sorts of policy intervention and avoid others. They do not consider or call for evidence that would point to material and social inequalities as causal in outcomes for children, and that would lead them to implement strategies for redistribution, such as income support, affordable and secure housing, and so on. They can put that difficult task aside and focus down on where they see the responsibility lying – that is, the more politically convenient target of how parents, or more specifically mothers, bring up their children and determine their brain architecture.

Policy rhetoric about evidence-based practice and strictures about adhering to 'what works' directs early intervention and binds professional practice. Yet there are some serious and fundamental problems with the evidence that is marshalled in support of early intervention. The brain-based claims that have pervaded education, social work, health and a host of early years fields, and the evaluations that are supposed to underpin programmes and services, are increasingly subject to question, as we indicate below and draw out in detail in this book.

Brain scan images and neuroscience as evidence

As noted above, the Perry brain scan images that have been used so freely in government policy documents and intervention training materials have been taken as indisputable proof of the effects of poor parenting on young children's brain development. Several studies have shown that 'brain science' images lead people to accept the accompanying assertions, however irrelevant or misleading (McCabe and Castel, 2007; Weisberg et al, 2008). Although there are challenges to the conclusions reached (Farah and Hook, 2013), the quote from a Children's Centre worker earlier in this Introduction shows that the Perry brain image can provide practitioners with a sense of solid evidence and, at the very least, reinforce their commitment to early years intervention.

More pertinently, the neuroimages reproduced in Perry's article raise a number of questions. Neuroscientists and social researchers who have tried to trace their source (for example, Wastell and White, 2013; Rose and Rose, 2016) found that the *Brain and Mind* journal in which they were published was rather short-lived (2000 to 2003). They have looked in vain for details about the children reported on in the paper beyond the information that they were neglected and had been referred to Perry's Academy clinic. These researchers were perplexed by the brain image resembling a walnut. What was the level of sensory deprivation and lack of interaction that the child involved was subject to? Was it the effect of malnutrition, massive birth trauma, or a genetic or physiological condition? Given that 'normal' children don't have identical brains, what was the range of measurements involved for the children in the study and why wasn't the 'extreme neglect' image compared with a smaller 'normal' scan? Other neuroimaging research on children, such as that seeking to show the effects of psychotherapeutic interventions on children's and young people's brains[8] (see Ramus, 2013), has not produced any startling results. Indeed, the inability to replicate neuroimaging results has been a focus of recent concerns. Neuroscientists from the USA and UK have identified some of the key challenges that neuroimaging research will need to overcome if it is to fulfil its promise of providing insights into how human brains work (Poldrack et al, 2016). Questionable research practices that they identify include small sample sizes that lack the statistical power to make generalisations (see also Button et al, 2013), not using corrective statistical tests (as in the infamous 'dead salmon' study, where an fMRI scan of a dead Atlantic salmon seemed to demonstrate that its brain was actively reacting to stimuli – a false positive result: Bennett et al,

2009), and errors built into some of the software packages that are used for analysing the neuroimage data (Eickhoff et al, 2016; Eklund et al, 2016). Similar sorts of errors may also occur in evaluation studies of early years interventions, as we discuss below.

Neuroscientists and social researchers working with them also have pointed out that current neuroscientific knowledge highlights the long-term plasticity of brain structures and functions; brains are constantly reacting to stimulation across the lifespan; forming, embedding and discarding synaptic connections (Bruer, 1999; Rose and Abi-Rached, 2013; Schmitz and Höppner, 2014). This forms quite a contrast with ideas that the first '1001 days' are crucial in an infant's brain development and in determining their future development. Further, while neuroscience as a discipline is full of exciting potential, the state of neuroscientific knowledge across such a broad and complex field is far from settled, with inconsistent results and provisional findings that are far from 'policy ready' (see assessments by O'Mara et al, 2016). Neuroscientists have taken to online social media to draw attention to examples of what they refer variously refer to as 'brain porn' (for example, Marcus, 2012) and 'neurobollocks' (@neurobollocks and #neurobollocks), with the science blogger Neurobonkers asking of the Perry brain images, 'Is this the most misleading image in neuroscience?'[9] Even the man whose brain scans image and work is cited in the policy reports, Bruce Perry, has criticised the overblown conclusions about the size and development of children's brains, poor parenting and crime that it has been used to support[10] (see Rose and Rose, 2016: 78). As David Wastell and Sue White (2012, 2013) identify, the main problems in extrapolating from the emergent knowledge about infant brain development are that most of the studies that claim relevance to the impact of parenting are on animals (rats in particular) and, where they concern humans, either deal with children who have experienced extreme institutional abuse or are on adults in traumatic circumstances. The slippage from findings in these sorts of studies to prescriptions in policy documents is widespread. Yet to transfer any knowledge from such studies directly into social policy interventions addressing poor and marginalised families is opportunistic and tendentious to say the least.

Evaluation studies as evidence

As well as neuroscientific evidence, evidence from a range of social science research approaches is drawn on to support early intervention (Macvarish et al, 2015), but with a particular emphasis on evaluation studies and longitudinal measurements. The results are often equivocal and short term (Bruer, 1999; Wastell and White, 2013), with some arguing that the turn to brain science is because the evidence from intervention studies is incomplete (Howard-Jones et al, 2012). Indeed, in contrast to the positive findings of a small-scale pilot study of the initial introduction of the FNP programme (Barnes et al, 2008), the findings from a randomised controlled trial (RCT) of the brain-based FNP intervention with first-time teenage mothers showed that it had little benefit over and above the usual, routine provision from health and social services across the four-year period covered by the evaluation, and thus was not cost-effective (Rohling et al, 2016). Of course, this is not to say that mothers who received the FNP programme may not have been enthusiastic about it and felt that it had made a difference, but the RCT did not find much in the way of the specific, measureable outcomes that government investment in the intervention was supposed to produce, such as reduced smoking, higher birth weight and reduced attendances at A&E (accident and emergency) hospital departments.

Generally, there are increasing concerns about the replicability of studies; that is, whether or not findings of success in outcomes from a parenting intervention in one study can be duplicated in a subsequent study. Science is undergoing what is called a 'replication crisis' – research that attempts to reproduce original studies is not coming up with the same results (Open Science Collaboration, 2015)[11] leaving researchers, policy makers and practitioners unsure about what to believe. There are two types of explanation put forward by statisticians for problems with replicability of results: cultural and historical context, and poor statistical practice. In terms of context, where and when an intervention and study takes place may mean that it is difficult to recreate the exact conditions of the original study (Van Bavel, 2016). This was one explanation put forward for why the RCT of the FNP intervention did not replicate the positive results of the FNP implementation pilot or the NFP evaluation studies in the United States (which are often carried out through service delivery rather than independently). The research team surmised that comprehensive welfare state health and other supportive services available to young mothers in the UK, unlike their US peers, may have made a difference. In relation to the other explanation, Peter Rossi, a renowned US government evaluator of social interventions, developed a 'stainless steel law of evaluation': the better designed the impact assessment of a social programme, the more likely is the resulting estimate of net impact to be zero (Rossi, 1987) In other words, this 'law' implies that estimating impacts through RCTs is more likely to show zero effects than other less rigorous approaches. Whatever the explanation at the time of writing, the central FNP website continues to highlight the very positive findings from the initial UK pilot study and only mentions a link to the RCT findings,[12] while clicking on the 'proven results' link on the website takes you to a description of the USA evidence.

Context is important with respect to RCTs. Commonly described as 'gold standard' evidence, RCTs claim an unbiased objectivity by randomly assigning subjects to a treatment or control group and measuring the results. They offer the benefit of standing outside of vested interests and the attraction of unequivocal truth about whether or not an intervention works. Their validity may be high in specific contexts where the experimental questions are narrow in scope and the interventions are precisely measureable, such the effect of statins on middle-aged men with coronary disease. This strength has less purchase where what is being evaluated are complex social services. Nancy Wolff (2000) points to the necessary assumption of equivalence in RCTs in relation to (a) the intervention, (b) the populations in the study, and (c) the environment of the study. In contrast, as we note in Chapter Two, parent-based interventions involve confounding contextual factors of different family characteristics and concerns, variable circumstances and access to resources, and the patchy provision and involvement of other services and support systems. Further, RCTs are not so appropriate for research with a broad social remit – such as improving opportunities, relationships and social mobility – as they are in medicine.

With these caveats in mind, the FNP RCT evaluation study was careful to clearly define the particular measures and levels of significance that would indicate that the FNP intervention was making a difference. The study also ensured a sample size that meant it was not beset by the 'power' problem described in relation to neuroimaging above, and which is another of the problems identified by the other explanation for the crisis of replicability in science: poor statistical practice. For example, the Heckman equation (invest + develop + sustain = gain) is an economic statistical model that asserts that investment in the early years is more effective than later remedial intervention and pays off in economic and social returns to society. Much of the evidence in this field does not substantiate such social investment claims, with what effects there are often being temporary (Bruer, 1999). Importantly, where studies do purport to offer proof of the Heckman equation, they may be subject to statistical flaws. One such study asserted early childhood interventions could increase young adults' earnings either by a jaw-dropping 42% or a slightly less staggering 25%, depending on which version of the published research you access (Gertler et al, 2013, 2014). The experimental study involved a comparison of early years children in low-income families in Jamaica who received parenting skills interventions with an equivalent group who did not. Follow-up on the groups 20 years later found that the average earnings of the intervention group were vastly higher than those of the group who had not received intervention, and in fact had caught up with those of their better-off peers. Children in the intervention group were also more likely to emigrate to wealthier countries in adulthood, thus broadening their educational and professional opportunities. In other words, the early intervention was successful and the Heckman equation operated. The published research methodology for the study was examined by the respected statistician Andrew Gelman (2013, 2014), who provides a note of caution. He pointed to problems associated with the small sample size (129 children), the correlating of the key outcome of earnings with emigration (contextual and statistical issues), and some speculative overestimating of the size of effects (statistical flaws), as well as remarking on the equivocal evidence base for early intervention generally.

As most careful researchers will be quick to point out, all our scientific and social scientific knowledge is provisional – and a questioning stance is part of good practice, it is what drives science forward (Pickersgill, 2016). In contrast, a range of poor practices including (i) asserting that something has been unequivocally 'proven' or 'found', (ii) referring to evidence from a particular method of investigation as unquestionably of high quality, and/or (iii) extrapolating from one sort of study population or environment to another, have been labelled 'scientific bullshit' (Earp, 2016; with 'epistemic ostentatiousness' providing a less colloquial version: Pickersgill, 2016). So, statements that begin 'We know that …' in the brain science and early intervention field, and projecting from the impairments to babies' physical and emotional development resulting from extreme institutional abuse in orphanages in Romania to the risks to the babies of young mothers living in disadvantaged conditions in England, might well be examples of scientific bullshit. In other words, it is wise to be cautious with the 'evidence' claims to certainty. And, of course, we want to be clear about the evidence that we are drawing on in this book.

The 'Brain Science and Early Intervention' research project

This book draws on a two-year study that we undertook: the 'Brain Science and Early Intervention' research project. The research investigated how biologised accounts of the formative impact of early experience on brain development have come to shape politics, key social policy legislation, and early intervention initiatives and practice, as well as the consequences for everyday practices among health care providers and early years educators. We looked at how key interest groups that promote the use of brain science to drive early years intervention – such as politicians, policy makers and political advisers; intervention lobbyists, consultants and evaluators; and chief executives and directors of statutory and voluntary sector services – engage with and draw upon what are evidently partial and misinformed versions of neuroscientific knowledge. We were concerned with how these versions of brain science are adopted by early years health care providers and early years educators to understand their intervention in ways that position the parenting practices of the mothers they work with as deficient. And we were worried about the implications for marginalised mothers and their families, and for the entrenching of wider social inequalities.

As part of our research we conducted an extensive review of key documents shaping political and policy engagement with neuroscience in relation to early years childrearing. We collated and analysed early years policy reports and manifestos, and gathered published materials from leading early years intervention programmes (although we could not access the materials that FNP nurses use with mothers they visit because of Olds' copyright restrictions). We attended events promoting early intervention and obtained transcripts of talks by key advocates in the field. We also accessed and reviewed relevant academic publications, and kept a watching brief on critical blogs by neuroscientists. To help us understand the current state of debate and reach of neuroscientific knowledge in the field we consulted with well-respected neuroscientists. We provided them with examples of key brain science claims in the early years intervention field, and an annotated list of significant publications and initiatives, so that they could evaluate the assertions made about the formative development and characteristics of areas of the brain in early years intervention policy statements and practice materials. We do not refer directly to the expert discussion in this book, but we want to acknowledge the invaluable help of these neuroscientists in providing us with background scientific information and assessment to inform our analyses and conclusions.[13]

In addition to this careful review of literature in the early years field and checking of their claims about neuroscientific knowledge, we also mapped the complex synergies and linkages of interest groups involved in promoting brain science as an evidence base in early intervention, and their discursive devices of persuasion. Our investigations have also led us to look back in time, to consider the history of interventions in family and parenting, to uncover the recurrence of old themes and the emergence of new ones about the biological and cultural deficiencies of the poor, and the culpability of mothering practices in reproducing them.

As well as our analysis of literature on brain science and early intervention we conducted two sets of interviews. The first set was with four influential public figures who have promoted the application of neuroscience as an evidence base in child and family intervention policy and practice: Camila Batmanghelidjh, then CEO of the now-defunct Kids Company (House of Commons Public Administration and Constitutional Affairs Committee, 2016); Frank Field MP (Lab.), author of early intervention reports (for example, Field, 2010) and Chair of the Foundation Years Trust;[14] Andrea Leadsom MP (Con.), author of relevant reports (for example, Leadsom et al, 2013) and then Chair of Parent Infant Partnerships;[15] and Matthew Taylor, CEO of the Royal Society of Arts and former policy adviser to the New Labour governments (for example, Taylor, 2009). We asked them to talk about their understandings of brain science processes, parenting practices and the consequences for policy interventions. These advocates of brain science and early intervention agreed for their views to be 'on the record' so we have not anonymised them when we quote from their interviews in this book. We sought interviews with several other leading advocates such as Graham Allen MP (Lab.) and George Hosking, CEO of the Wave Trust, but, either because they were too busy or because they became aware of our critical approach, they declined to participate in our research. Their views are publicly available in documents and speeches, and are included in the book in this form.

The second set of interviews was with 17 health and early years practitioners based in services in the south-east of England: FNP practitioners, Children's Centre workers and health visitors. We asked them about their understandings of brain science processes, their views on parenting practices and what they saw as the consequences for their practice interventions. In order to protect the identity of these interviewees, we have not included their names and location, or identified their role beyond the generic service indication in this book. For the most part we have included direct quotes from particular practitioners, but where a few of our FNP interviewees explained that they were not happy for us to use their words directly we have summarised their views.

The literature and transcripts of talks and interviews were subject to an in-depth discourse analysis, broadly involving close reading of the written text to identify recurring terms, metaphors and references that create and constitute understanding of an issue or set of issues (Gee, 2012).

Structure of book

In the report *Parenting matters* (Paterson, 2011), with its first chapter on 'Building the brain', the CentreForum thinktank excitedly exhorts government to throw aside traditional views of family as a private matter and take the 'bold' and 'brave' step of influencing what parents do (2011: 5). This notion of a break from a past where statutory and voluntary bodies left parents alone and did not interfere in family life is, however, far from what was actually the case. Aspects of children's biological and social development, parents' part in this, and what is to be done about it, have long been the concern of policies and interventions – although the why and how of these have changed over time. In the next chapter of this book (Chapter Two) we explore the history of ideas about intervention in family, highlighting attempts to shape children's upbringing for the sake of the nation's future. A consistent and influential idea has been that undesirable attitudes and actions, and the propensity for deprivation, are transmitted down the generations through the way that parenting shapes children's minds and brains. We consider the relationship between interventions designed to address fears about the state of the nation in the form of poverty, crime and disorder, and understandings of the role of parents and families as they link to shifting emphases of the capitalist system across time. We detail how 19th-century concerns about children's moral development gave way to a preoccupation with their physical health and genetic heredity, which then transmuted into anxieties about their physiological development. We establish the shift to contemporary preoccupations with the quality of infant neurological architecture to lay the groundwork for the Chapter Three.

Chapter Three takes us deep into the latest diagnosis of the problem that early intervention aims to address, focusing on the quality of parenting and infant brain development; it explores how brain claims came to define and propel to the fore early intervention in how mothers bring up their children as a logical expression of social investment models of social policy. We pick up the context for, and concerns about, the use and misuse of developmental neuroscience and of evidence for the early years being formative indicated in this Introduction, to open to question the detail of the five key biologised motifs – critical periods, maternal attunement, synaptic density, cortisol and the pre-frontal cortex – that are mobilised to make the case for intervention in the parenting of young, disadvantaged and marginalised mothers.

Earlier we introduced the notion of scientific bullshit or epistemic ostentation. In fact, bullshit has been theorised more broadly as a concept for understanding a lack of concern with 'how things actually are' coupled with the cultivation of vested interests in the policy field (Belfiore, 2009). In Chapter Four we consider the vested interests that are involved in the gap between actual evidence and representations through selective and partial use of information. We trace the intricate network of interests and their agendas that characterise social policy provision generally, focusing down on social investment in children's services and the early intervention field. In particular, we look at three key stakeholder groups with interests in early intervention: business, politicians and professionals, and their interlinked alliances and partnerships. We then build on this review of the interests at play in the early intervention field in the next chapter (Chapter Five) to examine them in operation, through case studies of three high-profile initiatives. Our first case study focuses on the Wave Trust, a campaigning and policy advocate organisation that has been highly influential politically in promoting brain-based early intervention in the UK. It claims a 'business-centred' approach to breaking damaging intergenerational family cycles of abuse and violence. The second case study subjects the origins, delivery and evidence claims of the FNP early intervention programme to scrutiny. The programme has been centrally placed among a network of stakeholder interests as the vehicle for providing high returns on social investment. The third case study explores the nodal network position of Parent Infant Partnership UK, which advocates for an emphasis on attachment between primary caregivers and babies. Its campaigning activities span political, service delivery and corporate interests.

Chapter Six explores the way that brain science and neoliberal ideas infuse and shape the understandings and practices of those working in the early years field. We consider the evangelical mission that they believe guides their work, which is to save children from the perils and consequences of inadequate parenting. It is brain science discourse that provides practitioners with what they regard as the unchallengeable 'truth', made visual through brain scans, which justifies their interventions and the ways that they intervene in parenting. Underlying practitioners' enthusiasm about saving children are ideas about optimising both children and mothers, and notions of intergenerational cycles of deprivations that reproduce low attachment and deficit parenting in families and localities.

We then move on to detail the ways in which social divisions and inequalities around gender, social class, race/ethnicity and poverty are embedded and reproduced through early intervention initiatives, especially those invoking brain science (Chapter Seven). We show how mothers are envisioned as a risky environment for their children and their outcomes, and held personally accountable for inculcating a 'biological resistance to adversity' in their children, able to act as protective buffers between them and harsh social conditions through practising intensive attachment. Poor working-class and minority ethnic mothers especially are positioned as the source of individual, social and national problems, and as the solution to them, and we note the international spread of such ideas.

The misrepresentation and misinterpretation of neuroscience conceal the deeply political and moral nature of decisions about what is best for children. The current early intervention logic is rooted in simplistic notions of cause and effect, with the ends of improved human capital justifying the interventions to ensure its production. In the final chapter of the book (Chapter Eight) we explore potential future directions. We contrast the 'brave new world of prevention science' and its instrumental economic logic, with a socially just approach to increasing family income and reducing material deprivation, and more collectivist ideals of supporting families, reducing social harm and humanely addressing the social good for its own sake.

Notes

[1] www.early-education.org.uk/sites/default/files/CREC%20Early%20Years%20Lit%20Review%202014%20for%20EE.pdf

[2] We received a copy of the transcript of the entire proceedings of the conference as part of our payment for attending the event. The Westminster Social Policy Forum requested that we point out that speakers have not had the opportunity to make any corrections to the transcript and that it does not represent a formal record of proceedings.

[3] http://fnp.nhs.uk/news/2015-03-26/life-changing-early-support-available-more-young-families

[4] http://solihullapproachparenting.com/

[5] www.anddrealeadsom.com/early-years-intervention/early-years-intervention

[6] http://fnp.nhs.uk/sites/default/files/contentuploads/fnp_information_pack_-_the_evidence_for_fnp_-_appendix_11.pdf

[7] www.eif.org.uk/

[8] For example, www.annafreud.org/pages/the-parent-infant-project.html

[9] http://bigthink.com/neurobonkers/is-this-the-most-misleading-image-in-neuroscience

[10] http://www.theguardian.com/politics/2010/apr/09/iain-duncan-smith-childrens-brains

[11] See also http://compare-trials.org/

12 http://fnp.nhs.uk/evidence/research–england
13 The arguments in this book are the responsibility of us alone of course.
14 www.foundationyearstrust.org.uk/
15 www.pipuk.org.uk/

TWO

Citizens of the future[1]

Introduction

Policy and practice debates around social policies are often oblivious to the way that similar themes and solutions echo down the centuries. The idea that deprivation is transmitted through the generations is particularly influential. The belief that early childhood experiences profoundly shape the personality, behaviour and destiny of individuals has exerted a potent allure across time, mutating and adapting to fit the political and cultural contours of the day (Kagan, 1998). Interventions focusing specifically on how children are brought up can be traced back to a religion-inspired reclamation of young souls from their dissolute poor parents in the 19th century. Such initiatives were concerned with promoting the virtues of productive citizenship and were rooted in the economic liberalism of the time. Attention then shifted from the soul to the body and mind as theories of child development emerged in the late 19th and early 20th centuries. These theories eventually were to endorse embedded liberal ideas about what was 'normal' in family life and children through psychoanalytic models of family functioning in the 20th century. Today, incarnations of infant determinism are conveyed through the language of cutting-edge brain science as having transformative potential, invoking new morally infused prescriptions for family relationships. Characterising each of these eras is an institutionalised effort to initiate behaviour modification in the name of prevention.

In this chapter we explore the history of ideas about intervention in the family, highlighting attempts to (re)engineer children's upbringing for the sake of the nation's future. We show how the specific goals of intervention in the upbringing of children shift over the centuries to reflect politically grounded representations of what is good for the nation. Taking the sort of long-term perspective we adopt in this chapter unsettles current assumptions and reveals the way that social concerns and remedies play out cyclically, across time, through attempts to advance, manage and regulate the social good through targeting and intervening in how children are brought up. We consider the relationship between programmes and activities that are designed to address social problems of poverty, crime and disorder, and understandings of the role of parents in the context of shifting emphases of political systems across time. We detail how 19th-century concerns about children's moral development gave way to a preoccupation with their physical health and genetic heredity, which then transmuted into anxieties about their psychological development and, more latterly, the quality of infant neurological architecture. While the rationale for and related modes of family intervention shift, a conviction remains that optimally formed minds and bodies can prosper within a capitalist system.

Saving the children

Family responsibility for the welfare and moral profile of children has long been assumed. But specific targeting of children and families for intervention can be traced back to 19th-century efforts to address the human suffering and social costs associated with the laissez-faire liberal capitalism of the time, which saw the market as best left alone to work for the benefit of society. Earnest conviction that free trade and the pursuit of self-interest upheld the best interests of all led the powerful and privileged to seek explanations for the misery and dysfunction that surrounded them. Deprivation and destitution were acute while crime and social disorder remained a constant threat, particularly in London where many of the wealthy elite resided. Victorian efforts at social reform were funnelled through the dominant framework of understanding associated with classical liberalism. This system of ideas identified the dubious moral character of those struggling to survive as the cause of their difficulties. Hardship and privation were viewed as temporary wrinkles in an otherwise benevolent system that could be ironed out through strengthening the moral fibre of the nation (Rooff, 1972). Reflecting the tenets of liberalism, the state was to play a minimal role in managing those who were not managing themselves. Bolstered by the growing influence of evangelism, philanthropy and charitable activity took on a new significance as a way for the Victorian rich to understand and control the unwashed masses, through the issuing of relief to alleviate poverty alongside moral surveillance and counsel (Stedman Jones, 2013).

Christianity played a central role in fashioning modern Western conceptions of personhood (Rose, 1999). As religious experiences came to be located in the hearts and minds of individuals, this relationship with God was identified in the qualities of the self. As such 'character' emerged as an early preoccupation, heralding the influence of ideas in shaping how we understand what a child 'is', and opening up mind and behaviour to public scrutiny, self-evaluation and redemption. Victorian philanthropists sought to inculcate self-governance as a moral sensibility that could overcome the social ills blighting their towns and cities. Poverty was approached as symptomatic of a lack of drive, resilience and self-respect. Worse still, extreme destitution and reliance on the State through the provisions of the Poor Law, which provided a barely minimal institutionalised safety-net, marked a shameful lack of foresight and self-control.

The second half of the 19th century saw an unprecedented proliferation of private charities and relief agencies, and significantly the singling out of children as the focus for moral ministry. Commonly represented by their philanthropic benefactors as innocents who could be saved from the bad character, degradation and degeneracy that had befallen their parents, children began to feature prominently in a range of social and religious associations. Many contemporary children's charities, including Barnardo's, Action for Children and the Children's Society, have their roots in what became known as the British child rescue movement. Propelled by a heady romantic vision of childhood and an imperialist concern with purifying the race and strengthening the nation, these organisations succeeded in extending legal protection to children. Crucially, they did this through the depiction of an abusive debauched underclass at the bottom of society routinely exploiting or abandoning their children. The broader social and structural context framing childhood and family experiences of deprivation and risk were overlooked for a sensationalist focus on the sins of the parents. Children of the poor were depicted as little barbarians; victims of their cruel, depraved parents and in need of assimilation into the ranks of respectable British society.

Thomas Barnardo is among the best known of the child rescuers, having set up the first of his homes for 'waifs and strays' in Stepney, east London, in 1870. Combining a flamboyant celebrity image with evangelical self-righteousness Barnardo did considerably more than simply provide for orphans. He actively constructed the children of the poor as a category apart, embodying the savagery of the degenerate classes but also the potential for deliverance. As Lydia Murdoch (2006) outlines, Barnardo skilfully developed the equivalent of missionary conversion parables, drawing on popular melodramatic tropes to raise money and justify the removal of children from their families. At the Stepney institution, a photographic studio was installed in 1874 with images of 55,000 of Barnardo's charges captured. Striking 'before and after' publicity shots were produced from there, as well as other fundraising material. To ensure the children looked convincingly neglected many had their shoes removed, clothes deliberately torn, hair tangled and dirt smeared on their faces. The post-'rescue' photographs showed the children transformed by Christian education and honest toil, depicted as tidy, shiny faced 'little workers', holding a broom or engaged in a useful trade.

Reflecting the imperialist sensibilities characterising Victorian Britain, the ability to rescue and redeem children's bodies and minds was viewed through a distinctly racialised lens. The children of the poor were identified as a risk to the hereditary superiority of British stock but also as a malleable resource born with a kernel of racial superiority that could be nurtured or left to degenerate (Boucher, 2014). Child rescue narratives commonly drew on explicitly racialised imagery, describing missions to civilise little 'street Arabs', 'urban savages' or 'ragamuffin tribes', depicting them as 'specimens' with darkened skin and exaggerated facial features. According to Barnardo, this physiognomy could undergo complete 'metamorphosis' under the auspices of his training, marking the child's newfound purity and religious salvation (cited in Murdoch, 2006). This narrative thus posed a link between the psychological and the physical; a transformation of the soul became evident and evidenced in a transformed appearance.

The notion that the British character of the young poor could be developed to shore up world supremacy was not confined to the high-profile philanthropists of the day. Deep faith in the power of British children to reform the colonies eventually drove a systematic migration programme, resulting in tens of thousands of the rescued 'waifs' being sent to underpopulated settler colonies in Australia, New Zealand, Canada and South Africa. The philanthropist Maria Rye was among the first to send regular parties of 'gutter children' to Canada to work as indentured servants, estimating that the 'expense of taking a child out of the gutters in London, and placing it in Canada ... may be roughly reckoned at £15 per head' (Liverpool Maritime Archive and Library, 2014: 3). This practice of finding and transporting suitable child migrants was legislated for and part funded by the British state right up until the 1950s. The investment was regarded as mutually beneficial, delivering the children from wretchedness, demoralisation and temptation, while extending the reach and strength of the British Empire. By the late 19th century over 50 charitable organisations were regularly dispatching poor children abroad including the Church of England Waifs and Strays Society and National Children's Homes. However, the substantial numbers of children shipped out of the country were dwarfed by the numbers that were institutionalised, ultimately because their families lacked the resources to care adequately for them.

Thomas Barnardo was by far the most enthusiastic and prolific perpetrator of what he termed 'philanthropic abduction'. This phrase hints at the harsh reality lying behind this systematic programme of salvation and the severing of family and community ties it entailed. His campaign literature was filled with lurid accounts of violent tussles with drunken, bestial mothers determined to keep their neglected urchins as exploitable property. But while the philanthropists were at pains to represent their targets as abandoned, abused and unloved, most institutionalised children had been embedded in family networks. As Murdoch (2006) has demonstrated, parents could make considerable efforts to stay in touch with their children and monitor their welfare. Destitute relatives often temporarily placed children in charitable institutions while they got back on their feet, subsequently returning to find they had been sent away without any warning or notification. The practice of isolating poor institutionalised children from the perceived bad influence of their family, was vigorously defended by the child-centric philanthropists, often in court custody battles with their relatives. Parents were portrayed as wicked, immoral and brutal, and their children as suffering 'worse than orphans' (Barnardo, 1885).

Yet ideals of home, family and hearth continued to exert great influence over Victorian consciousness (Behlmer, 1998). Other philanthropists, regarded 'the family' as a sacred wellspring of personal responsibility and British character, focusing their efforts on remoralising poor families as a whole through strengthening their character and resilience. This family-centred approach to poverty was to evolve eventually into statutory social work practice (Lewis, 1995). In line with the cultural sensibilities of the day, the child rescuers also expressed great faith in the redemptive power of family love, but instead privileged an artificial operational framework of domesticity over any blood or community relations. For example, Barnardo established substitute family settings styled as 'family cottages'. Administered by 'foster mothers' and housing between 20 and 40 children, these 'cottages' and 'village homes' were located away from urban squalor and the corrupting influence of the adult poor. While these provided a distinct contrast to the regimental conditions of the workhouse or state orphanage, the ideal of family promoted was largely reduced to a training in 'British character' and moral citizenship (Swain, 2011).

The science of reform: strengthening British stock

By turn of the 20th century, the fervour and conviction powering the 'philanthropic abduction' of poor children was waning. Severe and prolonged economic instability and the rise of socialist ideals saw the foundations for the welfare state laid, while the tenets of classical liberalism came under prolonged attack. A key catalyst for this reformist agenda was the unexpected struggle British forces faced in winning the Boer War (Kuchta, 2010). The conflict was expected to quickly establish the might of the British Empire, but it dragged on for nearly three years, provoking fears over 'national efficiency'. The appalling physical condition of young men in the army recruitment pool became evident, triggering panic about Britain's imperialist supremacy. Laissez-faire principles fell from favour as the state began to link the health of its children with national competitiveness.

The organisations established by the child rescuers continued to run residential homes for children but within a context that saw increasing involvement of the state in overseeing child welfare. As part of the Liberal government reforms, medical inspections of children in schools were introduced and free school meals were provided for the poor. Classes in 'mothercraft' were also founded to encourage the raising of fitter children, through providing advice on feeding and physical care (Kent, 2002). By this point, the general consensus positioned children as raw material to be shaped in the interests of the nation. This moved beyond the introduction of welfare reforms and a compulsory education system as attention began to converge around new scientific accounts of human development. In 1907 the Child Study Society was set up, followed by the medically orientated Childhood Society. The proponents of these organisations were informed by a range of circulating theories and ideas about childhood, not least influential debates about the social consequences of inheritance and bad breeding (Behlmer, 1998).

Conceptions of heredity and the laws of biology found particular resonance with the Social Darwinist instincts of the elite, inspiring a new generation of philanthropists and social reformers to rally around eugenic reasoning. Founded in 1909, the Eugenics Education Society sought to inform the public about the principles of selective breeding while lobbying the government for controls on fertility. The new 'science' of eugenics had wide and broad appeal across the political spectrum of the establishment, but proved particularly attractive to those on the political left and those who considered themselves radical reformers. Between the two world wars, eugenics belonged to the political vocabulary of virtually every significant modernising force in the Western world (Dikötter, 1998). In comparison with the US and Scandinavia, Britain was among the more cautious adopters of eugenic legislation, but support for the prevention of in-breeding through segregation of 'defectives', 'inebriates' and those with venereal disease was passionately discussed in Parliament. In 1913, the Mental Deficiency Act was passed with relatively little opposition, allowing the compulsory detention of those deemed 'unfit' despite them never having committed a crime or been certified.

The early advancement of British child psychology was grounded within this eugenic paradigm, under the auspices of the educational psychologist and now-discredited champion of intelligence testing, Sir Cyril Burt. Particular emphasis was placed on the development of intelligence testing and the ranking and sorting of children. Indeed, after the passing of the Mental Deficiency Act, Burt was appointed by the London County Council as their official education psychologist, with the aim of classifying children and weeding out the 'feeble minded' for admission to schools for the mentally defective (Stewart, 2013). But this period also marked a more general interest in defining and policing the parameters of normal child development. Sensitised to any manifestations of abnormality, officials and charity agencies increasingly began to refer children to the new psychiatric professions. As concern shifted from the moral development of children to their physical health and then to the inner workings of their minds, the Maudsley psychiatric hospital in London was forced to set up a separate children's department to deal with the rapid growth in numbers of children being treated during the interwar years (Evans et al, 2008). Most of these referrals concerned children living in deprived conditions, with many suffering from malnutrition and general poor health. Details collected about the child's physiology, habits, personality and family relationships were used to form diagnoses, primarily of physical or neurological abnormalities, 'moral disorder' or mental deficiency.

The psychological models drawn on to categorise and treat children grew in sophistication through cross-fertilisation with new behaviourist and psychoanalytic models, and, more specifically, the emergence of the child guidance movement in the United States. This precipitated the expansion of psychological horizons beyond the constraints of abnormality and deficit to encompass the risk of 'maladjustment' faced by otherwise normal children. Child guidance proponents came to emphasise their preventative function in promoting emotional and psychological development through 'the dangerous age of childhood' (Stewart, 2013: 14). Efforts were to be focused on early indicators of disturbance, which included a broad range of behaviour such as bedwetting, misconduct, shyness and other manifestations of non-conformity. These were viewed as symptoms of deeper dysfunctions rooted in the child's family relationships, ensuring that normal development became imbued with a sense of fragility (Rose, 1999). But, crucially, children were regarded as uniquely mouldable and responsive to treatment through the provision of expert advice to parents.

Again, philanthropy played a role in establishing child guidance clinics on both sides of the Atlantic. In the USA, large philanthropic donations from, among others, Rockefeller and the Commonwealth Fund, helped establish a network across the states to pursue the study, treatment and prevention of juvenile psychological disorders. Reflecting a more general post-war secularisation of philanthropic activity away from religious-informed principles and towards ideals of science, donors placed their faith in the power of therapy to uplift the human condition (Rosenberg, 2002). Alice Smuts (2008) has documented how the generosity of the philanthropists was underpinned by their conviction that shaping the mental, physical and moral development of the child was a way of controlling and directing their future, and that of the nation. This notion was widespread and shared by many in government positions. In 1930 President Herbert Hoover convened a White House conference with over 3,000 in attendance to discuss the issue of child health and wellbeing, declaring: 'if we could have one generation of properly born, trained, educated and healthy children a thousand other problems of Government would vanish' (cited in Smuts, 2008: 4).

US philanthropy was similarly instrumental in sponsoring the child guidance movement abroad. Following requests from British advocates, the Commonwealth Fund extended finance to support exchange observation visits and the setting up of clinics, supplementing the smaller scale investments of British philanthropists committed to further developing child mental health services (Stewart, 2013). After the Second World War, the child guidance system was expanded and became part of accepted state provision in the post-war reconstruction effort. Concern over the traumatic impact of the Blitz and evacuation on the psychological wellbeing of children led to demands for an integrated service that was to be administered through local education authorities. This was in a context where a vision of 'the family' was broadly promoted as an essential mechanism of reconciliation and order after an extended period of chaos and uncertainty (Thomson, 2013).

During this period, psychoanalytic accounts of child mental health rose to ascendancy, propelled by the psychiatrist John Bowlby's theorising around maternal deprivation and attachment. While working at the London Child Guidance Clinic during the war, Bowlby came to believe that the key to normal development was located in the warmth and consistency of mother–child relationships. Drawing on examples of clinic cases, he attributed the development of deviant personalities to maternal separation or poor quality relational bonding (Stewart, 2013). Attachment theory found great resonance among those who positioned the traditional family as the essential civilising force driving the development of the nation and social democracy. Mounting anxiety about increasing divorce rates in the aftermath of the war and the incidence of child neurosis was offset by a broader optimistic conviction that state intervention had the capacity to solve all social problems (Shapira, 2015). As such, the emotional as well as the physical welfare of children became incorporated into the development of post-war policies that were informed by Keynesian ideas of state intervention in economic policy and investment in public welfare provision to contain and ameliorate the excesses of market forces.

Mathew Thomson (2013) argues that Bowlby's attachment theory was pivotal to the development of a limited welfare state that depended on the caring labour of women in the context of full male employment. Thomson also describes how, in the process, a new 'landscape of the child' was carved out, reconfiguring the parameters of the state, the home and urban space. Development of the young was to be fostered through a state-maintained framework of education, medicine, social services and economic policy, a nurturing infant-centred home and the provision of specially designed protective spaces (such as playgrounds and children's TV) away from risky adult environments. However, this new cradle of social citizenship was predicated on a so-called 'Golden Age' of the industrial economy that, by the early 1970s, was lurching towards crisis. The manifest gender hierarchy and oppression underpinning embedded liberal ideals of the nuclear family also came under systematic attack from second-wave feminists who exposed the darker side of patriarchal family as a common site of abuse and violence against children.

By the 1980s the New Right was railing against the impact of welfare benefits and the 'nanny state', invoking among other things the negative impact on children's moral development. This marked a 'rolling back' of the state; Keynesian models of social security were attacked as dysfunctional and for encouraging a growing underclass dependent on state handouts (Peck and Tickell, 2002). A proliferating 'rabble' of crime-prone sons and promiscuous daughters was predicted unless state handouts were cut back (Murray, 1994). Instead, it was argued, the family should be recognised as the bedrock of civilisation and left to fulfil its social responsibilities. The then Conservative Prime Minister Margaret Thatcher was among the more notable advocates of this view. In a speech in 1988 she pronounced:

> The family is the building block of society. It's a nursery, a school, a hospital, a leisure place, a place of refuge and a place of rest. It encompasses the whole of society. It fashions beliefs. It's the preparation for the rest of our life and women run it. (Thatcher, 1988)

But this traditional model of the dutiful family fitted neither the changing cultural attitudes of the day nor the transformation of the economic and social order that the Thatcher government was to usher in. Deregulation, free marketeering, privatisation and a diminished state were promoted through a championing of ideals of freedom and liberation that cut across old, expectations and obligations. Rather, there was a concentration on the self-determining, networked individual, liberated from gendered and classed expectations and ties.

Through the 1990s the discrediting of Keynesian welfarism shifted into a new logic of state interventionism (Peck and Tickell, 2002). By the time the New Labour government came to power in 1997, children were firmly positioned at the centre of a new neoliberal-inspired paradigm of social investment. Rather than supporting families to raise 'normal' minds and bodies, children became viewed as future assets that could be maximised for the good of all (Jenson, 2004). The state's role was no longer to act as an agent of social security, but instead to enable personal responsibility and, crucially, to manage and prevent the social risks that might undermine children's future life chances. In the process, conceptualisations of family shifted away from the 'essential building block' metaphor towards a more contingent designation as, at one and the same time, a strength and a risk factor to be monitored and regulated.

Economic theorising around human capital was particularly influential in shifting the axis of concern away from a protective embedding of well-adjusted social citizenship towards the management of children as investment portfolios. Gary Becker (1981), for example, conceived of families as small factories, held together not by obligation or sentiment but by mutual interest in the human commodities they produce. Children came to assume a much greater significance within this market-based ethic as raw material requiring extensive investment to secure their futures as self-serving and self-producing individuals. And increasingly social problems, like poverty and inequality, became framed in terms of lack of human capital, attributable to poor parenting. Amid rising rates of divorce, cohabitation, birth outside of marriage and same-sex parenting, definitions of family became more flexible and inclusive. But, crucially, this occurred through a focus on childrearing as the primary moral concern. The replacement of male breadwinner models of family with norms around dual-earning households was promoted as the progressive solution to gender injustice, while the female-dominated practice of childcare was redrawn as a motor of meritocracy.

Cognitive development was the core component of dominant conceptualisations of human capital at the beginning of the 21st century. Intensively parented children, it was argued, would be better able to navigate and capitalise on post-industrial opportunities. But the job of cultivating competent minds, fit to compete in the global knowledge economy, was regarded as too important to be left to untrained parents. The New Labour years were characterised by a massive expansion of public and state-sponsored third sector initiatives directly targeting families under the rubric of 'parenting support' (Edwards and Gillies, 2004). A new interventionist policy ethos began explicitly to position family life as a public rather than a private concern through the linking of parenting practices to broader narratives of social justice. As the minutiae of everyday relations with children came to be seen as directly determining their future outcomes, good parenting was made synonymous with maximising a child's cognitive potential and inculcating aspirational neoliberal values. Family households were rebranded as home learning environments, child care became early education, and political consensus converged around the notion that parenting was the key to increasing social mobility.

Policy makers were particularly impressed by the theorising of the US Nobel Laureate economist James Heckman. Arguing that human capital is cumulative rather than fixed, Heckman and colleagues proposed a formula that they summed up in the phrase 'skills beget skills and abilities beget abilities' (Cunha and Heckman, 2007). This economic reasoning, which we introduced in Chapter One, is known as the 'Heckman equation' and asserts that return on human capital is very high in the early years of life and diminishes rapidly thereafter. In developing this model, Heckman and colleagues produced a graph that was to have huge influence in social policy making circles, inspiring New Labour's focus on early years provision as well as the subsequent

Coalition government's social mobility strategy and continued investment in pre-school nursery provision (*The Guardian*, 2012). Showing projected 'rates of return on investment in human capital by age', the hypothetical image was widely reproduced as if it were proof in itself of Heckman's contentions (Howard-Jones et al, 2012).

In 2006 the New Labour Prime Minister Tony Blair promoted his government's £17 billion investment in the Sure Start programme, in a speech titled 'Our nation's future'. He stated that 'the Nobel economist James Heckman famously showed that the return on human capital was very high in the early years of life and diminished rapidly thereafter'. Trailing a range of public service reforms he concluded 'more than anything else, early intervention is crucial if we are to tackle social exclusion' (Blair, 2006). The subsequent policy focus on early childhood reflected the broader shift away from welfare state principles of shared responsibility and universal protection towards a preoccupation with identifying and managing individual risk factors (Featherstone et al, 2014a). More coercive policy approaches began to explicitly target disadvantaged mothers, positioning them as the essential mediators of their children's high-risk profile. Intensive family support initiatives were introduced, promising to tackle recalcitrant parents and force them to parent more effectively (Gillies, 2011).

Beyond the economic theorising there was little concrete evidence to support claims that altering parenting practices and maximising childhood investment could reverse structurally engrained inequality, or even address educational attainment gaps. As we noted in Chapter One, longitudinal evaluations of interventions produced disappointing results. Further, cohort studies have highlighted the significance of income and maternal education above and beyond parenting styles (Hartas, 2011, 2012; Sullivan et al, 2013). But concern over this lack of verification from social research findings was overtaken by a new interest in psychologically inflected economic theorising associated with behavioural economics and, more specifically, models that grounded human behaviour in an emotional and social nexus (Jones et al, 2013). Efforts to maximise the cognitive capacity of children were instead viewed through the lens of a more nuanced engagement with the psychological foundations of achievement.

Emotion regulation, resilience and empathetic connection became positioned as fundamental precursors to learning. Disadvantaged parents were accused not simply of insufficient cultivation of human capital, but of failing to equip children with a rational mindset capable of learning. Social and Emotional Aspects of Learning (SEAL) programmes were introduced in primary and secondary schools in an effort to address this perceived deficit, with the aim of encouraging personal control, motivation and 'empathy skills'. Simultaneously, the policy focus on parenting intensified through new conceptualisations of emotional impoverishment (Macvarish et al, 2015). A reanimated version of attachment theory readily explained this perceived emotional and intellectual impairment in terms of insensitive early years parenting (Thornton, 2011a). More significantly, attachment as a process began to be articulated as an observably biological process, engraved into the structures of the developing brain.

Rescuing the infant brain

While parenting support was being developed as a key plank of New Labour's policy reforms in the 1990s, social investment spending in the USA was coming under increasing attack. Evaluations showed that long-standing programmes like Head Start (the model for Sure Start) had little impact on measurable outcomes for children and many on the political right were dismissing the model as waste of money. Advocates for childhood investment countered that interventions must begin at an earlier stage of development in order for them to be effective. Philanthropic organisations, such as the Carnegie Corporation and the Rob Reiner Foundation, made this argument by drawing on the language and imagery of neuroscience to suggest too much brain development had taken place by the age most interventions kicked in.

John Bruer (1999) has documented the way that this pseudoscientific explanation captured the public and political imagination, inspiring a 'common sense' attribution of social problems to deficiencies in infant brain development. Neuro rhetoric dovetailed with a broader cultural fascination with the brain and was to drive a remarkably effective public relations campaign, attracting more wealthy philanthropists, charitable foundations and high-profile public figures. Another White House conference was convened in 1997, this time by the then US President Bill Clinton and First Lady Hillary Clinton, to discuss early childhood development and the brain. In her opening address to the conference Hillary Clinton stressed the importance of new insights into the contingent biological influence of the early years noting:

> That the song a father sings to his child in the morning or the story a mother reads to her child before bed, help lay the foundation for a child's life, in turn for our nation's future.... These experiences can determine whether a child will grow up to be peaceful or violent citizens, focused

or undisciplined workers, attentive or detached parents themselves. (cited in Bruer, 1999: 4–5)

Largely disconnected from a rapidly developing academic discipline of neuroscience, US child advocacy groups sprang up claiming to 'synthesise' and make accessible the latest biological research to highlight the unique potential and risks of the first three years of life. Sensitive mothering within this window of opportunity was promoted as making or breaking a child's future, 'hardwiring' them for success or failure.

By the mid-2000s, references to infant brain development were beginning to creep into UK policy documents, often lifted wholesale from the US advocacy groups (Macvarish et al, 2015). Such claims supplemented an already thriving policy consensus around the social and economic significance of parenting. Their apparent grounding in science carried its own momentum, proving irresistibly appealing to a variety of UK-based philanthropists, politicians and public figures. Camila Batmanghelidjh, founder of the ill-fated charity Kids Company, was inspired to spend millions of the organisation's funds on brain scan research after receiving a 'sheaf of papers' from Prince Charles suggesting that childhood neglect changed brain structure (White, 2015). Her aim was to prove that the deprived young people who used Kids Company were psychologically damaged by their parents and required specialist therapeutic help. She was vocal and passionate in her promotion of this theory and lack of evidence from her scanning studies did little to dent her conviction.

Also captivated were the Conservative MP (later Work and Pensions Minister) Iain Duncan Smith and the Labour MP Graham Allen. Sharing Batmanghelidjh's belief in a culturally and biologically damaged underclass, both politicians found accounts of infant brain science compelling. As the first rumblings of the global financial crisis were being felt, Duncan Smith and Allen were brought together by the Wave Trust, a philanthrocapitalist organisation, to co-produce a paper attributing violence, low intelligence and poverty to the brain-stunting consequences of poor 'maternal attunement' (Allen and Duncan Smith, 2008). As instigators and ghost authors of this publication, the Wave Trust began an unobtrusive but highly effective campaign to promote and spread this biologised cycle-of-deprivation narrative. They urged that 'root causes' of social disorder rather than its symptoms be tackled. As we discuss in more detail in Chapter Four, the Wave Trust campaigned within the higher echelons of power, promising that saving the brains of disadvantaged infants would slash costs to the public purse (Wave Trust, 2005).

Austerity and early intervention

In the wake of the financial crisis and under the auspices of a new Conservative-led Coalition government, economic theories became further psychologised and embedded within policy making (Davies, 2012). New attempts were made to envisage and commandeer the social and emotional as underpinning 'judicious' choices that sustain the political equilibrium. More specifically, educational initiatives to embed emotional and social skills in the school curriculum morphed into a Victorian-flavoured preoccupation with the development of 'character'. This notion was a slippery, inchoate vision of purposeful determination, self-direction and restraint, with a 'military ethos', most often projected on to white, public school boys (see DfE, 2014). At a broader level, public policy experimented with psychologised techniques of 'soft paternalism', for example through the commissioning of a 'Behavioural Insights Team', widely known as the 'nudge unit' (Jones et al, 2013).

But in the realm of family policy 'nudge' became shove as an austerity that was driven by moral and political ideas resulted in brutal cuts to New Labour's social investment spending (Edwards and Gillies, 2016). Efforts to regulate the minds and brains of children became more assertive and explicitly targeted on disadvantaged mothers of under-2-year-olds. As funding for children's centres and other universal services was slashed, creative appropriations of neuroscience were systematically worked into key Coalition government child and family policy documents, justifying a narrowing down and intensification of intervention (for example, see Field, 2010; Allen, 2011a, 2011b; Munro, 2011; Tickell, 2011). Envisaged in terms of an inoculation against irrationality and personal pathology, early intervention was firmly directed at those viewed as most likely to raise problem children.

A government commission review on 'Child Poverty and Life Chances' concluded 'the development of a baby's brain is affected by the attachment to their parents' and that brain growth is 'significantly reduced' in inadequately parented children (Field, 2010: 41). Similarly, the highly influential Allen review into early intervention called for urgent government action on the basis that 'brain architecture' is set during the first years, inside and outside the womb, with the 'wrong type' of parenting profoundly affecting children's 'emotional wiring' (Allen, 2011a: xii). After the English riots of 2011 were diagnosed by the government as a 'crisis in parenting skills', a 'Troubled Families Unit' was established, with the aim of 'gripping' and 'turning around' parents identified as the wellspring of social disorder (mainly the sick, poor and disabled). In addition the Family Nurse Partnership programme (FNP – see Chapters One and Four) was tasked with breaking intergenerational cycles of deprivation. It was massively expanded in the wake of the riots to train targeted mothers to parent 'sensitively' for the sake of their children's neural development.

These and other simplistic misappropriations of neuroscience, rooted in the strategically developed claims of the US child advocacy groups, rapidly acquired the status of unchallenged fact in political, policy and practitioner circles. In 2013, an All-Party Parliamentary Group 'From Conception to Age Two' was founded, with support from all the major political organisations (co-chaired by Caroline Lucas from the Green Party). The Wave Trust acted as the group secretariat, producing a cross-party manifesto that called for 'every baby to receive sensitive and responsive care from their main caregivers in the first years of life' (Leadsom et al, 2013: 8). The group's recommendations essentially amounted to greater monitoring of new mothers and intervention for those deemed insufficiently 'attuned'. Without these safeguards, the group warned there would be 'another generation of disadvantage, inequality and dysfunction (BBC, 2015). The manifesto included a foreword from Sally Davies, the Chief Medical Officer, decrying the 'cycle of harm' and declaring that 'science is helping us to understand how love and nurture by caring adults is hard wired into the brains of children'.

Infant brain determinism calcified into policy orthodoxy, impervious to the dubious provenance and misleading nature of the 'science' in question (see Chapter One). Risk, as opposed to need, became the key justification for family services, with the defence of children's future prospects driving increasingly fervent and uncompromising forms of action. As Brid Featherstone and colleagues (2014a) outline, an 'unholy alliance' formed between early intervention and child protection, shored up by neuroscientifically embellished narratives of 'now or never'. This approach chimed with broader austerity-inspired caricatures of the feckless poor, and children from disadvantaged families increasingly became subject to a morally charged level of state surveillance. Concern that poor parents might wreak permanent damage on their children has since been reinforced through legislative changes criminalising an ill-defined category of 'emotional neglect' (Williams, 2014), and the introduction of timescales to speed up care proceedings (Featherstone and Bywaters, 2014). Following these changes and several high-profile child abuse cases, a steep increase began in the numbers of children taken from their families and placed into state care, with official statistics reaching new records year on year (DfE, 2015).

Meanwhile, government ministers have pursued a strategy designed to accelerate and escalate the numbers of children made available for adoption. New guidance and funding promoting the swift removal of 'at-risk' children and their resettlement with a new family was issued to local authorities in 2011. Michael Gove, then Conservative Education Minister in the Coalition government responsible for crafting legislative reforms on the issue, emphasised the need for 'social workers to feel empowered to use robust measures with those parents who won't shape up'. Hailing the transformative powers of adoption he pledged to address the 'cruel rationing of human love for those most in need' (Gove, 2012). A new 'foster to adopt clause' was enshrined in the 2014 Children and Families Act, requiring looked-after children to be placed with prospective new families before the onset of legal procedures.

Rates of adoption initially rose to record levels, only to fall back sharply when the Court of Appeal issued a stern judgment rebuking inattention to human rights (*Family Law Week*, 2013). Brid Featherstone and Paul Bywaters (2014) point out that an ideological commitment to adoption is being pursued alongside unprecedented cuts to family support that have left many parents without adequate resources to care for their children. Particular criticism has been directed at the UK from the European Council for removing children from mothers who had experienced domestic violence and depression. Nevertheless, the subsequent dip in numbers was widely described as a 'crisis' by the media, and as a 'tragedy' by the then Prime Minister, David Cameron (*The Guardian*, 2015). Under the 2016 Education and Adoption Act, the government can intervene directly to speed up local authority adoption services. In the context of austerity, adoption is promoted as financially prudent, morally right and transformative for the children concerned (Narey, 2011). Alternative, humane models of child protection addressing the economic, material and social support needs of struggling families have been increasingly marginalised in the context of 'shape up or ship out' ultimatums (Featherstone et al, 2014a).

Back to the future? From risk to resilience

As the neoliberal paradigm that stresses the primacy of the market and government support for it has been buffeted by global economic crises, children have been increasingly targeted as a core resource through which market-based rationality can be anchored. This has played out through a revival of Victorian themes about the importance of nurturing personal traits of determination and resilience, alongside a renewed mission to rescue poor children from their irredeemable parents. This represents more than a harking back to another age. A different political agenda as well as more contemporary sensibilities and concerns around the psychological development of the young, the prevention of permanent harm and the responsibility of parents and the state, has positioned children as national capital. In turn, this has rendered them public property, justifying the policing of parents in the name of early intervention. As such the state is mobilised on behalf of the market to secure the production of clear thinking, flexible, self-directed brains able to withstand the pressures of a global competitive system.

More significantly, 21st-century neoliberalism has become entirely detached from the classical liberal belief that market-based logic is rooted in human nature and realisable only when free from the distortions of the state (Soss et al, 2011). Instead market behaviour is perceived as learnt rather than natural, requiring the firm hand of government to secure the future though childhood intervention. Evaluations of personhood that were once essentially moral have since been re-presented in terms of emotional and cognitive capabilities. Traditional understandings of 'character' conveyed strong notions of moral virtue, whereas contemporary invocations denote personal competence and wellbeing. Meanwhile the process of childhood development itself has become deeply moralised as an aspirational goal rather than an end in itself. Kathryn Ecclestone (2012) notes that the imperative has shifted to the process of acquiring traits defined as character, with the onus placed on the development of appropriate capabilities. Laissez-faire optimism that poverty and destitution would be eradicated through a strengthening of moral fibre has been replaced by a more pessimistic drive to equip developing minds and brains with the psychological tools to endure uncertainty, hardship and distress.

This reconfiguration and redeployment of Victorian morality in relation to children has followed through into old-style practices of child rescue. Tussles are now over brains rather than souls, but the impassioned justifications for action remain remarkably similar in tone if not content. Legislative efforts to increase adoption have been widely described as a 'crusade', with a 'loving home' offered by a white middle-class family uncritically presented as best for the child (Barn, 2013). Leading the call for greater numbers of children to be taken from their unsatisfactory parents was Martin Narey, a chief executive of Barnardo's until he retired to become the government's 'adoption tsar' in 2011. Unlike his predecessor Thomas Barnardo, Narey's mission is pre-emptive rather than rehabilitative, aimed at increasing the removal of babies at birth to prevent them being damaged beyond repair by inadequate parents. This reflects the particular significance accorded to time and risk within the rationale of building human capital. Concern is projected onto what children will become in the future rather than what they are experiencing in the here and now. While child-centric Victorian reformers expressed moral repugnance at the suffering of vulnerable children, contemporary child savers denounce the negative effects deprivation will have on their later life chances. Narey is explicit about this in his 'blueprint' for adoption reform (2011, 1.11.11):

> I have intentionally talked about productivity even though I'm aware that many practitioners object to the application of such a term to an issue as sensitive as a child's future. But this is very much about productivity because delay is so damaging to children.

As this chapter has demonstrated, children's development has been targeted as raw potential since the late 19th century, with varying political and economic models driving frameworks of intervention. Consistent across time has been the notion that family relationships can be re-engineered, optimised or replaced to tackle social and structural problems. Wealthy philanthropists and social reformers, in particular, have been instrumental in championing simple solutions that promise to breed out poverty and crime at the level of the family without recourse to redistributive solutions. Theorising around degenerate character, physical weakness, genetic inferiority and psychological maladjustment represents efforts to tackle the shortcomings of capitalism by nurturing stronger, more resilient citizens for the national good. The contemporary policy preoccupation with sub-optimal infant brains is merely the latest incarnation of a long-standing conviction held by the rich and powerful. In the next chapter, we delve deeper into the claims about brain development by proponents of early years intervention.

Note

1 This chapter is a revised version of material from Gillies, V. and Edwards, R. (2017) '"What about the children?" Re-engineering citizens of the future', in J. Pykett, R. Jones and M. Whitehead (eds) *Psychological governance and public policy*, Abingdon: Routledge.

THREE

Rescuing the infant brain

In this chapter we examine the rationale underpinning early years intervention and subject the claimed evidence base to deeper critical scrutiny. Highlighted in particular is the use and misuse of developmental neuroscience as a justificatory framework for family intervention. We explore how brain claims came to define and propel a campaigning movement for early intervention in the UK. We begin by examining how early intervention functions as a logical expression of social investment policy models. As principles of need and mutual obligation have given way to an emphasis on building capacity and managing risk, the minutiae of infant experience has acquired a central significance in policy. This is despite the sparse evidence to support the formative influence of early years parenting.

The quiet revolution: social investment and the 'Third Way'

When New Labour were swept to power in 1997 social investment policy models were taking hold unobtrusively in a quiet revolution across Europe (Hernerijck, 2015). In the UK social investment became a core component of Tony Blair's 'Third Way' politics, articulated as a need to re-direct government expenditure from traditional welfare towards productive policy investment in human capital. Children assumed a new strategic importance as vectors of a sustainable capitalism in which economic growth would remain high while risks became opportunities. The young would be enabled to drive a flexible knowledge-based service economy, while managing their own risks (low pay, precarious contracts, shifting demands for skills).

After the sustained 'roll back' of the state engineered by previous Conservative governments, New Labour's social investment model was widely embraced as progressive and egalitarian. In 1999 Tony Blair pledged to eliminate child poverty by 2020, reflecting a conviction that targeting interventions at poor children would secure a more flexible economy in the future (Lister, 2006). This instrumental goal also framed New Labour's broader concern with tackling social exclusion and raising educational attainment. At the centre of this policy rationale was a redefining of parenting as a key determinant of children's future life chances, and as such a legitimate focus for state intervention. This meant cutting across traditional understandings of family life as outside the remit of state involvement in all but extreme circumstances.

Under New Labour a powerful moral argument was fashioned on the grounds of promoting both social order and justice, with parenting portrayed as holding the key to a safer and fairer society. This relied on a common-sense framing of parenting as a 'skill' that must be learnt. Detached from any appreciation of structural context, culture or values, good parenting was presented as set of neutral and natural techniques that could reduce crime, anti-social behaviour and poverty while increasing the social mobility and life chances of poor children. Following this reasoning the state has a responsibility to regulate and enforce good parenting for the sake of the nation and its vulnerable children. The guiding policy principles of prevention and early intervention began to take shape.

New Labour's emphasis on children was characterised by a passionate rhetoric about social justice. But rather than addressing inequality they sought to responsiblise the excluded and promote social mobility. Poor families were to be coerced back into the ranks of the included by reforming their motivations and personal qualities to suit a low-wage, insecure job market. Parenting interventions were intended to regulate children's development and inculcate particular skills, knowledge and values. Policy interventions were directed at families to secure a future return on state investment rather than to address social injustice in the here and now. As a result the yardstick for measuring the value of particular policies became more technical and economic focused, based on cost–benefit analysis and calculating future projections. Policy evaluations took on a greater significance as Tony Blair committed his government to 'evidence-based policy' as part of a modernising agenda: 'What counts is what works,' he asserted in the 1997 Labour Party manifesto.[1]

In this rhetoric, evidence-based policy and practice are presented as self-evidently positive and progressive, thereby silencing any dissent before it can even be formed. Behind this appeal to 'common sense' is a managerialist approach to governance. Social values and moral issues are reduced to matters of technical rationality and every social problem is assumed to have an evidence-based solution within reach. As Martyn Hammersley (2007) points out, accepting that research has value for practice is not the same as accepting the logics of evidence-based practice, but the two are conflated to the extent that it becomes difficult to critique the latter without sounding irrational (who could possibly object to basing decisions on evidence?). The effect is to shift the terms of debate subtly but definitively away from any consideration of the merits or detriments of tying policy and practice to 'evidence', towards a concerted focus on what the evidence says and how best to implement it. Central to this manoeuvre is the lauding of an apparently objective realm of research capable of generating incontrovertible truths. This in itself is a problematic concept, but at a more fundamental level policy and practice can never simply mainline knowledge in this way.

Facts are always filtered through a politically grounded value system, guiding assessments of whether an action or intervention 'works' (Rutter, 2013). Before policies are informed by 'evidence', parameters are already drawn, problem narratives are constructed and any 'facts' must fit within this ideologically contained agenda. In the process evidence becomes cut adrift from political debates involving interests and power, while social justice, material conditions and social inequalities are obscured (Edwards et al, 2015a). More specifically, political aims have been increasingly disguised as 'hard science' through an appropriation of the language, methods and rationale of biomedicine. Attempts to transcend messy, contestable ethical and moral dimensions of social policy have largely centred on the establishment of a hierarchy of evidence and the valorisation of a particular technique: the 'gold standard' randomised controlled trial (RCT).

RCTs have a long and distinguished history in the field of clinical medicine, but as many scientists have pointed out they are severely limited in their application to real-world complexity (Wolff, 2000; Cartwright, 2007; Pearce et al, 2015). As well as the crisis of replicability due to the vagaries of changing context or statistical practice that we pointed out in Chapter One, policy interventions tend to be staffed by a variety of individuals with varying skills, characteristics, experience and motivation – and thus unlike administering a carefully calculated dose of an active chemical substance. Further, social policy initiatives tend to be delivered in the community, and often in completely different settings, contexts and buildings. Fundamentally, no amount of training can standardise human relationality and indeed many would argue that contingent, responsive engagements lie at the heart of effective family support (Cottam, 2011; Featherstone et al, 2014). While these constraints do not preclude the careful and contained use of RCT models in a social policy context, they do expose the dubious grounds upon which the 'gold standard' claim is based.

In 2013, the National Institute for Health and Clinical Excellence (NICE), the national body originally set up to assess which drugs and treatments should be made available through the NHS, had its remit extended to social care. In the same year the Conservative-led Coalition government announced the introduction of a 'what works' network of policy evidence centres covering health, education, crime reduction, local growth and early intervention. Designed to act as a 'NICE for social policy' (Puttick, 2012), the network is hailed as promoting 'effective and efficient services across the public sector at national and local levels' (Cabinet Office, 2014). Within the politically grounded objectives predefining what it means to 'work', however, the inductive remit of the centres promises self-validating policies. The value of a policy direction itself is rarely in question. The very first designated 'What Works Centre' was the Early Intervention Foundation (EIF), founded not to establish whether early intervention works – that is a pre-given assumption – but to gather evidence to support the effectiveness of particular programmes.

The EIF was first proposed by Graham Allen in his 2011 government-commissioned review as a method of embedding the philosophy of early intervention (Allen, 2011a, 2011b). Launched in 2013 with a £3.5 million grant from the Department for Education,[2] the EIF swiftly assumed charitable status, receiving donations from a range of government departments, philanthropists and businesses as well as the Economic and Social Research Council. Unlike the other 'What Works Centres', the EIF assumed a twofold role combining a proselytising of the merits of early intervention with assessing evidence for the programmes. This objective is described on their 2016 national conference programme under the strapline 'Right for Children, Better for the Economy':

> Our three core functions are to assess, advise and advocate. We assess the evidence that exists on Early Intervention, provide information and tools to enhance knowledge and add to the existing evidence base ... We advise local areas on 'what works' in local policy and practice through bespoke advice, support and events ... We advocate to local and national decision-makers and make a strong case for Early Intervention.[3]

The 'vision' of a future defined by early intervention set out in the 2011 Allen report was structured around the introduction of rigorous new methodology to establish cost-effective programmes. Services should be evaluated by at least one RCT or two quasi-experimental designs.[4] To meet this requirement services were advised to become commensurable with this particular experimental paradigm by ensuring their design and content are amenable to measurement. As Brid Featherstone and colleagues bluntly observe: 'The interventions must be made to fit the method, not the other way round. This is not science this is dogma' (2014b: 68). The EIF applied their 'rigorous methodology' test to produce an online guidebook for commissioners, listing programmes that are deemed to work. Most are international, trademarked models with an RCT evidence base located abroad (predominantly in the USA). Home-grown, locally rooted programmes of many years standing did not make the grade because expensive RCT trials were beyond their capacity.

As we noted in Chapter One, however, several of the apparently best evidenced programmes lauded by the EIF have been subject to UK-based RCTs, notably the Family Nurse Partnership (FNP) programme, and found to have little benefit in a British context. Another disappointing result emerged from a recent independent UK-based trial of the 'Promoting Alternative Thinking Strategies' (PATHS) programme, which had also been awarded top marks by the EIF on the basis of multiple US-based RCTs. PATHS is designed to develop social and emotional competences and reduce aggressive behaviour in children. Yet a cluster RCT covering 45 Manchester primary schools concluded that PATHS did not have a positive impact upon children's attainment and could not be considered value for money[5]. Regardless, the EIF continues to validate and promote the 'evidence base' for both the FNP and PATHS. This is testament to the powerful and ingrained ideology of social investment driving early intervention as political solution.

Commandeering infant brains

The 'evidence' for the concept of early intervention (as opposed to particular programmes) is placed beyond question through the appeal to biological science. This is the contention that children develop faulty 'brain architecture' if they receive sub-optimal nurturing that we have already discussed. Hard science is invoked to override and delegitimise alternative understandings of social problems and their solutions. Assertions about the imperative to intervene early to ensure that babies' and children's brains are not damaged by poor parenting, and thus prevent poverty and disadvantage, seeped into policy literature across government departments, political parties, thinktanks and professional guidance. As we show in Chapter Six, factoids about infant brain development now structure the training and everyday routines of a wide range of health, education and early years practitioners.

Given its extensive reach and influence on British social policy, this account of formative and fragile infant brain development deserves considerably greater scrutiny. As was outlined in the previous chapter, claims that the early years are determinative can be traced back to US child advocacy groups. Brain science was first appropriated to argue for American state funding where there was very little provision available. John Bruer (1999) meticulously details how a rhetoric of neuroscience was harnessed, almost accidentally, as a highly persuasive public relations (PR) vehicle. Tracing the policy origins of the 'myth of the first three years' to a report commissioned by the Carnegie Foundation, Bruer described how the insertion of a few paragraphs linking brain development to early care and future outcomes ignited public interest and came to wield significant political influence. Neuroscience was requisitioned to market a social investment model, with brain development illustrating the growth of human capital. Economic reasoning inspired by the Heckman equation described in previous chapters, combined with psychotherapeutic tropes and emotive appeals to child protection and a formidable lobbying group materialised as a result, comprised of philanthropists, celebrities, politicians and the media.

As Bruer (1999) recounts, the film director Rob Reiner was a key proponent of this early years movement. In 1997 he set up the I Am Your Child Foundation with his wife, with the objective of spreading the message about infant brain development and the critical 0 to 3 window for development. The Reiners, in partnership with major philanthropic foundations (Carnegie, Dana and Heinz), consulted PR specialists to assemble a persuasive business case designed to garner corporate, professional and public support. Great care went into a media strategy, communicating ideas in a simple and appealing way, using mechanistic metaphors of 'brain circuits' and 'hardwiring'. A website offering advice on parenting and brain science was launched, featuring tips on how to encourage early learning. For example, the children's TV channel Nickelodeon was commandeered to produce several 'I Am Your Child' public service announcements on the importance of the first three years, featuring characters from the popular *Rugrats* cartoon series.

The power of neuroscience to convince and motivate was well understood by child advocacy groups lobbying for greater state investment in the young. Chief among these was the Harvard Center for the Developing Child, founded in 2006 by an academic paediatrician, Jack Shonkoff. The centre has pursued an explicit aim of 'catalysing' biological evidence to support particular policy objectives in achieving breakthrough outcomes for children facing adversity. In partnership with the FrameWorks Institute, an organisation working to 'reframe' social and scientific topics to the benefit of policy advocates, the Harvard Center for the Developing Child set about developing 'simplifying models' to 'help plug cognitive holes' (Shonkoff and Bales, 2011). FrameWorks' polling established that there was a widespread belief among Americans that children can recover from abuse or neglect without lasting biological effects. Efforts were then directed towards correcting this 'cognitive mistake' (FrameWorks Institute, 2009) through high-impact images, videos and catchy metaphors to maximise the accessibility and persuasiveness of the message.

Wielding similar influence in the early years movement was Bruce Perry, a psychiatrist and founder of the ChildTrauma Academy, an advocacy organisation designed to 'translate emerging findings about the human brain and child development into practical implications for the ways we nurture, protect, enrich, educate and heal children'.[6] Perry's work features prominently in one of the first UK policy articulations of the brain science trope in 2008 (see Chapter One). Attributed to Graham Allen MP (Lab.) and Iain Duncan Smith MP (Con.), *Early intervention: Good parents, great kids, better citizens* (2008) embellished a broken Britain-style lament with a biological explanation rooted in the early years cause. This publication also provided the foundation for Allen's later review, which drew heavily on the carefully crafted promotional messages emanating from the Harvard Center for the Developing Child. Allen's references to 'brain architecture', 'stress hormones', 'attunement', 'sculpting the infant brain', 'window of development' and many more were lifted from the slick PR campaigns charactering the US early years movement.

Examining the brain claims

The permeation of neuroscience language into English social policy and practice was rapid and deep, accelerating after the election of the Conservative-led Coalition government in 2010. But this was a very different mobilisation of the arguments formed in the US context. While US advocates of child investment campaigned for funding in the absence of state support, the UK government's agenda was brutal austerity and drastic revoking of family services. Neuroscience was appropriated in policy to justify more efficient targeting of resources towards monitoring and regulating the parenting practices of those deemed most likely to damage their baby's brains; that is, very disadvantaged mothers. Meanwhile universal services and benefits were culled. As Jan Macvarish and colleagues (2015) note, New Labour laid the groundwork for this neurobiologised approach through their construction of parenting as a pressing policy problem. With disadvantaged parents already marked out as failing their children it was a short step towards viewing this in terms of biological inferiority. As we will outline in the following chapters, the appeal of the infant brain development narrative went far beyond confirming right-wing suspicions about an underclass. Like the eugenic movement that came before, hopes and fears across a political spectrum were contained within it.

And like the eugenic movement, the science constituting the claims bear little scrutiny. In our analysis of policy and practice documents we identified five key biologised assertions repeatedly mobilised to argue the early intervention case.

Critical periods – 'Two Is Too Late'

In 2012 Conservative MP Andrea Leadsom convened a conference on early years intervention called 'Two Is Too Late'. The focus of the event was infant brain development and the social consequences of poor early relationships. The English riots of 2011 framed the discussion, with contributions from Iain Duncan Smith MP, Camila Batmanghelidjh (Kids Company) and George Hosking (founder of the Wave Trust) highlighting the magnitude of unaddressed attachment problems. As founder of Parent Infant Partnerships, a social enterprise providing attachment therapy to mothers, Leadsom was driven by her perception of the crucial need to improve mother–infant bonding. In a piece for the Conservative Home website written shortly after the event, she presents the riots as the sobering outcome of malformed brain development.

> The worst of the rioters are charged with being void of respect and values. It is a fair accusation, but this is not simply learned behaviour from TV shows or the selfish aspects of our social culture. It's far deeper rooted than that. In fact, from the first day of a baby's life, the quality of the affection and attention he or she receives from their adult carer (usually Mum) literally shapes the way the brain develops, with profound consequences for how they will develop later in life. (Leadsom, 2012)

Over 500 delegates attended the 'Two Is Too Late' conference, representing an impressive range of local authorities, services and charities from up and down the country. Tickets for the event quickly sold out, leaving a long reserve waiting list and illustrating the powerful pull of the imperative contained within the title. The notion that potential and future outcomes are determined during a 'critical period' for infant brain development was at the very core of the US child advocacy literature. As such it occupied a key strand of John Bruer's deconstruction of 'the myth of the first three years', first published in 1999. It is telling that critical-period proponents have resolutely failed to amass any more convincing evidence since, despite the rapid pace of growth in the discipline of neuroscience (Rose and Rose, 2016).

Bruer (1999) traced the concept of critical periods of infant brain development back to Nobel Prize-winning research conducted on kittens originating in the 1960s (see Hubel and Wiesel, 2004). It was discovered that deprivation of visual stimulus (suturing kittens' eyelids shut) could cause functional blindness if experienced during a 'vulnerable critical period' beginning shortly after birth and lasting for two months. As Bruer patiently explains, critical-period constraints exist only for very specific kinds of development, such as the formation of the visual cortex. Neuroscientists distinguish between two types of brain plasticity: experience-expectant and experience-dependent. Developing organisms are primed to expect particular kinds of stimuli around which neural responses can be shaped and refined. The visual system is a good example of experience-expectant development. Some form of visual stimulation is required for normal neural formation, with this basic environmental exposure enabling a fine tuning of neural development. As Bruer points out, experience-expectant plasticity and critical-period constraints apply only to species-wide and species typical traits, like vision and language. Very severe aberration (equivalent to suturing kittens' eyelids) would be required to inhibit this process.

Experience-dependent plasticity, however, refers at its most basic to the activity of learning, a capacity more recently discovered by neuroscientists to be retained throughout the bulk of an individual's lifetime. Early years advocates conflated experience-dependent learning in infants with experience-expectant development, extending critical-period reasoning to a variety of traits and behaviours. Moreover, they applied a seemingly arbitrary timescale of the first three years of life, regardless of the complexity of neuroscientific findings suggesting that critical periods for vision and language stretch over a considerably longer period. Faced with Bruer's critique, the US early years advocates largely abandoned the term 'critical period', replacing it with 'sensitive period' to make roughly similar claims. But in the policy transmission across the Atlantic the urgency of intervention was strategically re-hyped. The 'window of opportunity' was shrunk to just 18 months. 'Two Is Too Late' rhetoric warned of irreparable brain damage to emphasise the case for early intervention. For example, the Allen report reproduces a 'house building' analogy from the PR-proofed Harvard Center for the Developing Child:

> Just as in the construction of a house, certain parts of the formative structure of the brain need to happen in a sequence and need to be adequate to support the long-term developmental blueprint The estimated prime window for emotional development is up to 18 months, by which time the foundation of this has been shaped by the way in which the prime carer interacts with the child. (cited in Allen, 2011a: 14)

More explicit references to 'critical periods' featured in a review of evidence on child development and the impact of maltreatment, commissioned by the Department for Education and the Family Justice Council. The *Decision-making within a child's timeframe* (Brown and Ward, 2012) report was designed to advise professionals adjudicating over care orders. Claiming to examine the neuroscientific literature, the authors conclude there is a short window of opportunity for children:

> At certain times the impact of experience can be irreversible: these are a special class of sensitive period known as *critical periods*. Studies on cats, dogs, monkeys and geese as well as investigations of bird song and human language development have confirmed that critical and sensitive periods are a major phenomenon in brain and behavioural development. (Brown and Ward, 2012: 40, original emphasis)

The wording in this document is careful and slippery. Many researchers do believe there are critical and sensitive periods in emotional and limbic systems, but this is not on the basis of neuroscience. The reference to experience-expectant development in animals very effectively obscures the lack a scientific foundation for the claims being made. As Sue White and David Wastell (2013) contend, this kind of 'artfully packaged knowledge' may play well in policy and practice arenas, but potentially to the cost of children and families, particularly if babies are being removed from their families on the basis of misleading 'evidence'.

The brain-damaging consequences of poor maternal 'attunement'

At the forefront of the early intervention movement, here and in the US, stand attachment theorists keen to translate their work in to the hard currency of neuroscience. As we discuss in Chapter Four, their interests have coincided with a political and economic order, propelling a set of ideas that had largely fallen from favour back into the limelight. Bowlby's original formulation of attachment theory attracted considerable criticism, particularly in relation to its essentialist idealisation of mothering. Bowlby's archetypical nuclear family and the gender politics framing the post-war settlement became a focus for resistance as women campaigned for better nursery provision and greater employment opportunities. More fundamentally, Bowlby was also challenged on scientific grounds, with many social scientists detailing methodological flaws and lack of precision in his work (Wootton, 1959; Schaffer and Emerson, 1964; Rutter, 1972). The cultural universalism and ethnocentric assumptions inherent to the model were also exposed by US anthropologist Margaret Mead's (1962) observations that multiple caretaking of infants is the norm in many societies.

In response to these criticisms Bowlby and his colleague Mary Ainsworth reformulated attachment theory to encompass a wider range of caregivers, but in the context of increasing family diversity in the 1970s and 1980s attachment theory lost much of its influence. It was the rise of the social investment model that sparked a renewed and broad interest in attachment theory as part of the preoccupation with predicting and maximising the future outcomes of children. Theorists and practitioners began to revisit, modify and develop Bowlby and Ainsworth's work far beyond the original model. A huge volume of research has since been conducted into the broad concept of attachment, but the findings are complex and variable (for example, see Thomson, 2008: 348-65). Significantly, a considerable lack of consistency in attachment status over time has been observed, with fewer than half of children staying in the same attachment category over periods as short as six months (Meins, 2014).

Attachment status is still determined by the 'Strange Situation Test' designed by Mary Ainsworth in the 1970s, based on observing the reactions of babies or young children when their mother leaves the room. On the basis of their responses the infants are classified as either secure, avoidant-insecure, resistant insecure or disorganised. Not only is there considerable instability in these categorisations over time but also international studies point to differences across different populations. For example, high numbers of resistantly attached infants are found in Indonesia, Japan and the kibbutzim of Israel (van IJzendoorn and Kroonenberg, 1988; Zevalkink et al, 1999), while disorganised attachment is frequently found in parts of Africa and Chile (Waters and Valenzuela, 1999; True et al, 2001; Tomlinson et al, 2005). This likely reflects the variable ways children are raised in different cultures, but attachment research also highlights the significance of many other factors, including the social environment and characteristics of the child, such as temperament and genetic polymorphisms (Bernier and Meins, 2008; Clark et al, 2013). Indeed, from the perspective of Elizabeth Meins, a Professor of Psychology (and attachment expert) parent–child interaction is not a particularly good predictor of attachment (Meins, 2014).

Yet, a very particular, old-school model of attachment propels the early years intervention movement, papering over the intricacies of the research with an appeal to brain science. For example, the Allen review's emphasis on 'attunement' typifies the claims made in policy and practice literature:

> Sadly, for many parents attunement either does not come 'naturally' (because they did not receive the benefit of it themselves), or is disrupted by postnatal depression, domestic violence or other severe stresses. If a child does not experience attunement, their development is retarded, and they may lack empathy altogether.... A baby who is healthily attached to their carer can regulate their emotions as they grow older because the cortex, which exercises rational thought and control, has developed properly. Conversely, when the life of a child has been badly impacted, the cortex is underdeveloped – and the damaged child lacks an 'emotional guardian'. (2011a: 15)

But attachment as a theory cannot as yet claim an established basis in neuroscience, despite the biologised language used by proponents. As Hilary Rose and Steven Rose (2016) point out, there are no biomarkers that indicate whether a baby is or is not attached, let alone correlates for categories of attachment. As such, any association between poor 'attunement' and brain damage is highly speculative. Policy and practice documents making this claim tend to draw on four key sources to back up their arguments: the Harvard Center for the Developing Child, Bruce Perry, and psychoanalysts Allan Schore and Sue Gerhardt. Allan Schore is a psychiatrist and part of the 'neuropsychoanalysis' movement, which seeks to combine insights from neuroscience and psychodynamic theory. In particular, Schore draws attention to the maturation of neural systems associated with affect and self-regulation occurring in the right side of the brain, directly linking this to attachment. Schore and the neuropsychoanalysis movement have many eminent supporters, but it remains a controversial field, attracting criticism from neuroscientists and psychoanalysts alike. For example, Franck Ramus condemns vague analogies between psychoanalytical concepts and neuroscientific findings and wonders: 'is this not just an attempt to rehabilitate psychoanalysis by giving it a fashionable prefix and by attributing it the merits of other disciplines?' (2013: 170).

Sue Gerhardt is a psychoanalytic psychotherapist and author of the bestselling book *Why love matters: How affection shapes a baby's brain* (2004). Gerhardt draws extensively on Schore and other neuropsychoanalysts in her book, deftly weaving in the neuromyths identified by Bruer. This sundry mix of biologised concepts is embroidered with eclectic theorising, speculation, factoids and clinical anecdotes based on Gerhardt's patients. The end result is a deeply alarmist account of the fragile infant brain as dependent on assiduous, intently focused mothering for normal development. One wrong move and attachment becomes disorganised, with potentially terrible consequences such as lack of emotional regulation, depression, low self-worth and personality disorders. The violent children of the future are now babies, she notes in a chapter titled 'Original sin' (2004: 167).

Underlining and building on Gerhardt's biologised warnings about insufficiently attuned mothers was the much publicised *Baby bonds* report commissioned by the Sutton Trust, a philanthropic organisation seeking to improve social mobility through education (Sutton Trust, 2014). Released in 2014, it received mass media coverage, largely because the press release contained the startling claim that '40% of children miss out on the parenting needed to succeed in life'. The report contained no new research, but referenced a study from 2007 estimating the distribution of attachment categories in the USA. Reasserting familiar biologised tropes, insecure attachment was linked to poor prospects in later life. Meins (2014) publicly admonished the report's authors for a series of basic inaccuracies, describing it as dangerous and alarmist, but this did little to counter the hyperbolic media coverage. For example, the BBC ran with: 'The Sutton Trust study says children's early attachment to parents has far-reaching consequences for their ability to speak, learn and think.'[7]

Synaptic density and the role of stimulation

The claim that babies' brains require active, parent-led stimulation to grow adequately is often found in more directive, practitioner-based literature. It supports the provision of specific advice, for example to sing and read to babies, or to show them patterns or massage them. It also features heavily in biological accounts of health attachment. For example, in *Why Love Matters* Gerhardt states:

> The baby's brain is doing a lot of growing in the first year –
> it more than doubles in weight. The enormously increased
> glucose metabolism of the first two years of life [is] triggered
> by the baby's biochemical responses to his [sic] mother....
> Lots of positive experiences early on produce brains with
> more neuronal connections – more richly networked brains.
> We have all our neurons at birth, and we don't need to grow
> any more, but what we do need is to connect them up and
> make them work for us. With more connections, there is
> better performance and more ability to use particular areas
> of the brain. (Gerhardt, 2004: 42–3)

This process of connecting up neurones is commonly presented as a once in a lifetime opportunity to maximise the number of synapses and therefore increase intelligence. For example, the Solihull Approach training system designed for professionals working with early years and school-aged children makes the following statements:

> By the age of two years, the infant has as many neural
> connections as an adult. These early years of infancy
> are very important, as the final number of neural
> connections can increase or decrease by as much as 25%
> (Perry et al, 1995) depending on the levels of stimuli....
> We know that an adverse environment will lead to a child
> having 25% less synapses or connections in their brains
> than they could have had, while a stimulating environment
> can lead to 25% more connections. (Solihull Approach
> Resource Pack: The School Years: 73 and 99)

The striking figure of 25% does not trace back to the reference provided here. Perry et al (1995) makes no mention of synaptic density, but the 25% claim appears on websites all over the internet without any attribution or clue as to where it is derived from. More seriously, it promulgates a fundamental misunderstanding of developmental neuroscience. As Bruer explains (1999), the discovery of a developmental accumulation of synapses and a particularly rapid burst of synaptogenesis early in life was first made in the 1970s based on work with kittens and other animals. Significantly though, this process is followed by a protracted but substantial pruning of redundant synapses. Peter Huttenlocher and colleagues (1979) established similar patterns in humans by counting the synapses in 50 autopsied brains ranging in age from foetuses to 90-year-old adults. More indirect evidence for the overproduction and elimination of synapses came from measurement of glucose uptake by PET (positron emission tomography) brain scans (Chugani et al, 1987).

Babies have approximately the same synaptic densities in their cortex as adults, and the volume rises to a peak before surplus connections are eradicated. That these measurements say little about neural function in relation to learning or behaviour should be obvious given that 2-year-olds are not more intelligent than adults. Gerhardt's claim that 'with more connections, there is better performance' is deeply misleading. As synaptic density decreases learning improves, and if the pruning phase is insufficiently extensive cognitive ability is likely to suffer. For example, higher than normal synaptic densities have been found in inherited fragile-X syndrome, a genetic disorder associated with severe intellectual disability (Bruer, 1999; Scott et al, 2000). And, more fundamentally, this process of overproduction and elimination of synapses appears to be under genetic rather than environmental control. As Bruer concludes:

> Parents and caretakers should take some solace from this. Brainpower does not depend on the number of synapses formed before age 3. Environmental input, including stimulation provided by parents, neither initiates early synapse formation nor influences when or at what level synaptic densities peak. (1999: 99)

The corrosive effect of cortisol

Cortisol is the *bête noire* of the early years interventionists. It is a steroid hormone released in response to stress. Cortisol is identified within the policy and practice literature as a key mechanism inhibiting infant brain growth. The message communicated is that experiencing stress while pregnant and/or practising insufficiently attentive parenting is contra-indicated for normal development. For example, this claim is clearly set out by the Conception to Age Two All-Party Parliamentary Working Group report entitled *Building better Britons*:

> A stressful environment for a mother during pregnancy results in production of the stress hormone cortisol. This hormone crosses the placental barrier and circulates round the foetal body, overwhelming its capacity to regulate its own stress response. Professor Vivette Glover stated in her oral evidence that the impact of stress on foetal development rises in line with the 'dose' of stress experienced. Different people find different things stressful, and triggers range from quite normal everyday things to extraordinary events. Many of the effects of prenatal stress can be helped by sensitive caregiving, especially in the first year. If the mother is well attuned to her baby and responsive to his or her needs, this can help enormously with future development. (Wave Trust, 2013: 8)

The notion that such an apparently dangerous substance can be triggered by normal everyday experiences is in itself stress inducing. This works to underline the precarious nature of infant development and the need for mothers to demonstrate meticulous care and accept professional advice. And indeed professionals themselves are reminded that the biochemical effects of stress may not be immediately observable, as the Solihull Approach training system seeks to emphasise:

> Stress releases the hormone cortisol in the baby's brain, and the brain becomes sensitised to this between birth and the age of three years. Cortisol has a toxic effect on newly formed cells in the brain.... The stress hormone cortisol has been measured in the saliva of babies. Often people think that it is raised for the crying child and reduced for the passive child but the cortisol level is raised in the passive child as well, correlating inversely with the sense of felt security rather than observed behaviour. (Solihull Resource Pack, 2008: 102–8)

The reference to cortisol as 'toxic' is common (reflecting the language used by the Harvard Center for the Developing Child). It is also described as 'corrosive' and 'harmful'. You might be forgiven for thinking of cortisol as positively poisonous, but in fact the human body could not function without it. Cortisol has multiple purposes, from regulating blood sugar, salt and water balance, to learning and memory (Rose and Rose, 2016). Any stimulation, including excitement, running around a playground or laughing hard will likely elevate levels in the body. Conversely, low cortisol produces serious symptoms and has been linked to behavioural problems in some boys (for example, McBurnett, 2000). And, contrary to the impression given by the Solihull Approach, cortisol levels are actually very difficult to assess in children. Blood levels vary through the day and across the life course, and there are very large variations between individuals. As Rose and Rose note, 'baseline levels' measured mid-morning, may vary fivefold between one person and another' (2016: 74).

In flagging up the dangers of raised cortisol levels, the early interventionists are largely extrapolating from animal experiments suggesting that high cortisol triggers negative physiological and neurobiological impacts. But, as White and Wastell (2015) point out, this body of research has produced contradictory findings and there is limited agreed knowledge on the subject, with some scientists suggesting that high cortisol may actually foster resilience in monkeys (Lyons and Parker, 2007). Human studies have found that post-traumatic stress disorder can impact on brain structures, but this evidence comes from war veterans rather than infants (Wastell and White, 2012) and did not involve measuring cortisol. Research conducted on children suffering extreme neglect and abuse also suggests that in some cases neural pathways can be affected, but as Rose and Rose conclude: 'Measuring cortisol levels as an index of stress, is not dissimilar to looking for a lost key under a street light because nothing can be seen in the darkness' (2016: 75).

The stunted pre-frontal cortex: black holes and primitive brains

The iconic image of the 'loved brain' next to the 'neglected brain' that introduced this book is one of the most powerful representations of the pre-frontal cortex 'black hole' claim. Having placed the Perry image on the front covers of his reports Graham Allen underscores the narrative of damage, asserting:

> Specialists viewing CAT scans of the key emotional areas in the brains of abused or neglected children have likened the experience to looking at a black hole. In extreme cases the brains of abused children are significantly smaller than the norm, and the limbic system (which governs the emotions) may be 20–30 per cent smaller and contain fewer synapses.
> (Allen, 2011b: 16)

Gerhardt also describes the brains of Romanian orphans as having a 'virtual black hole where their orbitofrontal cortex should be' (2004: 38). Allen's statement carries no supporting reference so it is not entirely clear which children or brains he is referring to. Nevertheless, the reader instinctively connects his claim with the misleading image on the cover, although as Rose and Rose (2016) point out, the ill-defined Perry brains suggested a far more dramatic difference than anything ever seen in the desperately impoverished orphans.

Gerhardt does provide a reference to a paper by Chugani et al (2001) describing the results of PET scans measuring brain glucose metabolism in 10 Romanian orphans adopted by Americans. While the study pointed to dysfunction in a number of brain regions, the 'black hole' metaphor is a melodramatic description of this research. Evidence of brain damage in the context of these extreme conditions is not surprising, particularly since the children were also malnourished and commonly suffering from ill-health in the institutions (Wastell and White, 2012). What is surprising, encouraging and almost entirely absent from the early intervention literature is the dramatic recoveries made by the institutionalised children that were adopted. Follow up research at ages 4, 6, 11 and 15 suggests that those adopted before the age of six months experienced no ill effects at all, while only a third of those placed for adoption beyond the age of six months faced problems that warranted the intervention of professional educational, psychological or psychiatric services. A substantial minority of the children did experience severe developmental problems, but they too demonstrated very substantial catch-up after being adopted (Rutter et al, 2010).

More fundamentally though, it is difficult to see where the continuity might lie between infants experiencing such extreme adversity and mothers failing to properly 'attune' to children's emotional needs. That early interventionists so regularly resort to such a disingenuous comparison highlights the paucity of evidence available to them. Instead of engaging with challenging research findings a broader Heckman equation type of logic about brain growth is mobilised, tying the higher functional regions of the cortex to a cumulative foundational period of development. Each stage of development is claimed to be dependent on the quality of the preceding stage, as this quote from the *Decision-making within a child's timeframe* report asserts:

> The sequence of brain development follows a logical pattern. Development of the higher regions does not commence before the connections in the lower regions have been completed. This is because the higher levels in the hierarchy depend on reliable information from the lower levels in order to accomplish their functions. Impaired development in the lower regions of the brain will therefore have a negative impact on the development of the functions of the higher regions, such as language, empathy, regulation of emotions and reasoning. (Brown and Ward, 2012: 37)

This account is accompanied by a colourful, explanatory graph, reproduced with the permission of the Harvard Center for the Developing Child. The report goes on to claim that: 'extended exposure to threatening situations can compromise the development of executive function skills' (2012: 40), leaving children to rely on their 'primitive' limbic system. This notion of higher and lower brains is found throughout practitioner literature, featuring prominently, for example, in the Solihull Approach and Gerhardt's *Why love matters*. The term 'primitive' is used to imply an evolutionary order, with parts of the brain evolving from basic beginnings millions of years ago. Gerhard even describes a layered three-brained system in which a basic 'reptilian brain' (brain stem and sensorimotor cortex) was supplemented with a 'mammalian emotional brain' (amygdala and limbic system) and later topped with human neocortex.

At an elementary level this account promotes a misunderstanding of the process of evolution as linear and progressive, rather than a continual adaptation of organisms to their surroundings. The human brain did not evolve on top of a monkey's. Instead, monkeys and humans share a common ancestor, with both evolving some 25 million years ago. More importantly, distinctions between emotional and rational brains vastly oversimplify the complex interlinked structures characterising brain function, as the neuroscience blogger Jason Pipkin makes clear in an exasperated post:

> There is not just a 'primitive, emotional brain' and a 'complex, intellectual brain'. That is so ... wrong. Factually

wrong.... Let me be clear. You have ONE brain. One. It has many parts, which is to say that humans looking at brains have found ways to subdivide them into various areas and regions and structures and whatnot. Regardless of all that, the whole damn thing works together. It's one big circuit that does emotion, rationality, sensation, movement, the whole shebang. There isn't a simplistic 'emotion' part and an 'intellectual' part. The cortex is involved in emotions and feelings. The basal ganglia are involved in cognition. In fact, the whole idea of splitting emotion and reason into two separate camps is fraught, as emotion turns out to be critical in reasoning tasks like decision-making. (Pipkin, 2013)

Aside from these inaccuracies, the hierarchical account of brain development promoted by early interventionists vastly overemphasises the role parents play in securing normal function for their child. According to Gerhardt, 'It is not a matter of waiting patiently for your baby to develop an orbitofrontal cortex as a matter of course', after which she adds ominously, 'There is nothing automatic about it' (2004: 38). Of course if this were true there would be a significant number of the population lacking in this vital area of their brain, corresponding perhaps to the poorly attached 40% estimated by the Sutton Trust to have missed out on the parenting needed to succeed in life (Washbrook et al, 2014). Brain scans show no such damage, despite the contrary impression given by the misleading Perry brains. As Wastell and White incisively observe:

> The developing infant brain is not a uniquely fragile object, a medical emergency waiting to happen. The danger of such medicalisation is its crushing of the debate we need to have as a humane society about where and how the state should tread, and its limits. (2012: 409)

Prevention science: epigenetics and shrunken brains

While the early intervention movement was largely founded on the use and abuse of established neuroscience, a neoliberalised social investment paradigm has come to exert a powerful influence on the very direction of science itself. There is currently a vast amount of research exploring early childhood with a view to optimising development and preventing 'dysfunction'. Termed 'prevention science', much of this work is framed by broader rationales imposed by policy makers and philanthropists.

In the USA, budget cuts to publicly funded research have been offset by an influx of private donors, leading some to suggest that science is increasingly shaped by the particular preferences of individuals with huge amounts of money (Broad, 2014). Neuroscience in particular has been a clear beneficiary, receiving substantial sums from private as well as public sources. For example, Amazon CEO Jeff Bezos established the Bezos Center for Neural Circuit Dynamics at Princeton University with the aim of 'understanding deep behaviors, more effective learning methods for young children and neural disorders'.[8]

In the UK public funding has played a more explicit role in pursuing an early intervention agenda, with, for example, a research council investment of £3 million to explore formative social, biological and behavioural interactions in the early years.[9] Charitable money has also been directed towards similar goals by, for instance, the Nuffield Foundation[10] and the Big Lottery. But at a more diffuse cultural level, the 'common-sense' logic of early intervention inspires research questions and moulds interpretations of results. Scientists operate within culturally and politically specific frameworks, meaning they draw on normative contentions about the social world. Many have embraced the ideals of early years prevention science as a progressive development, viewing it as offering effective solutions to debilitating social problems. As such, increasing numbers of scientists are diligently seeking to reduce complex social phenomena like poverty to biomolecular levels.

There is now an extensive body of research seeking to root disadvantage in the biology of early years development. Strikingly few leads have emerged despite the volume of work. One area receiving much attention is behavioural epigenetics, with much of the enthusiasm revolving around the 'mothering' practices of rats. Epigenetics is essentially the study of inherited changes to the way genes are read by cells, with these changes affecting their expression rather than their genetic code. More simply, epigenetic changes are envisaged as environmentally driven biological mechanisms which can switch genes on or off. Michael Meaney (for example, 2014) and his colleagues generated much excitement when they demonstrated epigenetic differences in gene expression between rat pups who were licked and groomed frequently by their mothers and those that were not. This marked the beginning of what Greg Miller termed 'the seductive allure of behavioural epigenetics' (2010: 24). Controversies around the science rage, with many scientists decrying the 'hype' surrounding the field (Juengstemail et al, 2014). Martyn Pickersgill and colleagues note the uncertainty and ambivalence characterising epigenetic debates, pointing to the way 'tentative "coulds" and hopeful "mays" commonly steer these narratives' (2013: 434). The neurogeneticist Kevin Mitchell (2014) is less equivocal in his assessment of rat-based epigenetic findings, critiquing much of the science and challenging the conclusions drawn from them.

Despite the controversy, many have been quick to apply this emergent and unsettled field (based primarily on research with rats) to early years intervention. For example, the Big Lottery Fund has invested in an evaluation of early intervention initiatives via measurement of 'epigenetic changes' (alongside cortisol measures).[11] The premature rush to prescriptive policy uses has been roundly condemned by biomedical ethicists, who suggest it opens the door to 'epi-eugenics' and a 'vicious cycle of deterministic thinking' (Juengstemail et al, 2014: 428). Nevertheless, epigenetics is increasingly found in policy and practice literature as an adjunct to misinformed brain claims and seems likely to acquire a similarly prominent pseudoscientific profile. It has already been simplified and presented to early years practitioners, for example in a national conference organised by the EIF.[12]

Another area attracting considerable interest is the impact of poverty on children's brains. A significant proportion of neuroscientific research in the USA is dedicated to the search for differences between privileged and deprived children's brains. This is driven by the assumption that poor children's lower educational attainment must be reflected in a deficient brain structure. The findings, amassed over many years, are complex, span different forms of measurement and provide few unambiguous conclusions. The largest and most influential of these studies was carried out by a team of neuroscientists who scanned 1,099 US children and adolescents (Noble et al,, 2015). Their findings suggested that cortical surface was correlated with socioeconomic status as well as parental education (measured as the length of time spent in school). The research received major media publicity and was widely reported as confirmation that poor children's brains are smaller. For example, the journal *Nature* carried the headline 'Poverty shrinks brains from birth'.[13]

While this was a carefully conducted study, the enthusiasm it attracted masked the limits of the knowledge produced, and the fact that it raised more questions than it answered. While statistically significant correlations were demonstrated, this cannot be taken to imply that socioeconomic circumstances determine brain size. As the authors point out, marked variability was found in brain structure at all socioeconomic status levels, including among the most disadvantaged children. Variability and non-linear development is a recognised characteristic of developing brains (Gogtay et al, 2004), alongside a complexity of structure–function relations in cognitive development (Crone and Ridderinkhof, 2011). Analysis of these factors was limited in the study partly because it was cross-sectional, meaning it was conducted at one particular point in time rather than across time. It is also worth noting that cortical surface area was only related to the children's performance in some of the cognitive tests they undertook.

More specifically, it is not clear which aspects of poverty might have mediated brain surface area. There are many factors associated with lack of money, including poor nutrition, inadequate housing, fewer opportunities for physical activity and after-school programmes, stress, frustration, insecurity and, in the USA (where the study was conducted), a lack of health care (including ante- and post-natal care), inferior schooling and exposure to environmental pollutants. The researchers themselves acknowledge the multiple issues involved but point to a particularly strong negative association between very low income and cortical surface. Even very small incremental differences in income appeared to make a difference to the brain structures and cognitive performance of the most deprived children, leading the researchers to conclude that poverty alleviation would be the most effective way of improving development. This contention is supported by evidence that cash handouts to struggling families can generate significant advancement in the cognitive scores of children (for example, Fernald et al, 2008).

In short then, even if we adopt a social investment perspective and fetishise cognitive development and brain size, we arrive at the same conclusion – that providing economic assistance is the best way of reducing the effects of poverty. The influential interest groups at play in the early years intervention field, however, have investments in maintaining the status quo, as we discuss in the next chapter.

Notes

[1] www.politicsresources.net/area/uk/man/lab97.htm

[2] See Children and Young People Now, '4Children and LGA consortium to run Early Intervention Foundation', CYPN, http://www.cypnow.co.uk/cyp/news/1075349/4children-lga-consortium-run-early-intervention-foundation.

[3] http://www.eif.org.uk/wp-content/uploads/2015/02/Final-Conference-Brochure.pdf

[4] In quasi-experimental designs participants are not randomly allocated to the treatment and control groups.

[5] Manchester Institute of Education (2015) Promoting Alternative Thinking Strategies (PATHS): Evaluation report and executive summary, https://v1.educationendowmentfoundation.org.uk/uploads/pdf/PATHS.pdf

[6] http://childtrauma.org/about-childtrauma-academy/

[7]   'Poor parent–child bonding "hampers learning"', http://www.bbc.co.uk/news/education-26667036

[8]   See: http://molbio.princeton.edu/news/faculty-research-news/540-jeff-and-mackenzie-bezos-donate-15-million-to-create-center-in-princeton-neuroscience-institute

[9]   See: www.esrc.ac.uk/news-events-and-publications/news/news-items/new-epigenetics-research-to-understand-how-early-life-experiences-affect-health/

[10] See: www.nuffieldfoundation.org/childrens-resilience-non-supportive-parenting

[11] http://abetterstart.org.uk/

[12] www.eif.org.uk/event/national-conference-2016/

[13] www.nature.com/news/poverty-shrinks-brains-from-birth-1.17227

FOUR

In whose best interests?

Introduction

In previous chapters we have shown how contemporary child and family policy in the UK reflects a view of the world in which economics coupled with biology reigns supreme. Future outcomes and human capital are prioritised and conflated with the national interest, often at the expense of more humanistic values that could shape a different vision of the national good. The social investment logic that underpins this approach reduces social problems and solutions to technical and moral matters of individual capacity. It rules out and delegitimises alternative perspectives. So why and how has early intervention come to acquire the status of a virtually unchallengeable orthodoxy among policy makers and practitioners? In this chapter we step back from the focus on parenting and infant brain development, to look at the wider landscape of social policy delivery as social investment in which early years intervention is situated. We map out the intricate web of vested interests and agendas that are woven into the fabric of children's services generally, and, more specifically, early intervention. We demonstrate how social investment narratives have cultivated and buttressed these ulterior motives. We structure the chapter around the three key interest groups with a stake in the delivery of early intervention: business, politicians and professionals. Taking each in turn we show how the edifice of social investment initiatives is propped up by deep-rooted and interlaced interests in maintaining the status quo.

We begin by exploring the mechanisms of policy making in contemporary Britain, detailing how government reforms instituted over the last 30 years have prompted a diffusion of power and influence away from the public sector towards a range of private and voluntary sector actors. In examining this wider context, we show how strategic alliances, partnerships, informal allegiances and mutual interests have glued together an early intervention house of cards and rendered social investment logics beyond question. We then set out in detail the complex and contrasting political interests framing the current cross-party consensus on early intervention, revealing the underlying pragmatic, moral and broad-scale economic drivers. Tied to this unanimity, the inevitable pull of neoliberal political orthodoxies towards market-based solutions to social provision issues has created a set of substantial and lucrative business interests. We examine how corporate money, power and influence have pervaded a range of children's services, from child protection work to family and early intervention initiatives to education services. We show how this occurs through 'philanthrocapitalism' – an amalgam of an economic rationale of early intervention coupled with moral notions of social philanthropy. Finally, we consider practitioners' interests, outlining the emotional and pragmatic considerations underpinning adherence to early intervention models. As part of this, we reflect on the attraction of attachment theory for professionals as a seemingly radical counterpoint to the time-limited, rational-technical reforms that they are subject to within social work and child mental health services, as well as how this can be linked into academic agendas.

Policy networks and the 'polycentric state'

British governments have always relied on networks of actors to serve their ends and implement policy, but the power, control and status of interests involved in social policy has shifted dramatically over the last 30 years. The hierarchical and bureaucratic policy processes characterising state frameworks and controls generally, and the welfare state specifically, came under concerted attack during the 1980s as part of neoliberal restructuring. The corporate management and marketisation reforms instituted by the Conservative governments headed by Margaret Thatcher deliberately fragmented established policy dynamics and introduced a range of new interest groups and actors from the private and voluntary sectors (Rhodes, 2007). Since then governments have restyled themselves as facilitators and enablers of collaborative solutions, bringing together public, private and voluntary sector actors to 'innovatively' address ingrained problems that have defied previous efforts. The New Labour governments of Tony Blair, in particular, were defined by their commitment to policy making as an informal, decentred process ensuring that public services came to be largely designed and delivered through networks of interested parties.

This form of diffused network governance, described as a 'polycentric state' (Jessop, 1998), was advocated on the grounds that complex modern societies require more flexible and eclectic modes of policy delivery. The UK (especially England) is widely recognised as the pioneer of this polycentric approach (Skelcher, 2007), having developed a diverse policy landscape that encompasses business, social enterprise, philanthropy, celebrities, voluntary organisations and others. Stephen Ball and Carolina Junemann note that these networks operate outside of traditional hierarchical forms of government in 'a messy hinterland of influence' (2012: 9). It becomes increasing difficult to track and scrutinise decisions as the social dynamics of 'public' service responsibility and delivery play out across dispersed locations and through a complex set of asymmetrical relations between various interest groups. The state retains overarching power in a form of 'meta-governance'; 'self-organisation of governance systems through rules, organizational knowledge, institutional tactics and other political strategies' (Jessop, 1997: 575). 'Centres of calculation' (such as Ofsted, the Care Qualities Commission and the Early Intervention Foundation [EIF]) allow the state to performance manage seemingly at a distance through assigning responsibility for benchmarking, monitoring, target setting and so on (Ball and Junemann, 2012: 133).

This shift from government to 'governance' has occurred right across the public sector, but has had an accelerated trajectory in the delivery of education policy. In a detailed network analysis of this sector, Ball and Junemann (2012) highlight how new interests, actors and organisations have come to wield substantial power over policy processes and institutional sites of welfare state services. In particular, they document the increasing influence of philanthropy and business in determining educational values and the method, content and style of public provision. As we will outline in this chapter, early intervention initiatives are commonly channelled through these same rationales and mechanisms, and are often explicitly positioned in terms of early education. And, as we will see, early intervention initiatives increasingly are incorporated into and delivered within already established education policy networks.

Ball and Junemann's work reveals how specific kinds of knowledge operate as a core currency within education policy networks and beyond. Social capital (who you know) shapes access to the fluid domains of policy (projects, meetings, boards, committees, quangos and so on) as well as information about opportunities, events, structures and expectations. But this knowledge generation also drives and sustains a much broader ideological project. Network governance has injected new kinds of entrepreneurial values into the public sector, redesigning the welfare state to fit the contours of the market. Stephen Ball (2010) describes how policy networks are characterised by the commercialisation and commodification of two forms of what he calls 'governing knowledge'. The first is quantitative 'knowledge about'. This sort of knowledge is produced from monitoring, evaluating, inspecting or ranking existing services. With the institution of standards of accountability, efficiency and evidence have come new openings for organisations and companies that offer independent assessments. In the process, services and professional practice become compartmentalised, reduced to performance indicators and are then readily packaged for tendering purposes.

The second form of governing knowledge, 'knowledge for', describes the rise of consultancies and advisory bodies that are brought into the public sector to reform and innovate services and professionals. These organisations infuse a logic of economic enterprise through the promotion of clear, pragmatic and business-like solutions to long-standing social problems. We will explore the role of 'knowledge for' in some depth in this chapter and the next, because it has played such a crucial part in packaging early intervention as a policy panacea. Before we go any further though, it is important to acknowledge the impossibility of identifying and disentangling the interests of policy movers and shakers in any straightforward or linear way. As Ball and Junemann (2012: 11) note:

> The forms of exchange involved are often unclear or multifaceted. One of the interpretive problems involved in thinking about how these networks work is that of deciding at least in the case of some participants, where business ends and philanthropy or public service begins and to what extent philanthropy is a means of influence or a form of 'identity-work' (Breeze, 2007) or both.... Participation can lead to the receipt of awards, honours, appointments and positions in and around the state.

What we can do here, however, is to highlight the diverse stakes that influential groups, organisations and institutions hold in reproducing early years intervention narratives and the neat fit of the logic of social investment with private sector business requirements. We do this through considering, consecutively, political, business and professional interests and investments in delivery across the range of children's services. These various investments, though, are a close-knit, interdependent web of interests, as is clear from our discussion in the rest of this chapter.

Troubling the consensus: political interests

A striking feature of early years intervention as a significant and recurrent feature of social policy rhetoric and practice is the extent to which it draws almost unanimous support across UK party politics. As we saw in previous chapters, New Labour can lay claim to being the architects of the neoliberal social investment paradigm that drives British policy, while a commitment to improve parenting was ratcheted up under the Conservative and Liberal Democrat Coalition and the subsequent Conservative administration. In the process, there was a shift from the initial universal focus on parents generally to a muscular interventionist stance targeted at the poorest in society (Edwards and Gillies, 2016). Conservative, Labour, Liberal Democrat and Green Party MPs have stepped up to champion the '1001 Critical Days' campaign (Leadsom et al, 2013), promoted by the All-Party Parliamentary Group Coalition. Meanwhile, in Scotland, cross-party consensus has resulted in what many view as the most far-reaching and intrusive legislation to prioritise the development and wellbeing of children. The Scottish National Party, supported by the Green Party, has introduced the allocation of a state guardian to oversee the welfare of every child from birth to 18 years of age. Under the 'Named Person Scheme' the appointed guardian will be responsible for ensuring that families address any concerns as early as possible in order to prevent them becoming more serious.[1]

At a broad level, it is easy to see the seductive appeal of early intervention narratives for politicians. A social investment lexicon evokes a sentimental dedication to children's wellbeing for the good of the nation while simultaneously promoting a technical and apparently fully costed plan to eradicate pressing social problems. Politicians appear caring and competent while, as we have already shown, responsibility for poverty, inequality and crime is shifted onto the shoulders of poor mothers. If we take a more detailed look, however, we can see how party political adherence to early intervention models can operate in quite different ways. In the Labour Party, many still cling to the fragments of Third Way thinking, adopted by the Blair governments in their 'modernising' endeavour. Preventive spending was a key motif of the Labour Party's unsuccessful 'One Nation' policy 're-think'[2] in the run-up to the 2015 general election, with their manifesto promise to prioritise early intervention 'to give children and parents a better start'. For the Conservatives, rhetoric stressing the need for more initiatives targeted at the very poor and the very young are an effective driver for the narrowing of universal provision in the context of austerity. It also proves a useful vehicle to demonstrate their tough stance on crime and welfare, lending credence to wider attempts to blame and place responsibility on the poor.

At a superficial level, then, early intervention is a unifying policy tenet. Underneath it is a seething mass of political contradictions and contentions. Traditionalists in the Conservative Party have long opposed the laissez-faire stance towards personal relationships assumed by the economic liberal wing (such as the introduction of same-sex marriage). The influential Centre for Social Justice, the right-wing think tank set up by the Conservative MP Iain Duncan Smith, for example, campaigns for a radical intensification of early intervention to reverse family breakdown and reintroduce traditional family values (CSJ, 2014). But early intervention is a big enough tent to accommodate both those demanding moral retraditionalisation of the nation through support for marriage and sole-breadwinner nuclear-family structures, and those with economic preoccupations who look to reduce national expenditure and maximise human capital to better place Britain in competitive global markets. Early intervention marks an ideological convergence between the moral preoccupation of conservatism with traditional values and Conservative adherence to economic and social liberalism, papering over a long-standing fault line running across the issue of family (Edwards and Gillies, 2016). More specifically, the misleading brain claims that we detailed in the previous chapter were seized on by many in the Conservative Party as conclusive proof of the intellectual and moral inferiority of the poor, and the need to pursue a quasi-religious mission 'turn them around'. The distorted science bolstering early intervention is flexible enough to promote retraditionalisation narratives that stress the importance of stay-at-home mothering, while being simultaneously marshalled by those arguing for more and earlier nursery places to compensate for parenting deficits and to get more mothers off benefits and into employment.[3]

Analyses of the proliferation of early intervention tropes internationally reveal the political roots of the social investment paradigm (Jenson, 2010). As a neoliberal orthodoxy spread across continents, overriding and undermining collectivist agendas, the need for a strategic state to strengthen market compliance and protect business interests became obvious. Cuts to welfare spending and provision, deregulation, privatisation and structural reorganisations had deleterious effects in developed and developing nations alike. The resulting spiralling up of poverty rates and mounting social problems then meant that governments struggled to cut state expenditure. In this scenario, social investment proved to be the perfect bridge between laissez-faire neoliberalism and an active interventionist state. Through social investment the economic values of neoliberalism were maintained and the mechanisms of the state were appropriated to suit the needs of the markets. Thus, rather than undermining neoliberal philosophy, social investment approaches sustained and intensified it.

Jane Jenson (2010) demonstrates how commitments to tackle poverty through investment in children came to be articulated simultaneously as new policy directions in Europe and Latin America from the mid-1990s onwards. Although this idea was operationalised differently in the varying countries and regions, the notion that the young could be shaped to better fit market-based needs inspired new policy and political articulations. As we outlined in Chapter Two, this principle formed the basis of New Labour's 'Third Way' thinking. It was also actively promoted through the institutional spaces of the European Union (EU). For example, 'investment in human capital as a future orientated policy' was jointly recommended as a point of EU convergence by finance ministers, including those from Germany and Sweden and the UK (cited in Jenson, 2010). Meanwhile the Organisation for Economic Co-operation and Development (OECD), previously a supporter of roll back neoliberalism, began to publish and disseminate work by social investment economists such as James Heckman.

Jenson shows how social investment principles in Latin America progressed largely through the interventions of development agencies, with UNICEF (the UN children's charity) leading the way and setting the agenda – an issue we return to in Chapter Seven. The plea to invest in children to secure a greater social payback was accepted as radical and progressive in the context of the fundamental restructuring associated with the rise of neoliberalism. On both sides of the Atlantic (and beyond) policy statements began to revolve around the need to become more 'child centred', to break 'intergenerational cycles' and to make earlier investments to secure greater 'payback'. The campaign for early years funding in the United States (outlined in Chapter Three) highlights the extent to which policy debates were colonised by the constraints of neoliberal thought. In the UK, the myth Margaret Thatcher popularised as 'TINA' – there is no alternative – took hold.

Despite the economic and social failures of market-centred models having become ever clearer in the wake of the 2008 global financial crisis, TINA holds sway. Rather than poverty and inequality being regarded as dysfunctions of economic systems, these social problems are attributed to the biological and cultural inferiority of the poor and vulnerable. Social investment is the mantra and solution, but in the context of UK economic underperformance, it has now shifted ground to a preoccupation with curbing dysfunction and maintaining social order. Increasingly, the work of the EIF has become absorbed into the criminal justice services on the grounds that the police are 'uniquely placed to spot children, families or individuals needing support',[4] 'At-risk' populations are identified, monitored and allocated to short-term, often trademarked, interventions, which are themselves subject to evaluative monitoring. State efforts are galvanised to socially re-engineer the young who are still malleable and to control those who are beyond reformation. As concerns mount about weak economic growth and low productivity, early intervention is invoked by politicians as a remedy, promising to shore up national performance by streamlining the human capital production line. In the process, those promoting business-centred logics and intervention products have acquired a vested interest in protecting and promoting early intervention as a brand.

Financialising social welfare: business interests

A crucial context for understanding the stake the business sector has invested in early intervention is the rise of the public services industry. The market for outsourced public services in the UK quite simply is huge. Government expenditure on contracts in 2015 was estimated to be £120 billion, with the amount having almost doubled over the years of the Coalition government's rule up to 2014 (ISG, 2014). The size of this market is second only to that in the USA, and it is predicted to rise by a further third by 2020 (Pimmer, 2015). To place this figure into perspective, the public services industry outstrips value-added revenues from the private sector categories of Food, Beverages and Tobacco, Communication, Electricity Gas and Water as well as Hotels and Restaurants (cited in Huckfield, 2014a).

Children's welfare and services are among the most lucrative arenas for financial returns. The Audit Commission estimated that, in 2013, private equity had a 25% share in the foster care provision market (cited in Huckfield, 2014a), although precise details about procurement are hard to come by because of commercial confidentiality clauses. Polly Toynbee (2014) has highlighted the quite astonishing investment returns being made from residential services for looked-after children, the multiply disabled and secure placements for young offenders. The higher the need, the higher the profit. Plans to privatise child protection services also attract interest from hedge funds, asset management companies and private equity firms (Jones, 2015b). Fast implementation privatisation modes and methods have even a generated market in their own right, with British companies plying their solutions abroad with the help of the state, as was documented by the activist and academic Leslie Huckfield in 2014:

> Britain is now the world leader in exporting mechanisms, techniques and templates to fund and deliver public services 'on the cheap' – using private money and external contractors – with a babble of Social Enterprises and other organisations tripping round the world as global ambassadors in poverty and misery, with expenses paid by the UK Coalition Government and British Council. (2014b)

In this context of frantic privatisation and value extraction, the rationale of prevention and early intervention is carving out new frontiers for capital gain. For example, government efforts to encourage a new market in 'social investment bonds' and 'payment by results' schemes depends heavily on a 'stitch in time' mantra. Private financing of public services on the basis of returns on investment was hailed as way of cutting government expenditure. Infrastructure and indirect costs were to be offloaded, with the state paying only when initiatives can be proved to work. Predictions of huge cost reductions have been made. For example, a key recommendation of the Allen review on early intervention (2011b) was a substantial expansion of outcomes-based contracting funded by £1 billion of private investment, to unlock 'massive savings' to the public purse. But, predictably, businesses are reluctant to invest without clear pathways to profit. As a result initiatives have had to be rolled out to support investors through generous subsidies and tax relief. Global financial institutions such as Bank of America, Merrill Lynch, Goldman Sachs, JP Morgan Chase and Morgan Stanley are supporting and promoting these projects, anticipating a new 'asset class' (Whitfield, 2014).

Controversy also surrounds methods of measuring social impact and the loose, undefined way in which success is claimed. Stephen Crossley's (2015) research on intensive family interventions suggests that payback criteria are unlikely to be rigorous or hard to fake. But risks must be identified and performance indicators still need to be monitored and analysed, meaning that information management is an expanding market in its own right. It is little wonder, then, that Capita, one of the largest beneficiaries of public sector outsourcing, is extremely supportive of the early intervention mission. Capita One currently offers a whole range of software and data management products to assist in the monitoring of children and families as part of what they describe as an 'early warning system': 'With full visibility of a child and family's history you can profile, identify and target vulnerable groups. [Capita] One provides a clear picture of what is, and isn't going well – helping you intervene earlier and deliver targeted interventions.'[5]

Crossley (2015) notes that software companies and management consultancy firms are offering data-based solutions to the challenges of working with 'complex' families, amassing detailed information on behaviour, movements and compliance of families subject to interventions. For example, Capita One own a database operating within schools containing the personal details of around 8 million children. Information about age, sex, attendance, disciplinary records, absences and academic attainment are entered regularly by teachers without parents' knowledge. Capita One even hire photographers to capture images of the children for their database, which are offered for sale to parents before quietly being uploaded to the system.[6] Further, the Department for Work and Pensions has passed a regulation that allows it to share data on families receiving out-of-work benefits with agencies delivering the Troubled Families programme, without obtaining the subjects' informed consent (Bate, 2016). A policing of the poor through, and authoritarian co-opting of, surveillance biotechnologies looms on the horizon, raising questions about the potential of companies like Capita One to ride roughshod over basic civil liberties.

The conflation of charity with business interests is a prominent feature of the early intervention movement. For example, Capita One are in the business of providing both tailor-made and off-the-shelf consultancy services to local authorities and children's services. In addition, they organise and run over 150 public sector conference events every year, described as 'neutral cross-cutting policy forums for learning and networking'. This 'neutrality' does not extend to corporate interests, who are offered sponsorship opportunities to 'launch your service, demonstrate your products, build awareness and make important contacts in the public sector'.[7] Yet Capita One are keen to demonstrate their corporate responsibility and proudly proclaim their 'charity work'. Primarily this consists of working in partnership with the EIF and sponsoring their annual conferences 'to bring together leaders, decision makers and opinion formers from the public and voluntary sector organisations engaged with early intervention, including Directors of Children's Services'.[8]

Giving and taking: the rise of philanthrocapitalism

As we have outlined, social investment narratives acquire a sheen of munificence through pledges to reduce poverty and improve child outcomes. Philanthropic foundations, trusts, charities and social enterprises have played a pivotal role in assembling and disseminating the case for early intervention, and are integral to the delivery and evaluation of many services that are operating currently. Examining this role in more detail offers a crucial insight into how child and family welfare came to be reformulated as a business opportunity. Ball and Junemann (2012) point out that philanthropy has afforded capital investment a respectable face in public sector dealings, acting as a Trojan horse for new business–centred philosophies and values. While neoliberal reforms continued to wreak havoc, philanthropists developed their own model for ameliorating the worst effects. Exporting the principles of the market to non-profit operations they sought to reform the voluntary sector through applying business thinking to social problems. Social investment was promoted as an effective and efficient way to achieve sustainable social impact, while simultaneously creating new service markets in the name of the greater good.

This approach has been referred to as 'philanthrocapitalism' and sometimes as 'new philanthropy', although as Lindsey McGoey (2015) demonstrates that there is long history of the application of profit maximisation strategies to achieve philanthropic goals. She traces the conflation of private interests with public benefits back to the 18th century and Adam Smith's contention that the invisible hand of the market would transform self-interest into social good. And as we suggested in Chapter Two, 19th-century liberal capitalism was pursued as a deeply moral endeavour with its tenets inspiring Victorian efforts to build the character of the poor and rescue and reform their children. Contemporary philanthrocapitalists tend not to share the religious beliefs of their forefathers, but they lack none of the moral zeal. They are instead powered by a conviction that an application of market methods can save the world. Michael Edwards (2008) attributes three key characteristics to the 'new' philanthrocapitalism: (i) the devotion of large sums of money to philanthropy (gained from huge profits); (ii) a belief in the natural superiority of business methods and their capacity to solve every social problem; and (iii) a claim that these business methods can achieve social transformation without the need for any kind of wealth redistribution. Michael Bishop and Matthew Green effectively illustrate these themes in their high-profile book, *Philanthrocapitalism: How the rich can save the world*:

Their philanthropy is 'strategic', 'market conscious', 'impact orientated', 'knowledge based' often 'high engagement' and always driven by the goal of maximising the 'leverage' of the donor's money. Seeing themselves as social investors not traditional donors some of them engage in venture philanthropy. As entrepreneurial 'philanthropreneurs' they love to back social entrepreneurs who offer innovative solutions to social problems. (2008: 6)

The economic rationality and market potential of early intervention has attracted substantial interest from philanthrocapitalists. For example, New Philanthropy Capital (NPC), an organisation guiding wealthy donors towards 'high-impact social investments', emphasises the huge financial and public benefits of tackling the 'root causes' of social problems. In a report published by Barclay's Wealth, a leading global fund manager, NPC presented an economic analysis of the potential financial gains associated with favoured child and family interventions,[9] echoing many of overstated claims in the Allen reports (2011a, 2011b). Donations and investments commonly are made in private so it is difficult to establish the exact extent of philanthropic investment in actual early intervention initiatives. The promise that private finance would plug financial gaps in the public sector and inject entrepreneurial solutions has fallen well short, however, delivering modest investment amid high sensitivity to risk (McGoey, 2014). Despite this, philanthrocapitalists are now to be found at the centre of governance, occupying prominent positions in policy networks, while social investment from private capital remains largely dependent on state supports, subsidies and any potential monetisation opportunities.

Wealthy philanthropists have played a commanding role in reshaping and corporatising English education policy generally, as detailed by Ball and Junemann (2012). These same wealthy individuals and trusts are influential in funding and promoting early intervention initiatives and rationales. For example, the founder and director of both the Sutton Trust (which describes itself as both thinktank and 'do tank') and the Education Endowment Foundation (an education charity), Peter Lampl, describes himself as practising 'strategic philanthropy' through policy and practice reform. His work is focused on increasing social mobility through education by seeking to raise the performance of disadvantaged children. In particular, Lampl has sought to promote 'evidence-based' initiatives to break the link between educational attainment and family background. The Sutton Trust and the Educational Endowment Foundation have received substantial government funds to pursue this objective. They have also been jointly designated as a government 'What Works' centre for the policy area of education, complementing the role of the EIF. There is, of course, much crossover between the two 'evidence centres'. For example, the Sutton Trust partnered with the venture philanthropist organisation Impetus to invest in early intervention projects to improve 'school readiness', receiving £125 million in government funding to institute it.[10] It is also worth noting that the Sutton Trust was responsible for the inaccurate and inflated Baby Bonds research described in Chapter Three, and the claim that 40% of children miss out on the parenting required to succeed in life.

Philanthropic individuals and organisations are advocating and campaigning for early intervention initiatives using a variety of mechanisms. They act as advisers, lobbyists, sponsors and, as we will explore through case studies in the next chapter, they are increasingly involved in commissioning, delivering and evaluating services on the ground. For example, another significant player in the field of education policy and early intervention, the Garfield Weston Foundation (GWF) is the charitable arm of Wittington Investments Limited. Its assets include Associated British Foods, British Sugar, Primark and high-end department stores such as Fortnum and Masons. GWF was an initial investor in Explore Learning, the private tutoring centres that have spread across British high streets and supermarkets. They are large donors to the Conservative Party and fund two right-wing thinktanks: the Policy Exchange, which has published reports setting out the case for early intervention, more extensive nursery education and longer school hours, and the Institute for Economic Affairs, which is devoted to the promotion of free market economics. GWF is clearly keen to promote the case for early intervention, funding both the EIF and the Wave Trust, as well as charities and social enterprises running the 'evidence-based' programmes.

The boundaries between charitable endeavours, not-for-profit organisations and commercial interests are becoming increasingly blurred. Ball and Junemann (2005) show how GWF has been influential in shaping the direction of public education and the move to academy schools in particular. While academy schools cannot, as yet, be run for profit, they are most commonly sponsored by businesses, philanthropists or charitable trusts (GWF sponsors several in partnership with the wealthy de Capell Brooke family). Once approved, sponsors receive money from the government to fund the establishment and running of the school. The sponsored academy is then accorded charitable status. The academy is not-for-profit in that no dividend can be paid to shareholders, but there are more subtle ways to capitalise on this arrangement. Many academy trusts are now run by extensions of multinational companies which then buy services for the school from their parent business.

Public interest and self-interest can now be made to converge. For example, the Aurora Academies Trust (AAT), made up of four primary schools in East Sussex, was established by Mosaica Education. Mosaica is a global education services company that sells a patented social sciences curriculum called Paragon. AAT buys Paragon from Mosaica for an estimated cost of £100 per pupil per year.[11] Consequently Mosaica is in effect charging for and profiting from curriculum development that is routinely provided by teachers in other schools at no extra cost. Further, Paragon, which centres on teaching character, empathy and self-esteem, has been criticised by Ofsted for lacking a local dimension[12]. More commonly, trusts buy packages of services, including human resources, legal advice, catering, cleaning and leadership training (Johnson and Mansell, 2014). Another example of this conflation of the public interest and the profit interest is Bright Tribe Multi-Academy Trust. Run by venture capitalist Mike Dwan, Bright Tribe made nearly £2.9 million in payments to businesses owned by Dwan himself over the course of two years.[13]

A similar direction of travel can be seen in child and family services. Government efforts to outsource social work services and decision making for children in care to private companies were robustly resisted in 2013 (Jones, 2015a). But since ostensibly backing down on this issue the government has pursued a stealth privatisation agenda, allowing companies to bid for contracts by setting up a non-profit subsidiary. As with academies, the parent company will be able to bill for the provision of basic services like accommodation, IT and administration. And business ambitions extend well beyond capitalising on 'non-profit' subsidiaries. There may be opportunities to be exploited further down the pipeline through apparently benevolent, charitable efforts. For example, a not-for-profit consortium called Tablets for Schools has been set up by Carphone Warehouse, Dixons and Google to donate the 'Nexus 7' devices to schools across Britain and provide a 'blueprint for them to adopt tablet technology'.[14] There is significant commercial interest beneath the rhetoric about corporate responsibility and bridging digital divides. It might also be noted that David Ross, a co-founder and major shareholder in Carphone Warehouse (the main supplier of the tablets), is also the sponsor of an academy trust consisting of 25 schools.

Over the last 30 years the public services landscape has been transformed dramatically. Privatisation, social entrepreneurship, social enterprise and related chimeras have been key vehicles of ideologically driven neoliberal government reforms. Those working within the public sector now have a reduced role in policy making and strategic management, but face increased demands to reduce costs, increase efficiency and meet targets. The offloading of service responsibilities through outsourcing has led to worsening pay and conditions and increased job insecurity across a variety of sectors (TUC and NEF, 2015). At the same time, voluntary and community organisations are made increasingly dependent on contract funding from central and local government, and find themselves in direct competition with commercial operations and their 'not-for-profit' subsidiaries. In this pressurised and competitive environment, the rationale for, and cost-cutting potential of preventive action wields considerable influence. Businesses, charities, public sector professionals and governments seeking social investment all build their cases around the apparently unassailable logic of early intervention, leaving little scope for critical judgement.

Strategy, power and justification: professional interests

While the motivations of politicians and businesses are generally contingent and tactical, professionals tend to have a more emotional stake in early intervention narratives. In the days of New Labour, a commitment to social investment was translated into increased government spending on children and families. Sure Start children's centres were rolled out and there was a major expansion of state-sponsored and third sector initiatives directly targeting families under the rubric of 'parenting support'. This expansion generated a new taskforce of 'parenting professionals'. The principle of early intervention was assimilated across the education, health and social care sectors as progressive common sense. The subsequent execution of a hard austerity agenda by the Coalition government from 2010 onwards provoked a passionate defence of social investment in an attempt to preserve services and jobs. The arguments reinforced the narrow, instrumental economic focus – fund early intervention services or pay more later for the consequences of social dysfunction. Alternative professional and public service values, ethics and models were largely silenced in an effort to dig in and defend a problematic service structure. As Brid Featherstone and colleagues (2014a) point out, general apprehension about the survival of state services hindered critical engagement and intensified hard-line interventionism among family practitioners.

And, significantly, the overblown and misleading brain science claims outlined in the previous chapter worked to delegitimise any doubts. The mobilisation of apparently hard scientific evidence cemented the orthodoxy, directing the focus of practice towards the saving of future generations from the sins of their parents. As we show in Chapter Six, many practitioners enthusiastically endorsed biologised constructs, building them into professional training and practice techniques with targeted families. By adopting the language of neuroscience, early years practitioners can demonstrate knowledge and proficiency, augment the status of their professions and a construct a compelling case for continued state funding (McDonald, 2003). And many have welcomed the conviction the common denominator of biology provides in navigating the murky real-life ambiguities of culture, diversity and difference.

While some professionals may retain doubts about the veracity of the claims being made, the instrumental value of the brain science rhetoric tends to curb critical challenges. Professional bodies and charitable organisations have benefited from weaving neuroscience-informed accounts of child development into their public relations material, funding bids and claims to expertise. Family intervention programmes carry the biological claims to emphasise the efficacy and trade upon the persuasive impact of science. In a context of accelerating marketisation, where services are put out to tender and programmes, models and professional disciplines are forced to compete, professionals require a convincing business case. There is no place for equivocation, complexity or humility in the commissioning of services. Providers must be able to speak the language of costs, benefits and (neuro) evidence or they will be replaced by those who do.

In Chapter Two we noted that an early advocate of the infant brain claims in Britain was the founder of the charity Kids Company (now in liquidation), Camila Batmanghelidjh. Kids Company is a good example of the power of claims that weave together brain science ideas, early intervention and financial interests. Batmanghelidjh may have passionately believed in a biological basis for social deprivation, but she was also cognisant of the power of neuroscience to convince policy makers and politicians to invest money. Her depiction of the young (mainly black) users of Kids Company services as a brain-damaged underclass prone to violence resonated with the beliefs of Conservative ministers, including then Prime Minister David Cameron.[15] The organisation received at least £46 million of public money, much of which was received outside of the competitive process that charities are expected to conform to. It is generally accepted that this was an extraordinary amount of public funding for a small charity that operated, for the most part, in just two London boroughs. Dependence on government financing eventually led to the downfall of Kids Company (National Audit Office, 2015). But in the run-up to its closure, government ministers and civil servants were warned that serious social disorder would be unleashed if Kids Company's work was to be discontinued. The chair of the charity's trustees sent the government an email alerting them to the high risk of looting, rioting and arson, suggesting that the communities served by Kids Company might descend into 'savagery'.[16] The use of brain development rationales to present working-class and minority ethnic parents and children as primitive is an issue that we will pick up on again in Chapter Six.

As Batmanghelidjh acknowledged during her interview for our research, brain science was pursued by Kids Company as the holy grail of evidence. She discussed the wide variety of neurobiology studies the organisation had commissioned and/or supported:

Batmanghelidjh: We've got, UCL [University College London], Cambridge's neuropsychiatry department, we've got the Institute of Psychiatry, Kings and then we've got stuff going on at Bristol and Southampton. It's a range.

Gillies: Yeah, and what do you think the benefits are of pursuing that kind of research?

Batmanghelidjh: They want some kind of evidence and so I'm using – for us the reason we're doing it is to get a paradigm shift, because my motto is unrelenting love is the real intervention. Now those people who believe in that will understand it and support it. But there's a cohort of people who don't. They want some kind of evidence and so I'm using, I'm using it in a very practical instrumental way. I'm learning things as I go along. It's giving me a vocabulary to be able to create a narrative that is comprehensible for people who can't rely on intuition.

Kids Company's doomed efforts to secure scientific substantiation of its methods illustrates the high stakes in play. Batmanghelidjh's 'intuition' chimed well with government reasoning around prevention and intergenerational transmission of deprivation, securing a lucrative channel of state support for her charity. General mismanagement led to the downfall of Kids Company, revealing the hidden interests and incentives driving its research agenda, and its close links to government.

Other voluntary organisations have pursued a similarly politically bounded agenda in the name of protecting children. Echoing the child rescue sensibilities of their 19th-century antecedents, a variety of long-established children's charities have enthusiastically embraced the social investment cause, campaigning for child-centred reforms and services. For example, Action for Children, Barnardo's and the NSPCC all draw heavily on dubious interpretations of neuroscience to promote their early intervention services. As in the past, these and other organisations position children's needs and rights as largely independent from those of their parents, with family construed as an intrinsically precarious location for vulnerable children. Campaigns generally focus on protecting children's wellbeing from the potential threat posed by careless, ignorant, neglectful or abusive parents. The severe structural and economic pressures affecting families rarely feature in their demands for change.

Despite the fact that social services referrals in the UK are clearly associated with desperate hardship and vulnerability (Bywaters et al, 2014), material factors do not merit a mention in this campaign to prioritise the wellbeing of babies and children. For example, the NSPCC (National Society for the Prevention of Cruelty to Children) is calling for a new emphasis to be placed on infant mental health and is piloting the New Orleans Intervention Model (NOIM). Named after the city in which it was developed, NOIM is designed to reduce abuse and neglect of infants by placing attachment at the centre of social work interventions. Detailed assessments are made of the quality of mother–children relationships and intensive therapeutic support is provided. After a final assessment the child is then either permanently removed or returned to the mother. The aim is to speed up intervention to avoid potential brain damage, focusing primarily on attachment rather than the material circumstances contextualising parental behaviour. So, while many disadvantaged parents are now deprived of the basic economic and practical resources required to care for their infants, the large children's charities continue to cling to the 'child-centred' principles of social investment. It is also worth noting that the chief executives of these charities tend to be closely linked in to central government through advisory posts, honorary positions and titles.[17]

Therapy wars: the institutionalisation of attachment

Attachment theory wields a huge influence in contemporary child and family services. But as we outlined in Chapter Three, the gap between complex empirical research findings on attachment and their translation and implementation in professional practice and services required an active process of bridge building. Few question the basic tenet that human development depends on babies forming attachments, but the claims framing early intervention doctrines and practice extend well beyond established evidence and depend instead on creative interpretations of neuroscience. The hooking together of brain science and attachment was driven in part by disciplinary struggles between mental health clinicians over the aetiology, substance and appropriate response to psychological problems.

Psychoanalytic and humanist approaches dominated public health provision up to the 1980s when cognitive behavioural therapy (CBT) began to mount a serious challenge to treatment orthodoxies. CBT eschews deep-rooted drives and emotions for a more prosaic focus on managing thoughts, beliefs, attitudes and behaviour in the here and now. It entails a detached psychometric approach, consisting of easily reproducible techniques and coping strategies as opposed to the deeper analytic probing associated with more traditional forms of therapy. In the context of neoliberal restructuring, CBT rose to ascendancy. It was cheap, time-limited, formulaic, promoted no-nonsense rationality and it could claim a strong evidence base. The apparent cast iron case for CBT left many therapists struggling to justify the more intensive relational work they pursued. In the USA a fightback began to coalesce around the concept of attachment as a theoretical justification for a deeper, more connected form of practice. Inspired by Bowlby's belief in the power of therapeutic relations to compensate for poor attachment in childhood, therapists began to emphasise the importance of developing close, empathic bonds with clients to address unresolved attachment disorders. Meanwhile, the work of neuropsychoanalysts such as Allan Schore provided a 'hard science' justification. As Mary Sykes Wylie and Lynn Turner perceptively suggest:

> At a time when brief, technical, pragmatic therapies were all the rage, attachment research seemed to offer genuine scientific validation for a deeper, emotion-focused approach that took infancy and early childhood seriously. The rich, evocative descriptions of attachment theory, the basic allure of it (what could be more appealing, more psychologically

nourishing, than mother-love?), the very fact that such a pretty package was gaining scientific heft made it almost irresistible to many therapists. While attachment theory in itself didn't provide an accompanying toolbox of tactics and techniques, it did offer a new therapeutic attitude, justifying deep, soul-felt work, which would offer the client a genuinely new beginning. (2011: 4)

In the UK, the CBT revolution was slower to influence child and family mental health services. But as child guidance clinics became Child and Adolescent Mental Health Services (CAMHS) and were incorporated within primary health care trusts, new pressures came to bear. Attachment theory allowed psychoanalytically informed child psychiatrists and psychotherapists to retain an expertise and power base as they worked alongside CBT-trained psychologists and systemic family therapists. And the body of empirical research on attachment accumulated through the 1980s and 1990s allowed them to claim their own evidence base.

At the same time the profession of social work was subject to a whole series of managerial reforms in the name of raising standards, modernising the profession and safeguarding children. A rational-technical conception of social work came to prevail, with concern centred on making practice accountable and transparent within a broader remit of early intervention (Parton, 2005). Brid Featherstone and colleagues argue that this led to a ramping up of pressure on families and social workers:

New Labour created the conditions for the perfect storm of today, catch them early, focus on children, treat parents either instrumentally or render them invisible and identify and treat the feckless and risky. While they were spending money the consequences were not quite so obvious. However, under the Coalition government and its enforced austerity, matters are rather different. The residualism requires that parents be held to blame for their own predicaments and has increasingly involved the conscription by policy makers of a range of 'expert' discourses to validate increasingly unforgiving interventionist practices in relation to (primarily poor) families. (2014b: 27–8)

Attachment theory, grounded in a persuasive rhetoric of neurodevelopment, provides a practical framework to guide and warrant these unforgiving practices. It also endows the struggling and beleaguered profession of social work with an apparent scientific mandate, reducing uncertainty and relieving disquiet.

Clinicians, social workers and other practitioners tend to receive their training in attachment-centred principles from independent organisations which often have their own distinct agendas. An influential example of these is the Anna Freud Centre (AFC), a charity that describes its objective as 'campaigning for and creating mental health services for children'. The AFC offers a good example of the links between early intervention provision, the provision of an evidence base through academic research, and policy-making bodies. It provides treatments and training in therapy, research and service delivery, conducted in partnership with UCL. AFC's Chief Executive, Peter Fonagy, is a Professor of Psychoanalysis at UCL, specialising in early attachment relationships. Most of the rest of the senior leadership of AFC are also associated with UCL, while the board of trustees are largely from the finance industries. The AFC exerts considerable influence on policy and practice in the area of child and adolescent mental health, shaping service delivery and designing, piloting and evaluating initiatives. For example, Fonagy contributed to the development of National Institute for Clinical Excellence guidelines, and shaping the 'Improving Access for Psychological Therapies' Initiative, a government programme aiming to increase clinical provision for depression and anxiety. AFC income comes from treatment and assessment fees, the training portfolio, publishing and substantial donations from philanthropists and corporate industry. They also accepted a contribution from Kids Company shortly before it was liquidated, to search for brain-based biomarkers for early stress and ameliorative therapy (one of several neuroscience-based studies they are pursuing). Overall then, this organisation is key in resourcing, researching, evidencing, disseminating and promoting particular therapeutic approaches that link attachment and brain science, and inform early intervention.

As we noted in Chapter Three, a social investment paradigm exerts a significant influence on the direction of academic research. A normative undercurrent is intensifying across disciplines as a result of what Nikolas Rose and Joelle Abi-Rached (2013) have termed the 'translational imperative', that is, the pressure to satisfy funders by producing meaningful, applicable findings. Since 2009 academics seeking funding from research councils have been required to provide a detailed assessment of the likely 'impact' of their work on society and the economy. In the context of increased competition and shrinking funds researchers are expected to demonstrate effective links with policy makers, voluntary organisations and industry to maximise the reach and influence of their work. Any promised impact must then be measured and evidenced through highlighting specific changes to policy, practices or culture. This stipulation works to narrow research agendas down to suit the particular interests of dominant organisations and powerful individuals (Back, 2015). In the process, symbiotic relationships have been created between academics keen to increase the reach and impact of their work, and organisations looking for validation and support. The result is a proliferation of research which reinforces rather than challenges established orthodoxies and the status quo, while dissenting voices are silenced or are confined to academic conferences and journals.

There are critical voices raised in relation to attachment theory however. Despite achieving near hegemonic status among child and family practitioners in the UK, routine reliance on attachment theory does not go uncontested. Sykes Wylie and Turner describe a 'barely visible fault line between true believers in attachment and its doubters' in the world of psychotherapy (2011: 2). They cite concerns raised by the family therapy pioneer Salvador Minuchin that a preoccupation with attachment can mask compelling social and racial issues:

> It can take us back to the heyday of psychoanalysis and deny the full familial and social reality of children's lives, as well as obscure our understanding of the context in which they grew up.... These days therapists too often talk as if child therapy is the same thing as 'trauma therapy'. (cited in Sykes Wylie and Turner, 2011: 12)

Other sceptics include the eminent developmental psychologist Jerome Kagan (2011), who provides a scathing assessment of the evidence underpinning theory and practice. Even attachment therapists themselves may express alarm at the tenuous assumptions, misdiagnosis and mislabelling of families that has followed from the proliferation of attachment-inspired interventions (Zilberstein, 2014). In the current climate, however, doubt, dissent or even hesitation risks being interpreted as incompetence. Vested interests have tightly stitched explanatory narratives together to discourage critical analysis.

In whose interests then?

We end this chapter with the observation that, after 20 years of a social investment state, children's prospects are considerably worse than before. Young people are the age group most likely to be living in poverty and have the least access to decent housing and well paid jobs (EHRC, 2015). Youth unemployment is at a 20 year high[18] and more than half of UK graduates can now expect to end up in non-graduate jobs (CIPD, 2015). The reconceptualisation of children as human capital and the resulting emphasis placed on early development and sensitive parenting has done little to mediate these risks; rather, it has coincided with an apparent rise in depression and anxiety among young people.[19] As we have elaborated in this chapter, many powerful institutions, industries, groups and individuals benefit from a doctrine of early intervention, but children, young people and their families do not seem to be among them. In the next chapter, we detail case studies of the links between some of the key interests at play in the early intervention field.

Notes

[1] 'What is the named person scheme?', www.bbc.co.uk/news/uk-scotland-scotland-politics-35752756

[2] See for example One Nation Fizz, www.yourbritain.org.uk/uploads/editor/files/One_Nation_Fizz.pdf

[3] On the one hand see www.dailymail.co.uk/femail/article-2296567/Scientific-proof-stay-home-mothers-benefit-children-So-coalition-Budget-tax-break-working-mothers.html, on the other http://www.savethechildren.org.uk/2016-03/leading-scientists-warn-failure-stimulate-toddlers%E2%80%99-brains-could-affect-quality-life-whole

[4] See www.eif.org.uk/our-work-with-the-police/

[5] www.capita-one.co.uk/why-one

[6] http://schoolsimprovement.net/warning-over-secret-capita-one-database-featuring-8m-schoolchildren/

[7] www.capitaconferences.co.uk/sponsorship-exhibition.html

[8] www.capita-one.co.uk/why-one/our-charity-work

[9] https://wealth.barclays.com/content/dam/bwpublic/global/documents/wealth_management/Early-Interventions.pdf

[10] www.suttontrust.com/newsarchive/125-million-boost-attainment-poor-children/

[11] 'How the coalition is privatising state education', http://leftfootforward.org/2014/10/how-the-coalition-is-privatising-state-education/

[12] www.theguardian.com/education/2013/may/18/academy-pays-for-us-curriculum

[13] www.theguardian.com/education/2016/jun/12/academy-schools-cash-cow-business?CMP=share_btn_tw

[14] www.campaignlive.co.uk/article/1174153/govt-approves-carphone-warehouse-tablets-schools-drive#

[15] www.theguardian.com/uk-news/2016/feb/12/kids-company-camila-batmanghelidjh-denies-mesmerising-david-cameron

[16] www.bbc.co.uk/news/uk-34572934

[17] For example, the CEO of the NSPCC, Peter Wanless, was previously a high-ranking civil servant. He was awarded the Companion of the Order of the Bath (*CB*) and was appointed by the Coalition government to lead a review into historical sex abuse claims. The CEO of Action for Children, Sir Tony Hawkhead also acts as a non-executive director at the Department of Environment, Food and Rural Affairs. The government links associated with the former CEO of Barnardos, Martin Nary, are discussed in Chapter Two.

[18] www.theguardian.com/society/2015/feb/22/youth-unemployment-jobless-figure

[19] www.youngminds.org.uk/about/whats_the_problem/mental_health_statistics

FIVE

Case studies of interests at play

In the previous chapter we provided an overarching view of the interests involved in early years intervention, focusing on the key interest groups of politicians, business and professionals. In this chapter we present case studies of three high-profile organisations in the field of early intervention that illustrate and elaborate on the interlinked nature of interests and ideas. The first case study foregrounds the activities of the highly influential campaigning and policy advocate organisation, Wave Trust. As we have demonstrated already, the Wave Trust has played a formative role in promoting brain based early intervention narratives in the context of British politics. Here we reveal the nature and extent of their involvement across the three interest groups, exemplifying what Stephen Ball and Carolina Junemann's classify as 'boundary spanning':

> Some people (or organisations) who occupy multiple positions and who are adept in the arts of networking act as nodes; they join things up and "span boundaries".... In doing so they accumulate valuable information and move ideas and influences between sectors. (2012: 10)

We explore in detail how Wave Trust assumes the role of a nodal actor in embedding and diffusing early intervention policy narratives.

Our second case study centres on a linked early intervention programme: the Family Nurse Partnership (FNP). The proclaimed success of the FNP has been key to the growth of early intervention as a policy doctrine. The FNP present themselves as having 'one of the strongest evidence bases of any childhood preventitive [sic] programme.'[1] This claim to proven impact has made it the programme of choice for a wide range of early intervention advocates including the Wave Trust, the Early Intervention Foundation (EIF), the Sutton Trust, Labour MP Graham Allen, as well as the consecutive Conservative Governments. In this sense, the programme spans sector and political boundaries. In this chapter we take a closer look at the FNP's origins, operating structure, practices, network of supporters and evidence claims in the context of underwhelming results from a UK-based randomised controlled trial (RCT).

Our third case study explores the prominence of the charity Parent Infant Partnerships United Kingdom (PIPUK) in early intervention prescriptions – another nodal actor. PIPUK provides specialist therapeutic services to mothers and babies, based on an attachment model, while also advocating for greater emphasis to be placed on the quality of the relationship between caregivers and babies to ensure 'the child's subsequent developmental trajectory is as favourable as is possible'.[2] We highlight the politicised nature of PIPUK's campaigning activities, trace the roots of the organisation back to the Conservative Party and highlight the extent to which a distinct moral and political framework is concealed beneath an apparently uncontroversial mission to help mothers and babies.

Case study 1: Wave Trust

Curious George and the rising tide

Wave Trust ranks among the most influential boundary spanning advocates of early years intervention in the UK. It operates as a charity 'finding solutions to the root causes of damage, before it happens'.[3] More specifically, the core of Wave Trust consists of a husband and wife team of business strategists driven by an unshakeable belief in the transformative powers of philanthrocapitalism. Clearly inspired by the campaigning strategy of the Harvard Center for the Developing Child, Wave Trust seeks to take on a similar mantle, drawing on a scientific discourse to warrant policy recommendations. Using parallel language to the Harvard Center, Wave Trust presents itself as a synthesiser and mediator of science. It claims to 'connect the dots between multiple strands of global scientific research into various forms of social dysfunction' and to 'Develop a cohesive overview of the scientific findings about solutions to social problems.'

Wave Trust positions itself as assembling and translating scientific findings into policy as part of a troubleshooting model: 'We bring together the best of international scientific understanding of both root causes and solutions. We then use this to create practical, effective action plans to break the cycles of childhood abuse and neglect.'[4]

In its business-centred approach, science is presented as holding apolitical answers that can neutrally be applied to produce measurable results. Academic specialisms and literature are eschewed for a more pragmatic focus on getting the job done. Wave Trust invokes science as pure knowledge in its own right, with facts emerging to speak for themselves. Business experience, the Wave Trust claims, has taught it that causes need to be understood before solutions can be found. And for Wave Trust, bad mothering is the origin of most evils in the world. In various articles and reports produced since 1999, the organisation draws heavily on an appropriation of brain science to emphasise the importance of sensitive maternal attunement in eradicating violence and enabling a child to become 'socially efficient'.

Given that Wave Trust's key publications are authored by a business strategist rather than experts in the field, its influence has been quite remarkable. On its website, Wave Trust describes itself as an educational charity aiming to 'make the world safer by breaking damaging, inter-generational family cycles'. According to the blurb, it was founded in 1995 by their current CEO, George Hosking, following his 'discovery' that 'despite the best efforts of children's charities and the government, levels of child abuse and neglect had not decreased since 1950'. Believing his career as a Unilever executive and business consultant equipped him with the necessary troubleshooting acumen, Hosking set about conducting his own research. A more detailed account of this epiphany is provided in a self-published article from 1999, titled 'Digging up the roots of violence' it is worth reproducing at some length:

> About eight years ago, my life was changed. Two separate cases of child murder by parents or step-parents filled the newspapers, one quickly after the other. What caught my attention was not the deaths. It was that for a year or two before their deaths these children suffered systematic torture at the hands of their parents, so extreme that death itself must have been a release. I was shocked to the core. I had not previously realised that children could (and often do) suffer so at the hands of their parents. At that moment I made a decision – more accurately, a decision made me – that I could not live in a world where such things occurred while I did nothing about it.… I knew that to change how businesses perform it was crucial to understand the root causes of their cost and profit structures.… Could the same approaches be applied to the problem of child abuse? My first thought was, yes, it could. I then began a voyage of exploration to understand the root causes of child abuse. For some weeks I trawled the internet seeking advice, opinions, evidence, references, experts and material relevant to my search. One of my first discoveries was that there were almost as many theories about what causes child

abuse as people to hold them.... I was bombarded with ideas by people, every one convinced they held the sole true understanding of the problem. I resolved to base my conclusions only on verifiable scientific evidence.[5]

On the basis of his internet search, Hosking, who refers to himself as an 'economist, accountant, psychologist and clinical criminologist', concluded that violence is caused by harsh discipline experienced in the early years. He set out to 'end abuse of all children, everywhere, period'.[6] 'Digging up the roots of violence' appears to be the first elaboration of Hosking's thoughts on child abuse. It is a curious mix of anecdotal evidence, personal reflections, cherry-picked expert opinion and studies. While making no reference to the established body of practice-based knowledge informing health and social work training, Hosking prescribes parenting and relationship interventions as a preventative measure 'to resolve the problems of broken marriages, failed relationships and aggressive, violent children'.

A year later, Hosking produced another, short, reflection called 'An ounce of prevention', echoing (though not acknowledging) a USA-based childhood investment campaign. In this piece he warns of rising levels of violence, repeats his assertion that the root cause lies in early life experience, and suggests research is tracing pathways to violence from poor parent–baby interactions. Another year on in 2001 and Hosking's next address, 'Nursery crimes',[7] makes a first explicit reference to the malformed infant brain as the origin of violence:

> Babies brought up in violent families are incubated in terror and their brains may be permanently damaged. The brains of abused children are significantly smaller than those of non-abused children. The limbic system (which governs emotions) is 20–30% smaller and tends to have fewer synapses. Similarly, the hippocampus (responsible for memory) is also smaller in abused children. There is also increased activity in the locus coeruleus (responsible for hair-trigger alert), as one might expect in violent families.

In 2003, Hosking wrote another self-published piece called 'The hand that rocks the cradle', in which he sought to bring together the conclusions from his 'seven years of research'. His first deduction was that violence is on the increase. He makes a vague reference to the 'horrifying' statistics on recorded violence, but provides no further details. Given that most criminologists at this time were documenting an apparent steep drop in violent crime from the early 1990s onwards,[8] this claim is odd. His next insight is that though violence derives from social and personal factors, little can be done about social factors. He does not explain why. He then reiterates his concerns about the effects of harsh discipline on infant brains, making the striking but unreferenced claim that three-quarters of babies are hit before they are 1 year old.[9] His proffered policy recommendations included parenting training for school children, greater monitoring of at-risk families and the introduction of evidenced-based intervention programmes (particularly FNP).

By 2005 Hosking's work had been transformed into an authoritative-looking 'Wave Report' on *Violence and what to do about it*, with his wife, Ita Walsh, as a co-author. In the preface Hosking is introduced as a business strategist whose consultancy work has added over £30 million per annum to his clients' profits. He is also described as a psychologist engaged in therapeutic work to prevent violent reoffending. The exact nature of his credentials remain unclear[10] but he claims a 100% success rate in his work inside and outside of prison. Ita Walsh is described as an international strategy consultant for blue chip clients with a vision for a world devoid of all cruelty. The report itself is a lengthy exposition of Hosking's thesis about violence and infant development. The first chapter repeats his alarming assessment of a rising tide of violent crime, its severity conveyed through starkly climbing graphs attributed to a Home Office statistical bulletin. The bulletin itself, however contains very different images and clearly documents a substantial 24% fall in violent crime between 1997 and 2003.[11]

Despite these inaccuracies, poor referencing and disconnection from an established academic body of criminological research, *Violence and what to do about it* was well received, particularly among influential philanthropists and policy movers and shakers who were attracted by its troubleshooting approach. At a launch for the report Hosking spoke of a 'cycle of aggression' caused by emotionally immature teenage parents. This was reported in several mainstream media outlets, including *The Guardian*, which presented Hosking as a 'leading criminologist' before describing his report as 'one of the largest ever studies into violence'.[12] This would have been a remarkable feat if true, given he was simultaneously heading up a management consultancy while conducting it. Yet Hosking's adept nodal networking skills and contacts with wealthy, powerful philanthropists gained him entry to influential political circles.

In a *Wave Supporters Newsletter* published in 2006, Hosking is described as touring the UK on the back of his report, providing 'a non-stop response to interest and enquiries'. As the newsletter documents, this included addressing a conference organised by Graham Allen MP and organising talks to form a 'close' collaborative alliance with the charity Kids Company. Hosking's work was also embraced with enthusiasm by the Centre for Social Justice, inspiring Conservative MP Iain Duncan Smith in particular. By 2007 the Wave Trust was proudly boasting of meetings with a cross-party selection of other high-ranking politicians including Prime Ministers Tony Blair and Gordon Brown, former Home Secretary John Reid, then Conservative Shadow Attorney General Dominic Grieve, leading Liberal Democrat MPs Danny Alexander and Norman Lamb, as well as many other influential MPs.[13]

The Wave Trust's boundary spanning political manoeuvring was designed to build a broad consensus on the case for early years intervention. This motive was behind the bringing together of Labour and Conservative MPs Allen and Duncan Smith to produce the *Early intervention: Good parents, great kids, better citizens* report (Allen and Duncan Smith, 2008). Jointly published by the Centre for Social Justice and the Smith Institute, the report called for early years intervention to receive cross-party support and priority in government funding. Ita Walsh is credited with drafting most of the content, drawing heavily on previous Wave Trust publications and articles. Walsh quotes herself prominently at the beginning of Chapter One (without providing a source) claiming: 'The evidence overwhelmingly indicates that dysfunction strongly correlates with adverse experience in early life.' In Chapter Two, the Perry brain scans image makes an early public appearance (see Chapter One in this volume) just before the following claim is reproduced from page 18 of *Violence and what to do about it*: 'The early years are so critically important to the child's later social development that pathways to violence are often laid down by the age of two or three.'

Two references are provided to back this claim up. One to Hosking's 'Nursery crimes' piece, and the other to a study by Daniel Shaw and colleagues (2001), which focused solely on the behaviour of disadvantaged boys up to the age of 6. Hailing the husband and wife team of business strategists as experts, neither Allen nor Duncan Smith questioned the paucity of evidence supporting the claims being made in their names.

Moving, shaking and spanning

Although the Wave Trust remained a tiny organisation revolving chiefly around the activities of Hosking and Walsh, their influence grew almost exponentially from 2007. Their campaign for the introduction of David Olds' USA Nurse-Family Partnerships (NFPs) won the support of Prime Minster Blair's Strategy Unit and Cabinet Minister Hilary Armstrong. Funding of £15 million was announced for a UK version of the NFP, with ten FNP pilot studies in England and Wales beginning in 2008. Meanwhile the Wave Trust's contacts in Parliament saw it involved in a variety of other policy projects. For example, Hosking describes being invited by Prime Minister Gordon Brown and five other cabinet ministers, alongside a small group of people (including chiefs of police forces) to advise on how to tackle the problems of guns, gangs and knives'.[14] As the criminologist Simon Hallsworth notes, the Wave Trust began to feature as part of an eclectic 'gang control industry' within government, consisting of moral entrepreneurs, private industry and celebrities.[15] Hallsworth recounts how the Wave Trust narrative featured prominently in discussions at this time:

> To help develop its anti-gang response the Home Office commissioned private consultants. At a seminar convened at 10 Downing Street – co-chaired by the Prime Minister and the Home Secretary – a representative of the Wave Trust (a proselytising organisation steeped in biologically reductionist theories of crime) argued, in part that the problem of 'gangs' arose from the fact that the average gang member had an atrophied brain by the age of 3. (2011: 191)

This argument seems to have been well received. After a further a meeting with then Home Secretary Jacqui Smith MP, Hosking became part of a Home Office policy group on violent crime reduction. The extent of Wave Trust involvement in policy networks during this period is evident in a quote from Graham Allen MP, proudly reproduced by Hosking in his 2007 'CEO Message':

> WAVE's work with the Cabinet Office and the Treasury was invaluable in helping change Government attitude to the importance of early intervention in an overall violence reduction strategy. Their strategy of collaborative engagement with Ministers, MPs, Government departments, Police, Health, and Education services, Local Authorities and others has saved years in our journey towards a violence-free society.

During this period Wave Trust appears to have developed a particularly close relations with the Metropolitan Police force, contributing to their Youth Violence and Serious Violence strategies. The Met Commissioner at the time, Sir Ian Blair, is quoted by Hosking as stating: 'Other than the threat from terrorism, violence by young people on young people is the most significant cause of fear and concern about community safety. The WAVE Trust [is] part of the solution.'[16] With such support Wave Trust was appointed to lead the 'Programmes' strand of the Prevention component of a 'Five Boroughs Alliance' of Croydon, Greenwich, Lambeth, Lewisham and Southwark in London, working with them to design intervention programmes for young people at risk of gang involvement. A Hosking-devised therapeutic model to prevent violent reoffending was 'married together' with the 'know how' of a Californian personal development coach, Robert Razz. The resulting programme, named 'An End to Violence' was delivered by 'Wave representatives' to London teenagers convicted of violent offences and inmates at High Down prison in Surrey. No details are provided about 'An End to Violence' and there appears to be no independent evaluation of its effectiveness. Hosking, however, claims a £300,000 cost saving to the government was made from implementing the High Down intervention alone.[17] The boundary spanning Wave Trust also acted as adviser to a variety of local councils, third sector organisations and directors of children's services on the implementation of early intervention programmes, extending its influence beyond the criminal justice services and central government.

It seems, though, that the Wave Trust was promising, and expecting, a rapid decline in violence to follow immediately from a prioritisation of early years intervention. Believing his own hype, by 2009 Hosking was lamenting the unchanged incidence of child abuse rates despite all his efforts. Concluding that a new business strategy was required, Wave Trust drew up a plan for an 'achievable' 70% reduction in child maltreatment by the year 2030. The revised strategy revolved around extensive and faster implementation of early intervention programmes alongside a media campaign. Echoing the 'I Am Your Child' public relations blitz in the USA, the Wave Trust's 70/30 campaign sought to draw an influential cohort of politicians, chief executive officers and thinktanks to the cause:

> Our proposed approach has been to set a radical but achievable goal of a 70% reduction in child maltreatment by the year 2030 – we call this the '70/30' objective – and to create a coalition of supporters, spanning political parties,

charities, professional experts and grass roots, with the intention of creating an unstoppable momentum supporting and arguing the case for change.[18]

Iain Duncan Smith stepped up to take on the role of Wave Trust Patron, alongside Baroness Walmsley, the Liberal Democrat spokesperson for Children in the House of Lords, Baroness Hilary Armstrong, former Labour Cabinet Minister, and General the Lord Ramsbotham, the ex-Chief Inspector of Prisons. Promotional events for the 70/30 campaign were held at Kensington Palace and Guildhall (donated by the City of London Corporation). Select academics researching in the areas of early child development were also recruited as supporters, while funding for the campaign was received from the Joseph Rowntree Charitable Trust, Esmée Fairbairn Foundation, the Metropolitan Police and the Garfield Western Foundation.

A key feature of the Wave Trust's policy networking activities has been the maintenance of cross-party consensus on early years intervention. Hosking has been able to span across political parties, changing governments and shifting institutional dynamics, through foregrounding child rescue narratives. Before the 2010 election Wave Trust met key representatives from all three main political parties to 'educate them on the latest research findings on effective policies to improve outcomes'. When the Coalition government was formed, Wave Trust was well placed to consolidate its influence. The new Deputy Prime Minister Nick Clegg hosted a Wave Trust reception at 10 Downing Street, and Hosking began work as a key adviser to Graham Allen MP as part of his review into early intervention, helping him draft the first of his reports (2011a), while also contributing to a wide variety of policy reports and committees.

It is difficult to overestimate the influence of the Wave Trust since 2010. It has received considerable funding from various government departments including the Home Office, the Cabinet Office, Department for Education and Department for Health. George Hosking has assumed high-profile roles across a wide variety of policy networks. For example, he has played a formative role in lobbying for the preventive elements in the Children and Young People (Scotland) Act 2014 (with its Named Person provision), while also being contracted to provide consultancy support to a variety of local councils implementing early intervention programmes. As Hosking states in the 2012 Wave Trustees report, the organisation enjoyed prime access to parliamentary decision makers:

Between January and July 2011 the Government and civil service were actively engaged in considering their response to the reviews by Graham Allen, Frank Field and Claire Tickell. We were actively engaged throughout this period in providing relevant research and policy commentary to ministers, politicians and civil servants to inform them in judging their response.[19]

By 2013 Hosking was co-chairing a special interest group on under-2s for the Departments for Health and Education, and producing the detailed *Conception to age two* report emphasising a moral, 'scientific' and economic case for greater early investment in young children (Wave Trust, 2013). Recommendations included a universal 3–4 month assessment of the quality of parent–infant relationships, with a further follow-up assessment at 12–15 months alongside the existing developmental check for 2-year-olds. Mothers failing to demonstrate sufficient 'attunement' would then be referred for support and further monitoring, thereby allowing the 'growing brain to become socially efficient' (Wave Trust, 2013: 69). The report contained a detailed commissioning framework to guide service provision, funded by the CEO of a wealth management corporation offering social investment portfolios. Forewords were provided by the then Ministers for Education and Health, respectively Liz Truss and Daniel Poulter, with Truss declaring: 'As our understanding of the brain development of babies improves, so too must our policies, to reflect this critically important period of life' (Wave Trust, 2013: 6). On the back of the *Conception to age two* report, the Wave Trust went on to employ a 'Local Authority and Health Liaison Officer' to lobby key decision makers and persuade them to adopt the report's central recommendations.

A decisive proposal of the report was for the Big Lottery Fund (BIG) to invest £165 million in prevention-focused early years intervention. Shortly after, BIG announced the 'A Better Start' funding initiative claiming:

> There is strong evidence to show that what happens in the womb and through the first three years of life can profoundly affect a child's future. Tens of thousands of vulnerable babies who may be at risk of a future of long-lasting health issues, unemployment or even criminal activity will now have a better start in life following a £215 million Big Lottery Fund investment to five areas in England.[20]

Hosking was appointed to the steering group of the project, feeding into funding decisions. The BIG also invited him to provide training sessions on 'early years' to staff involved in appraising the quality of applications, as was the Dartington Social Research Unit, a group awarded BIG funding to develop science-based prevention strategies.[21]

Hosking was also invited, on behalf of Wave Trust, to become chair of a new All-Party Parliamentary Group (APPG) on Conception to Age Two, founded by Conservative MP Andrea Leadsom and Labour MP Frank Field. Leadsom was keen to produce a short manifesto version of Hosking's 2013 report, with the aim of appealing to MPs. The result was the '1001 Critical Days' manifesto, website and campaign. Meanwhile, Hosking was working his parliamentary contacts in an effort to secure a greater funding commitment to early years intervention projects:

> At the invitation of Iain Duncan Smith, in October 2013 I made a presentation on the importance of prevention in the early years to the Cabinet Social Justice Committee. There was no dissent about the principle of investing in prevention, but also no commitment to put resources behind this policy. The last of seven ministers to respond to my recommendations was Oliver Letwin, policy adviser to David Cameron. He presented me with the stark and challenging, but clear, political reality that he would not give his support unless we could prove its financial value *within a 5-year parliamentary term*. WAVE promptly turned its energies throughout 2014 to designing a robust pilot project approach ('Pioneer Communities') that could answer the challenge of that political reality.[22] (Hosking, Wave Trust Annual Report in 2014)

In the context of austerity cuts to social spending, public services and welfare benefits Hosking was successful in securing £15 million from the Treasury to pursue a pilot project. Match funding from local authorities of £12.5 million was agreed, and Pioneer Communities was launched at 11 Downing Street in November 2014. While details of the project currently remain unclear, the broad proposal appears to revolve around screening for risk for new mothers in four 'pioneer areas', referrals to attachment-informed services and ongoing monitoring of attachment status. The outcome, according to Hosking will be '1,280 rescued from consequences of Disorganised Attachment'.[23] This, he claims, will 'turn off the taps' of child maltreatment.

If implemented, Pioneering Communities would operate at a different level of scrutiny compared with previous Wave projects. It appears many of the county's leading proponents of attachment theory are listed as project contributors.[24] More significantly, as a condition of Treasury funding, the programme will be subject to rigorous independent evaluation by a consortium of universities. Hosking has promised dramatic and very specific impacts deliverable over the course of just five years. These include improvements in participating children's health, wellbeing and school readiness, fewer children in care or needing special support, reduced inequalities and, of course, a major reduction in child maltreatment.[25]

Hosking's long-standing conviction and commitment saw him awarded an OBE in 2014. Yet his concern for the wellbeing of children is curiously narrow. Hosking's evangelism about the prophylactic powers of maternal sensitivity has coincided with a steady deterioration of material conditions for disadvantaged children and families. He has stayed silent about the devastating impact of austerity on the lives of infants and their parents, despite clear evidence linking deprivation to child abuse and neglect (Bywaters et al, 2016). It remains to be seen whether or not an independent analysis will show that Hosking's efforts to better 'attune' mothers to their infants can compensate for persistently high levels of child poverty, sharp rises in family homelessness, destitution, hunger, dependence on foodbanks, and the decimation of services addressing domestic violence and other specialisms. In the meantime, some indication of the project's likely success might be gleaned from our case study of the Wave Trust's favoured intervention, the FNPs.

Wave Trust and Hosking are also keyed into early years intervention nodal networks internationally. For example, Hosking was invited to speak on promoting early childhood services at a conference held in Canada involving key international players and funders in the field, including UNESCO and the Bernard van Leer Foundation ('Models of Early Childhood Services' international conference, 5–6 June 2012), and Wave Trust is a member of the World Health Organization Violence Prevention Alliance. We consider some of the racialisation issues raised by initiating and funding 'universal' models of early intervention and child development in the West and applying them in developing countries in Chapter Seven.

Case study 2: Family Nurse Partnerships

Licensed for success

The FNP programme has always been more than a technical intervention model. Based on the original USA Nurse–Family Partnerships (NFP), it arrived in the UK with a readymade narrative backdrop, promising social and economic transformation through the salvation of disadvantaged families. It was hailed as a proven method of promoting the life chances of poor children and cited as key to securing the massive reductions in public expenditure promised in the Allen Reports (2011a, 2011b). While precious few of these miracles have come to pass, the programme remains the early interventionists' flagship initiative and sits at the centre of nodal networks in the field. Before exploring the implementation and characteristics of the British FNP we will begin by examining its USA progenitor as the source of the programme's reputation and evidence base.

The founder, advocate and guardian of the initial US-based NFP is David Olds. He has a story to tell about the origin of the programme and his part in creating a highly successful evidence-based intervention. In a published report melding together the foundations of the NFP and the life story of its creator, Olds describes knowing he wanted to help others from the age of 11. Harbouring 'romantic visions of going off to India or some exotic place' he began studying International Relations at Johns Hopkins University only to realise his calling to help people lay closer to home. Olds switched his major to Social and Behavioural Science after developing his interest in infant attachment. He cites his parents divorcing when he was 11 as formative, reflecting 'there is a part of me that has always wanted to recapture that sense I had of a happy family in my earliest years' (Goodman, 2006: 6).

Olds' first job after graduating in 1970 was as a teacher in a day care centre for pre-schoolers in inner city Baltimore. He notes disapprovingly how most of the activities in the centre were purely play-based. Concerned about the lack of aspiration and structure, Olds immediately set about introducing the infants to new curriculum. But he described eventually coming to realise that many of the children were suffering 'irreparable damage' from the poor quality of mothering they received. This inspired him to return to college to study for a PhD in Developmental Psychology. During this period he designed the prototype for NFP and, most crucial of all to its trajectory, sought and received funding to enable him to conduct a long-term RCT of the programme's efficacy. In Elmiram, New York, he allocated 200 pregnant first-time mothers to be visited by a nurse until their child's second birthday and 200 to a control group receiving standard pre-natal provision. His reported results were encouraging, with fewer pre-term births and a lower incidence of abuse and neglect in the treatment group.

These positive findings attracted the attention of philanthropic organisations and Olds was funded to conduct two further RCTs in Memphis and Colorado. Again clear health benefits accrued to mothers and infants participating in the programme, but it is important to note these effects were primarily confined to the first three years of the child's life. In a follow-up study ten years later, Olds struggles to identify long-term meaningful impacts beyond very modest savings in welfare expenditure on the most deprived mothers. No effects were identified in relation to the mother's marriage, relationship with the biological father, intimate partner violence, alcohol and other drug use, arrests, incarceration, psychological distress or reports of foster care placements (Olds et al, 2010). Instead, Olds points to indications of 'less role impairment' and a greater 'sense of mastery' among nurse-visited mothers.[26] Despite these disappointing results, Olds subsequently was able to claim significant decreases in self-reported criminal and anti-social behaviour among nurse-visited families in a further follow-up of the families 15 years later (Olds et al. 1998). These results were achieved in the context of assessing a wide range of outcomes however, without formal adjustment for multiple significance testing.

Inspired by the results Olds reported from the RCT, a range of philanthropists gave their backing to the programme, including the Bill and Melinda Gates Foundation, Kellogs Foundation, the charitable arm of Johnson & Johnson, and many others. The NFP then became incorporated as a not-for-profit business. Its headquarters in Denver pursued a plan to market its 'product' using a business approach to replication and monitoring 'fidelity to the model' (Goodman, 2006). The aim was to roll the programme out across the USA, but this required an active promotional strategy advertising the benefits of the programme to potential funders and commissioners. Philanthropic foundations, think tanks and social investment advocates began endorsing the NFP through often exaggerated claims. For example, the Brookings Institute published a description of the programme authored by Olds that concluded:

> Poor children and families in the United States deserve programs that work and taxpayers need to know that their dollars are being spent wisely. The NFP provides a model for

serving a segment of the population of vulnerable children and families at a critical stage in human development that can have long-lasting and far-reaching effects in reducing health and educational disparities.[27]

Claims to proof of efficacy and long-lasting effects proved to be particularly appealing to Hosking during his period of internet research on child abuse (see Case Study 1). In their first Wave Report, *Violence and what to do about it*, Hosking and Walsh identify the NFP as their top example of 'global best practice' and recommend large-scale implementation of the model in the UK.

Seemingly incognisant of the very localised differences between the USA and the UK, most notably the UK's NHS and universal health visiting service, Hosking lobbied hard for the introduction of the model in pilot areas, flying to Denver in 2004 to persuade Olds to extend his model to the UK. Olds agreed on the condition that funding would be committed. Drawing on his extensive political networks, Hosking found favour with a minister in the Prime Minister's Cabinet Office, Hilary Armstrong, a close ally of Tony Blair, and soon to become a Wave Trust Patron. In 2006, *Reaching out: An action plan on social exclusion* was published by the Cabinet Office. The report devoted a chapter to the early years, drawing heavily on Hosking and Walsh's 2005 Wave Report and claiming:

> Neglect in early childhood literally alters the physical and functional development of the brain – a powerful environmental effect. In extreme cases this can be dramatic, as illustrated by Figure 4.2, which shows CT scans of an average 3-year-old's brain compared to the brain of a 3-year-old child suffering from severe sensory-deprivation neglect. (Cabinet Office, 2006: 47)

'Figure 4.2' was, of course, the Perry brains in their first ever appearance in UK policy discourse (see Chapter One). The NFP programme was presented as a clear example of 'what works' to prevent such damage. In his book on political governance in Britain, Patrick Diamond (2013) gives a fascinating account of how the pilot for the British version, the FNP, was railroaded through the government at the behest of the Prime Minister's Office. Blair was in the final stages of his premiership and keen to establish the FNP as a legacy project. Armstrong was appointed to initiate it, but, despite acting from the centre of the government, she had no resources or infrastructure available to her in the Cabinet Office. Instead she was forced to scrabble around for money, exhorting other ministerial departments to provide support. This attempt to impose policy from the centre was resented by many in the government. Even a personal appeal from Blair to David Milliband, then Secretary of State at the Department of Communities and Local Government, to contribute a budget underspend was unsuccessful. As one of Armstrong's Special Advisers reflects in Diamond's book:

> I'm not sure Special Advisors can really do this, but I had to personally ring round officials in the departments, Home Office, Health, Local Government and Communities, to get £15 million for the pilots. As Special Advisor it wasn't really my role but as I say relationships with officials were not functioning and the Home Office was particularly obstructive. I had to ring Moira Wallace who was a Deputy Director, who I knew from my time there previously and basically managed to lever the money out of them. (Cited in Diamond, 2013: 159)

The £15 million raised was a far cry from the £60 million originally requested from Blair, but it enabled the FNP pilots to be initiated through Primary Care Trusts, with local consortiums bidding for funding. The pilot was defined by an overarching aim to reduce social exclusion. More specific objectives included improvements in health, educational success, and reductions in crime. Reflecting Hosking's particular concern over teenage parents, the FNP was targeted specifically at young disadvantaged mothers. At Olds' insistence, however, the model was to remain as faithful as possible to the US version. This was explained by likening it to medicine:

> The Family Nurse Partnership (FNP) is a licensed programme. One way of looking at this is to think about the comparison with prescription drugs – these are licensed to be used to treat specific medical conditions, to be given to a particular group of patients at a prescribed dose…. A complex community-based intervention such as the FNP programme has far more licensing requirements than just the eligible population and 'dose', but the principle is the same. If the programme is not delivered in the way that is set out in the license agreement, then it is also less likely to realise its intended benefit.[28]

The licensing requirements were extensive, demarcating the target client base, programme structure and nurse qualifications. Approved nurses were expected to complete an NFP-based clinical learning programme and deliver the intervention with careful conformity to the model.

Changing the world, one baby at a time™[29]

The lack of a clear ring-fenced programme budget made the FNP initiative vulnerable. But following on from Blair, the subsequent Prime Minister Gordon Brown was a passionate advocate of social investment and also embraced the model. Sharing Blair's conviction that transformational benefits for children would be forthcoming, Brown announced the expansion of the programme in his first speech to the Labour Party conference. He drew on a biblical reference to emphasise his commitment:

> 'We all remember that biblical saying: "suffer the little children to come unto me." No Bible I have ever read says: "bring just some of the children." Because no child should ever be written off, for mothers of infants, we will expand the help of Nurse-Family Partnerships.'[30]

This expansion was promised before the pilots had even got under way. An FNP National Unit was set up to lead national delivery, commissioned by the Department of Health and Public Health England who bought the licence from Olds at the University of Colorado. The FNP National Unit oversees its own licences to local providers and commissioners, and monitors adherence to the licence on behalf of Olds. Acknowledging the lack of a more localised evidence base, the Department of Health also commissioned a large-scale, independently administered RCT led by Cardiff University to provide a clear assessment of the effectiveness of the FNP programme.

The programme itself is offered to first-time young mothers early in pregnancy, with weekly or fortnightly visits continuing over the course of the child's first 24 months. Practice is informed by a detailed copyrighted curriculum, and FNP nurses are expected to collect extensive administrative data about mothers, children and the content of each visit to inform supervision and demonstrate programme fidelity. The actual content of the FNP curriculum is treated as commercially sensitive (despite being funded by public money) and is therefore not accessible for any detailed analysis. However, as we discuss in Chapter

Six, FNP practitioners draw on accounts of fragile developing brains to secure interest, support and compliance from the mothers they visit. FNP nurse practice is informed by attachment ideas combined with ecological and self-efficacy theory. The aim is to motivate mothers to change to become more attuned and aspirational parents. Further details can be gleaned from practice-based literature detailing for example, 'the use of life-sized dolls to model positive parenting behaviours that clients can copy and practise with their babies in order to understand better their baby's emotional states and cues and to respond appropriately' (Clayton, 2015: 2).

The hype surrounding the impact of the FNP programme grew through the 2008 global financial crisis and permeated the new Coalition government. Just before becoming prime minister in 2010, David Cameron declared, 'What matters most to a child's life chances is not the wealth of their upbringing but the warmth of their parenting,' before hailing the FNP as a programme that works for dysfunctional families.[31] Further expansion of the FNP programme also formed the core recommendation of the Allen reviews into early intervention (2011a, 2011b). A commitment from the government to double FNP places by 2015 followed. In 2013, Health Minister Daniel Poulter announced that a £17.5 million contract would be awarded to a new consortium to lead on the expansion of the FNP model, taking the programme outside the Department of Health. The consortium partners included the Tavistock and Portman NHS Foundation Trust; Impetus, a private equity foundation (and financial backer of the Sutton Trust); and the Dartington Social Research Unit, a charity 'advocating for evidence-based prevention and early intervention'.[32]

The involvement of Impetus in the FNP expansion consortium reflects a broader political agenda to 'free' the FNP from the bounds of the NHS by encouraging social enterprise 'spin-offs'. Derby FNP was the first to detach as an independent social enterprise called RippleZ. The move was supported by a grant administrated by an Impetus and Sutton Trust partnership, taken from the £125 million public funds entrusted to them by the Coalition government. Other FNPs have been similarly been disconnected from the NHS through annexation into 'not-for-profit' social enterprises that deliver a range of publicly funded health and social care services. The result is a compartmentalised and neatly packaged intervention ready for social investment and potential privatisation.

The evidence base amassed by Olds in the USA was influential in continuing UK government support and public funding. The FNP is rarely cited without mention of its proven efficacy by leading advocates of the programme, expecting similar benefits to be evidenced in the UK. Even the name of the RCT commissioned from Cardiff University by the Department of Health: 'Building Blocks', conveyed anticipation that the programme would indeed be built upon. As we have outlined in Chapter One though, the results published in 2015 were damming, concluding that: 'Adding FNP to the usually provided health and social care provided no additional short-term benefit to our primary outcomes. Programme continuation is not justified on the basis of available evidence.'

This 'gold standard' evaluation provoked protest from many early years intervention advocates, highlighting a somewhat contingent relationship with evidence. For example, in a Wave Trust press release, George Hosking queried the statistical interpretations of the study. Appearing not to understand the need to take account of effect size and of significance testing, he reproduced raw percentages from the research to argue small secondary effects of the programme were in fact very large.[33] In a blog posted on the EIF website, an FNP commissioner suggested that the primary focus of the RCT may have been misconceived and expressed concern that the evaluation had begun too soon after its introduction to the UK.[34] A statement from the Chief Executive of the EIF was more equivocal, claiming the results to be part of the normal and healthy development of an early intervention programme.[35] She also pointed out that the US studies tracked families for years, seemingly forgetting that the programme was sustained because clear benefits were evidenced in the first phase RCTs.

Broader level consideration of the reasons for the FNP's lack of impact reflect the social context/statistical practice explanations identified in Chapter One. Some have settled on the obvious conclusion that it offers little extra in the context of universal health care and health visiting. Others have also pointed to the more rigorous, independent nature of the British study: 'Scientifically, it's not ideal to have the same person who came up with a program trying to determine whether the program is any good.'[36] Nevertheless, the FNP project continues to be promoted by the 'What Works' Centre as evidence-based. Claims for its impact are mismatched with its actual impact in the UK. For example, an information pack for local authority commissioners carries the extraordinary claim that: 'FNP can transform the life chances of some of the most disadvantaged children and families in our communities, helping to improve social mobility and break the cycle of intergenerational disadvantage.'[37]

Meanwhile, the NHS and universal heath visiting in particular are vulnerable to the constraints and vicissitudes of spending targets. In

2015 services for children aged 0–5, including health visiting, were transferred from the NHS to local authority health care budgets. In the context of unprecedented cuts to local government funding, many councils have been forced to consider whether health visiting is any longer an affordable service. For example, the London Borough of Harrow put forward plans to axe its entire health visiting budget to achieve an estimated saving of £3.23 million.[38] Commissioning a narrow, targeted FNP programme could prove a more attractive option to cash-strapped councils, regardless of the evidence base.

Case study 3: Parent Infant Partnership UK (PIPUK)

'Restoring family life'

Parent Infant Partnership UK (PIPUK) was founded by the Conservative MP Andrea Leadsom in 2012. Before being elected to Parliament in 2010, Leadsom served as a trustee and 'Chairman' of the Oxford Parent Infant Project (OXPIP). OXPIP is a charity founded in 2005 by Sue Gerhardt (see Chapter Three) to promote infant mental health and child development through the framework of attachment theory and object relations. Leadsom has discussed publicly how her own experience of post-natal depression galvanised her interest in early years intervention.[39] In her interview for our research, Leadsom explained how her mother (formerly a midwife) became an OXPIP volunteer and asked her to write a business plan for the charity. In the process of acquiring funding for the charity, Leadsom says that she became 'utterly convinced' of the benefits of their attachment-based model and of the need to expand the service across the UK.[40] In 2011 Leadsom founded a 'sister' organisation in her constituency called Northamptonshire Parent Infant Partnership (NorPIP), before going on to establish PIPUK as a national charity and umbrella organisation. The substitution of the word 'partnership' for 'project' in the charity name is not explained, but lends a corporate air to PIPUK's 'vision' of 'a society of emotionally secure children who grow up to become socially responsible adults'.[41]

Leadsom secured funding for NorPIP and PIPUK chiefly from the Ana Leaf Foundation, a charity co-run by her sister Hayley de Putron, who is married to the Guernsey-based hedge fund manager Peter de Putron. The Ana Leaf Foundation is dependent on a single donor: Gloucester Research Ltd (latterly renamed GR Software & Research Limited). This company, owned by Peter de Putron, also engaged Leadsom's husband on its board of directors until 2014.[42] An investigation carried out by *The Guardian* in 2014, based on leaked identities of wealthy offshore clients of a private bank in the Channel Isles, established that the de Putrons had donated £816,000 to the Conservative Party via Gloucester Research since Leadsom was elected. This led the Labour MP Tom Watson to advise her to address suspicions of 'a cash for office' arrangement with the Conservative Party.[43] While Leadsom denied any knowledge of her brother-in-law's political donations, disquiet still surrounds the de Putrons' bankrolling of PIPUK. In 2016 it was revealed that Leadsom failed to declare the donations as 'related party transactions' in line with the standards guidelines drawn up for charities.[44]

More significantly, questions have been asked about the charity's high-profile role in Westminster politics. When Leadsom went on to co-found the APPG on Conception to Age Two, PIPUK was duly appointed as joint secretariat with the Wave Trust. The first clinical director of PIPUK, Miriam Silver, left after just six months in the job, expressing her misgivings in a blog post in 2014. She described the charity's 'Two is Too Late' conference launch as 'one-third professional conference, one-third stately home wedding and one-third party political broadcast for the blue party'.[45] Lambasting the charity's use of 'dodgy neuroscience', Silver revealed how mothers using the service had complained of feeling stigmatised. She also expressed doubt about the charity's real purpose, stating: 'I felt, cynically perhaps, that there was a second agenda, designed to promote the MP who founded the project and her political party, which was of more importance than our clinical goals, although this was never explicit.'[46]

Although she eventually stood down from her bid to become leader of the Conservative Party and prime minister in the wake of David Cameron's resignation in 2016, Leadsom's campaign prominently centred on the importance of early years intervention and attachment. Conservative MP Tim Loughton had by this point become the Chair of PIPUK. He also took on the role of Leadsom's leadership campaign manager. Shortly after she declared her candidacy, PIPUK sent a supportive tweet reading '@andrealeadsom puts social justice agenda of babies life chances as key priority for UKs brighter future'.

PIPUK has continued to grow and occupies a nodal network position that spans across political, service delivery and corporate interests. The charity now acts as hub for variety of local Parent Infant Partnerships across England, promoting 'model implementation for national replication, with recognition that early childhood development matters from a moral, scientific and economic perspective'.[47] While still primarily dependent on the largesse of the de Putrons, the charity has won significant contracts from local authorities to deliver infant mental health services. They are also in the process of developing a 'network of relationships with potential investors'.[48] This will no doubt be aided by connections to the finance industry through its trustees. For example, as well as Hayley de Putron, trustees include: Lady Fink, wife of the former treasurer of the Conservative Party, who is known for the controversy surrounding his Swiss bank account and his admission that he engages in 'ordinary tax avoidance'[49], and also Duncan McCourt previously of Morgan Stanley and Credit Suisse, who worked as Leadsom's office manager before becoming a special adviser to Philip Hammond, Chancellor of the Exchequer.

Underlining the political links, the 'moral' component of PIPUK's mission is pursued by its Executive Director Clair Rees, who also acts as a 'Parliamentary Early Years Advisor'. Echoing the traditionalist principles of many of the organisation's Patrons (Leadsom, Iain Duncan Smith, George Hosking, Frank Field), Rees is a passionate supporter of 'family values'. She has described how the Conservative Party's promise to tackle family breakdown through compassionate conservatism converted her to their political cause. Writing a blog titled 'Revolutionising the nation must begin with restoring family life' for the political website 'Conservative Home' in 2016, she states:

> It is within the family environment that an individual's physical, emotional and psychological development occurs. From our family we should learn unconditional love, understand right from wrong, and gain empathy, respect and self-regulation. These qualities enable us to engage positively at school, at work and in society. Let us restore stable family life, stability in community life for greater social cohesion and bring back into the social fabric of our daily lives increased life chances for all. This Government is making headway on tackling some of these entrenched issues of social justice and this needs to continue to be the cornerstone of compassionate Conservative policy.[50]

Rees presents a personal reflection on her own family background, highlighting her dysfunctional upbringing amid labour values and welfare dependency:

> Margaret Thatcher was not the icon in my family home growing up in the Eighties where negative perceptions of those who voted Conservative were rife. The bridge the

family car was driven under every week stated in large, bold letters 'fingers up to the poll tax'. Generational voting records emblazoned with the colour red prevailed from the legacy of coal miners and steelworkers on both parental sides of my house. Long hours of being in dark places in the earth and purgatorial furnaces does something to the mind. Such was that legacy for my family that one of my grandfathers had such an awful life down the mines that the message he passed on to the next generation was not to work if they didn't have to. Family narrative and labour values then became for my family welfare dependency.... I now have two in three members of my wider family who do not work to this day, and family breakdown exists in every corner.[51]

PIPUK's nodal actor and boundary spanning is evident in other links that it cements. Its chief function is to act as an umbrella organisation for a variety of locally based psychotherapy services. Like the FNP, PIPUK uses a trademarked strapline to publicise itself. In fact the two slogans are remarkably similar: the FNP asserts that it is 'Changing the world one baby at a time', while PIPUK is somewhat more specific in its claim to be 'Creating a better future for the UK – one baby at a time'. This slogan assists its campaigning role, advocating for a greater understanding of the importance of attachment and infant mental health. Its publicity drives have included designating a week in June 'Infant Mental Health Week'. As part of this particular PIPUK campaign, a conference titled 'Investing in Early Potential' was organised in Central Hall Westminster, sponsored by the parliamentary-based 1001 Critical Days campaign. The event featured speeches from a range of MPs (including Leadsom, Loughton and Field) alongside papers from practitioners and psychotherapists. The parliamentary links enjoyed by PIPUK also enable the organisation to offer 'bespoke' consultancy work to organisations looking for expertise in policy making, legislation and parliamentary research.[52]

★

As these three case studies have shown, interests and agendas converge and reinforce a social investment and early intervention orthodoxy. Each example illustrates how politicians, business concerns and practitioners have an investment in sustaining narratives about the transformative potential of mothering. In the next chapter we take a more detailed look at how practitioners working with families on an everyday basis interpret the 'evidence' for early intervention and explore, in particular, how misinformation about brain science has come to shape the practice of early years workers.

Notes

[1]   http://fnp.nhs.uk/about-us
[2]   www.pipuk.org.uk/what-we-do/perinatal-and-infant-mental-health
[3]   www.wavetrust.org/about-us
[4]   www.wavetrust.org/about-us
[5]   www.wavetrust.org/our-work/publications/articles/digging-roots-violence-1999
[6]   www.wavetrust.org/about-us
[7]   www.wavetrust.org/our-work/publications/articles/nursery-crimes-2001
[8]   www.ons.gov.uk/peoplepopulationandcommunity/crimeandjustice/compendium/
       focusonviolentcrimeandsexualoffences/2015-02-12/chapter1violentcrimeandsex
       ualoffencesoverview#summary
[9]   A general reference bibliography is provided but not explicitly linked to the text.
       It appears likely it this claim comes from a publication dating from the early 1970s.
[10] He does not appear to be registered as a psychologist with the British Psychological
       Society or the UKCP.
[11] http://webarchive.nationalarchives.gov.uk/20110220105210/rds.homeoffice.gov.
       uk/rds/pdfs2/hosb703.pdf
[12] www.theguardian.com/society/2005/oct/16/socialcare.childrensservices
[13] www.wavetrust.org/about-us/our-history/ceo-message-2007
[14] www.wavetrust.org/about-us/our-history/ceo-message-2007
[15] Such as Ross Kemp, whose expertise extended no further than being cast as a
       gangster in the popular BBC TV soap *EastEnders*, and fronting the Sky documentary
       series *Ross Kemp on Gangs*.
[16] www.wavetrust.org/about-us/our-history/ceo-message-2007
[17] www.wavetrust.org/about-us/our-history/ceo-message-2009
[18] www.wavetrust.org/about-us/our-history/ceo-message-2009
[19] www.wavetrust.org/sites/default/files/page/WAVE-Trust-Annual-Report-12-
       finance.pdf. The Wave Trust also fed into the influential *Parenting Matters* document
       published by CentreForum (Paterson, 2011).
[20] www.biglotteryfund.org.uk/global-content/press-releases/england/170614_nat_
       abs_a-better-start-in-life
[21] Hosking also provided his training in early years to staff at the EIF.
[22] WAVE Trust Annual Report, 31 October, http://apps.charitycommission.gov.
       uk/Accounts/Ends89/0001080189_AC_20141031_E_C.PDF
[23] www.1001criticaldays.co.uk/~ criticaldays/UserFiles/files/Building%20Great%20
       Britons%20Written%20Submission%20WAVE%20Trust%20250215(1).pdf
[24] www.wavetrust.org/sites/default/files/event/NCASC%202014%20-%20
       WAVE%20Trust%20-%20A%20preventive%20approach%20to%20creating%20
       a%20large%20scale%20step%20reduction%20in%20levels%20of%20child%20
       abuse%2C%20neglect%20and%20domestic%20violence..pdf
[25] www.wavetrust.org/sites/default/files/event/NCASC%202014%20-%20
       WAVE%20Trust%20-%20A%20preventive%20approach%20to%20creating%20

a%20large%20scale%20step%20reduction%20in%20levels%20of%20child%20 abuse%2C%20neglect%20and%20domestic%20violence..pdf

26 Yet self-reported criminal and anti-social behaviour was measured to be significantly lower in nurse-visited families in a 15-year follow-up. At the very least this raises questions about the reliability of self-report measures.

27 www.brookings.edu/~/media/Research/Files/Reports/2010/10/13-investing-in-young-children-haskins/1013_investing_in_young_children_haskins_ch6.PDF

28 http://fnp.nhs.uk/deliver/licensing-effectiveness

29 This FNP registered strapline reflects a consistent trope in corporate mission statements, with Johnson & Johnson 'Caring for the world, one person at a time', while Starbucks 'inspire and nurture the human spirit – one person, one cup and one neighbourhood at a time'.

30 http://news.bbc.co.uk/1/hi/uk_politics/7010664.stm

31 http://conservative-speeches.sayit.mysociety.org/speech/601554

32 https://dartington.org.uk/about/#goto1

33 http://wavetrust.org/our-work/publications/articles/press-release-wave-trust-comment-fnp-national-evaluation

34 www.eif.org.uk/the-fnp-evaluation-inconvenient-truth-or-a-bump-in-the-road/

35 www.eif.org.uk/eif-responds-to-evaluation-of-family-nurse-partnership/

36 www.theatlantic.com/health/archive/2015/10/nurse-family-partnership/412000/

37 http://fnp.nhs.uk/sites/default/files/contentuploads/fnp_information_pack_-_an_overview.pdf

38 www.cypnow.co.uk/cyp/news/1155119/entire-health-visiting-service-under-threat-at-london-council

39 www.dailymail.co.uk/news/article-2680082/My-baby-blues-nightmare-Tory-minister-New-mums-help.html

40 www.andrealeadsom.com/early-years-intervention/early-years-intervention

41 www.pipuk.org.uk/our-story/mission-vision-and-values

42 www.buzzfeed.com/jamesball/andrea-leadsoms-charity-is-bankrolled-by-her-offshore-banker?utm_term=.vxovPDeDZ#.dpM6RzWzG

43 www.theguardian.com/politics/2014/jul/08/andrea-leadsom-family-links-offshore-bank-donations-tories

44 www.buzzfeed.com/alanwhite/andrea-leadsoms-charity-has-not-declared-a-potential-conflic?utm_term=.sxvgDjojx#.wfRzbxMx9

45 https://clinpsyeye.wordpress.com/2014/10/02/high-on-scare-low-on-science-a-tale-of-charity-politics-and-dodgy-neuroscience/

46 https://clinpsyeye.wordpress.com/2014/10/02/high-on-scare-low-on-science-a-tale-of-charity-politics-and-dodgy-neuroscience/

47 Report of the Trustees and Unaudited Financial Statements for the Year Ended 31 August 2015 for Parent Partnership UK.

48 Report of the Trustees and Unaudited Financial Statements for the Year Ended 31 August 2015 for Parent Partnership UK.

49 www.standard.co.uk/news/uk/everyone-avoids-tax-says-lord-fink-after-he-was-named-by-ed-miliband-in-commons-row-10041040.html

50 www.conservativehome.com/platform/2016/02/clair-rees-revolutionising-the-nation-must-begin-with-restoring-family-life.html

51 www.conservativehome.com/platform/2016/02/clair-rees-revolutionising-the-nation-must-begin-with-restoring-family-life.html

52 www.pipuk.org.uk/what-we-do/legislation-and-policy

SIX

Saving children

Introduction

In this chapter we move deeper into the implications of early intervention. We look at the way that brain science and social investment ideas infuse the beliefs of practitioners who work in the early years field. We consider how it shapes their understandings and practices, with consequences for their approaches to and interactions with parents. Practitioners are no mean constituency; the UK has 'the most elaborate architecture anywhere for parenting support' (Daly, 2013: 164). There is an extensive workforce involved in early years provision in children's services, health and education. They include early years educators, health visitors, home visitors, nurses, play workers, social workers and therapists (Churchill and Clarke, 2009; Gillies, 2011; Lewis, 2011; Daly and Bray, 2015). Such practitioners work in public provision such as Children's Centres and primary schools, and most significantly in the home setting. They provide instruction and knowledge to parents as to how best to relate to and bring up their children, and they monitor babies' and children's development and parent–child relations. Mary Daly and Rachel Bray (2015) argue that this expansion has been stimulated by the coming together of concerns about 'risks' to children and society, the identification of deficits in childrearing practices as causal, and a set of interventionist policy 'solutions' that focus on individual behavioural change rather than structural interventions (see also Dodds, 2009, on the Family Nurse Partnership [FNP] specifically).

A key motif of early years intervention is the idea that children need to be 'saved' from poor parenting. It is sub-optimal parenting that is claimed to hold back babies' brain development and thus their future wellbeing and achievement. As we have seen in previous chapters in this book, through saving individual babies from the neuro-damage that deficient parenting can create, the world will be changed. The idea is neatly summed up in the FNP intervention programme's slogan: 'Changing the world – one baby at a time'. There will be savings in the moral sense. Enthusiasts claim that intervention before a child is 3 years old will save society from future crime, low attainment, teenage parenthood, and drug and alcohol abuse. Consequently, there will also be savings in the financial sense. Public expenditure on those social problems in the future will be reduced by investment in early intervention in the present it is claimed (for example, Allen, 2011b). We have examined how these individual, moral and financial 'savings' are underpinned by the involvement of new philanthropists and social entrepreneurs in promoting and providing intervention programmes within a neoliberal social investment paradigm focused on children as future assets.

In this chapter, we draw on our interviews with health and early years practitioners to look in more detail at the strong mission that they feel guides their work, to save children from the vicissitudes of poor parenting. We look at the way that brain science provides practitioners with the 'proof' that they feel justifies the methods of intervention they use, and their promotion of this form of knowledge. We consider two sets of assumptions that are implicit in practitioners' assertions – the idea of optimising both children and mothers, and notions of low attachment and deficit parenting intergenerationally that mean that children need to be saved.

Evangelical early intervention

A powerful factor in the general rolling out of early intervention is that policy makers and providers 'believe in it', as Daly and Bray term it (2015: 638). The expression of belief takes on a devout tone, with Jan Macvarish noting how the 'wondrous brain' is spoken of in 'reverential terms', with synaptic connections described as 'miracles of the human body' in her critique of 'neuroparenting' (2016: 22–23). In fact strong belief has always fuelled the proponents of early intervention. In Chapter Two we traced the targeting of children and families for intervention back to 19th-century earnest convictions that moral self-governance would overcome social ills, propelled by an evangelistic Christianity that chimed with liberal ideas. It is interesting to note that several of the most vocal contemporary advocates of early intervention and promoters of brain science as a rationale for it, also hold strong Christian beliefs. These include early intervention nodal actors from our case studies in the previous chapter: George Hosking, Wave Trust CEO; Andrea Leadsom MP, founder of Parent Infant Partnerships UK; and Frank Field MP and Iain Duncan Smith MP, authors of influential brain-based early intervention policy reports.

The ardent evangelism of early intervention has been noted by others reviewing the field. Professor Sir Michael Rutter (2002) has drawn attention to the way that claims about the extent to which early experiences determine brain development have been subject to what he terms a 'misleading evangelism' from people outside the field of neuroscience. Such evangelism involves 'false claims, mistaken inferences, and misleading enthusiasm' (Rutter, 1999: 169; see also Webster et al, 2002). Policy makers and practitioners however, are each somewhat differently placed in this endeavour (Horsley et al, 2016). High-profile advocates evangelising for early intervention at the policy level may use brain polemics to bolster their message instrumentally. For example, one of the early proponents of the value of brain science in social policy making, Matthew Taylor, CEO of the Royal Society of Arts and former adviser to the New Labour governments, explained to us:

> If you're asking to what extent does neuroscience and just neuroscience influence policy I would say in a very, very limited way ... there can be a tendency to want to put the neuroscience argument at the front because it's couched in science and, you know we generally speaking believe science has an authority that social sciences doesn't have.

Practitioners who were interviewed for our research, however, were sincerely committed both to early years intervention and the supposed explanatory potential of brain science as a means of saving struggling families from themselves and transforming the lives of parents and children. A fervent enthusiasm and belief in vocation characterised their descriptions of their work that could echo the language of evangelism and biology:

> I've always just had a fascination right from a child of babies, always loved playing with them ... how they grew, how they developed, it's just always – I suppose it's always been within my genes, I suppose.... I did a conference in London a few years ago and we had talks ... very much looking at the development of the brain. It was quite frustrating sitting there thinking it hasn't yet hit health visiting yet, it hasn't hit mainstream knowledge yet.... So finally, *hallelujah*, a few years later coming into our practice, and these books that we can quote and people that we can turn to in increasing our knowledge, and it's something that is vitally important. (Health Visitor interview 1, our emphasis)

> I can actually make a difference to people's lives. So I now have a passion, rather than just going through the motions.... I'm trying to persuade [the head teacher] to get the *Why love matters* book, the little *bible* of Children's Centre managers. (Children's Centre interview 2, our emphasis)

> I remember thinking what an amazing job to be in that early stage when you can make such a difference ... to enable [the parent] to have the best chance to give their baby the best opportunity really. To make it different. (FNP interview 7)

Many of the practitioners stressed the intensive nature of the work they were undertaking in building trust and saving children, conveying the extent of the deficit in parenting that they are attempting to overcome. Persistence was said to be necessary to engage and retain families in early intervention, in the face of lack of interest or disengagement. Effort was required if the message of the importance of the optimal form of parenting for babies' brain development, and of engagement with the intervention to promote it, was to get through to the parents who needed it. For example, one FNP practitioner (FNP interview 3) described her role as hard and challenging work that required a great deal of tenacity. She referred to a drip-drip approach where FNP nurses would not walk away if a mother did not want to participate in the voluntary programme, but would keep calling back and trying to offer the provision. Other practitioners talked about the need to draw mothers into services through attractive activities, such as pampering sessions, before addressing the issues and making the interventions that were on their professional agenda:

> Once you've got them ... we do, not always therapy, we do arts and crafts, sometimes it's just chin and chat, but then occasionally I will do a therapy thing on, it could be how they were brought up as a child, like their relationships with their families. (Children's Centre interview 5)

A passionate, persistent and maybe stealthy evangelical approach was required to deliver brain science-informed early intervention to mothers whose young children were at risk of deficit parenting. Further, other professionals needed to be made aware of the message and see the light of brain science. Professionals who did not have training in neuroscientific knowledge were regarded not only as missing out on important knowledge, but dangerously so:

> You go to a Children's Centre, you see the way they talk to mums, you see the way – they don't pick up what we think are the cues. I think a prime example is social care. For example some of the ways – I've just been to a meeting, some of the ways perhaps even independent reviewing officers talk to children and talk to mums.... How are we going to change the world? I mean we have poor attachment, we have poor – we have high crime, we have high drug use, we have poor ability to self regulate. Through all realms I don't think anybody working in, you know, professions such as health and social work should not be aware of these changes. I feel quite strongly about it … I'm quite passionate about the brain you can tell. (FNP interview 7)

Indeed, many of the practitioners believed that rapid development in scientific knowledge was placing their profession on the cusp of dramatic advancement. One FNP practitioner (FNP interview 3) remarked that the evidence about the critical importance of the period of pregnancy and the first two years was strengthening all the time because of the progress being made in neuoscientific knowledge.

Practitioners work in contexts where there is little internal questioning about the general endeavour of early intervention (Daly and Brady, 2015: 639). Indeed, despite us building opportunities for reflection on the drawbacks to a biologised approach into our interviews with them, the practitioners who we spoke to rarely expressed any reservations about the assumptions guiding their practice (Horsley et al, 2016). Nonetheless, while not questioning or challenging the brain science knowledge itself, a few expressed concerns that the messages about brain development could make parents feel guilty, or be overemphasised and sensationalised:

> Guilt as well, so being very skilful about the way [brain science's] incorporated in, you know, health and education. And also not thinking if you haven't got it right in the first two years, you know there's no kind of way back. (FNP interview 8)

As long as they don't compartmentalise, that's just the brain. I mean the child is a whole person, and there are lots of factors influencing them. Although it is important, but it has to be put in relation to the whole child, not just all about the brain. But that never used to be the case before. The brain didn't even come into it before, previously. As long as it's seen as another dimension of the child, yes, that's fine.... And it's not just a fad. Because you do get these young courses, and some things are just in at the minute, and then you have lots of training, and then it's out again, and something else has taken over.... As long as they introduce it research-based, so they can back up what they say with research, and the research is done properly and not sensationalised. (Children's Centre interview 3)

The rare caveat aside, several reasons for the enthusiastic acceptance on the part of practitioners are apparent. Brain science rhetoric in early years intervention is amenable to a seamless weaving into ideas about attachment theory as a core foundation of professional knowledge. Most practitioners in FNPs, for example, have Health Visitor qualifications and experience of working in the community in other roles (Robinson and Miller, 2013). For these and other early years practitioners, ideas about brain development and the specific sort of parenting that stimulates it resonate with their prior professional knowledge and practice experience, providing greater impetus to their belief and commitment:

It's very hard to separate how what I would just do anyway, no, it's more about, as I say, justification. That really gives me a reason, a clear reason as to why I believe x, y and z. (Children's Centre interview 2)

[In my work I am] putting some of the stuff around attachment and early brain development, you know all the stuff we know is important, into place.... Without that confidence in your own ability, I think it would be a very hard job to do. It's got to be a confidence backed by a good foundation of knowing you've been able to practise safely and well for a long time.... And a good programme with evidence base. (FNP interview 7)

Thus brain science backed up the rationale for and practice of early intervention. It provided practitioners with a sense of expert knowledge that shored up their professional status through the aura of authority conferred by science, as referred to above by Matthew Taylor. The revelatory knowledge that fuels and justifies early years evangelism is the research-based 'truth' of neuroscience.

Reliance on science: the truth

For the practitioners, brain science knowledge served as evidence and reliable proof of the solid foundations of their belief in early intervention to save children from poor parenting, with the Perry brain scan image (Chapter One) evoked as a confirmatory vision. Despite the false claims and mistaken inferences that characterise the evangelistic brain science claims in early years intervention policy and practice documents (Chapter Four), because it comes under the rubric of science, such knowledge generally was seen by practitioners as transformative in terms of truth status. It established veracity, reduced uncertainty, offered unarguable clarity and thereby closed down objections:

> I think that it gives it more clout, definitely. There's something structural that parents can actually hear about. They all want the best for their children. And it's something that is affecting the brain. It gives it more of – I suppose it gives something to hang on to, doesn't it, something more credible to hang on to. It's not as wishy washy as it used to be before I think. (Children's Centre interview 4)

> I think it's one more layer of knowledge that we have now that we didn't have before. I suppose it's more actual evidence, proof, you can see a physical structural change in the brain. (FNP interview 8)

> There is so much they've discovered and to know that what you are doing is actually affecting parts of the brain, and that's almost like evidence that what you are doing is making a difference, you know. I mean I don't know enough to absolutely lay it out like that but I know from what I've read and studied that now that they can actually look into the brain and see whatever they look at, there are areas and, you know ... you can see the effect of it.

That is real proof that it makes a huge difference. I think that helps me to know that. It backs up what I'm doing. That somehow it's not just something airy-fairy that we're doing, it's something that has profound effect, you know. (Children's Centre interview 6)

I think it's *the* most important thing. I think it's – you know, everybody looks for an evidence base and it's very hard to argue with some of the strong evidence that's out there. I think it informs everything. It's not an old wives' tale, it's not an old-fashioned way of practice, it's, you know, you're seeing the MRI scans, you're seeing the evidence out there of how babies develop, you know, when they have the input. I think it's absolutely vital that we continue to have the research that supports that to help inform our practice. (FNP interview 7, her emphasis)

The practitioners frequently described the mothers that they worked with as needing advice and support to optimise their parenting skills, with the core of their work as professionals focused on ensuring babies' brain development was maximised and their future potential reached. These ideas resonate with and key into the neoliberal ideas about social investment in children with future returns in the form of socially mobile human capital assets that we have discussed in previous chapters:

I regularly talk to parents about, and especially with dads as well, about talking to babies and how much the brain develops within that first year, really emphasising the point that what they put in now is going to pay dividends in the future. (Health Visitor interview 1)

Explaining to parents the importance of play, because if they don't know anything about it obviously they are going to think children just play and they won't realise how important it is to their development, their emotional development, and developing all the skills that they need later on in life, and that they need for pre-school and school, and all this thing around school readiness and brain development. A lot of parents just think it's only playing, just let them get on with it, and they don't realise how big a part they can play in it. Also it's skilling parents up with all of that, really. (Children's Centre interview 7)

You'd hope that during pregnancy [the baby's] not subjected to too much cortisol and stress, and so their brain can develop to its fullest potential. That they've got parents that are able to manage their emotions in a positive way, then that will have that knock on effect.... Sometimes play is not calm. You know, there's a lot of throwing up in the air and all that sort of thing. You know, it's an opportunity to talk about soothing and soft play that's helpful really in the long term. (FNP interview 8)

Mothers were also subject to this asset-driven social investment. Often they were portrayed as lacking basic understandings, common sense and values, so there was an emphasis on the development of the values of being productive and positive parents.

It was science in the form of randomised controlled trials (RCTs) and fMRI scans that provided the evidence for the efficacy and future returns of the early intervention programmes, and underlined the need for fidelity in implementing their particular curriculum package:

Hopefully, if the parent has taken [what you are teaching them] on board, the child will have a chance of succeeding. And having that lots and lots of repetition to connect that brain cognitively to what they are doing.... Not everyone is going to have an MRI scan, but I think it would highlight particularly parenting skills and it would reinforce what I was saying that actually if the parents haven't got those skills then the children are never going to gain those skills. (Children's Centre interview 4)

Science provides the justification for the methods of intervention that must be followed according to the steps in the programme instruction manuals, and for adhering to the bespoke package materials developed for it. As we noted at the start of this book, many of the standardised parenting support programmes are commercial enterprises (with consequences for any objective assessment of 'what works'). In the case of the FNP, this means that the manual materials that are used under licence cannot be shared with colleagues working in services outside of the programme – a situation that FNP nurses can find frustrating when they want to spread the good-practice news (Robinson and Miller, 2013), and which can give the feel of a cult-like quality to 'outsiders'.

Early intervention is also about spending money now to save money in the future (as in the Heckman equation discussed in Chapter One).

Again, the rhetorically convincing 'what works' element provided by scientific evidence affords the justification for belief in the endeavour of and investment in early intervention. Services stand and fall by the outcomes that they meet in reducing future spending on welfare and shaping human-capitalised worker-citizens:

> The reality is our service is expensive. We have to be clear that what we're doing works and there's a reason for what we're doing, so we have to justify it hugely. So it's [got to be] absolutely clear that this early period makes a huge impact to people's whole lives, prison populations, all those sorts of things in the future. (FNP interview 3)

Intergenerational cycles of deprivation

Early years intervention is premised on the belief that the condition of the poor and marginalised is a result of the quality of parenting that they received as children. In other words, poverty and disadvantage is alleged to be a characteristic that is passed down the generations in families. This understanding extends to the innate causes of poverty in developing countries (Moore, 2001), shaping policy responses that focus on individual behaviour. In the UK, ideas about cultural and biological cycles of deprivation, transmitted disadvantage and intergenerational continuities of dysfunctionality are a long-standing, recurrent feature of political pronouncements, where low aspirations, low intelligence, fecklessness and benefit dependency are said to be passed down in families and communities:

> The concept of an intergenerational underclass displaying a high concentration of social problems ... has been reconstructed periodically over at least the past one hundred years, and while there has been important shifts of emphasis between each of these reconstructions, there have also been striking continuities. (Macnicol, 1987: 296)

There is a long-held assumption about the causes of poverty and inequality being transmitted down the generations in low-income families. Hereditarian thinking about the poor and their deprivation is centuries old. It is there in ideas about pauperism and the child rescue movement in the latter part of the 19th century, and the growth of eugenic perspectives on the early 20th century. It is evident in a host of notions about problem families, cycles of deprivation, the underclass thesis and social exclusion in the second half of the 20th century, through to the deficits of attachment and brain development posited today. Also consistent across the years though, is the fact that solid and straightforward evidence to support contentions about pathological intergenerational continuities has been hard to come by. In 1972, for example, the then Secretary of State for Social Services, Sir Keith Joseph gave a speech on the 'cycle of deprivation'. He raised the issue of intergenerational continuities of problems in families rooted in dysfunctional parenting, and the benefits of early intervention to address this. The speech led to a major research programme on transmitted deprivation. One of the review outcomes of that research (Rutter and Madge, 1976) found that few of the many forms of disadvantage could be traced causally to failures of parenting and intergenerational familial continuities. The review pointed out that this was even more difficult prospectively – that is, predicting which families will face problems and benefit from intervention.

More recently, there have been repeated political and media assertions that 'worklessness' is passed down from parent to child, inherited culturally in families, and – most stridently – that there are families and communities in which 'three generations have never worked'. Yet, it is notable that research has been unable to substantiate such claims statistically or through qualitative enquiries (Gaffney, 2010; Macmillan, 2011; Shildrick et al, 2012; MacDonald et al, 2013). Even two generations of extensive or permanent worklessness in families was a rare phenomenon. Although the existence of families where generations had not worked was often talked about by local practitioners, the inability to actually identify them through strenuous local recruitment strategies led one team of researchers to dub their search as equivalent to 'hunting the yeti' (MacDonald et al, 2013). More generally, evidence that unemployed parents entrench attitudes and behaviours in their children that perpetuate welfare dependency was also scant.

Despite this, claims of intergenerational dysfunction have taken on a biological as well as cultural hue. Much media attention accompanied psycho-biologist Adam Perkins' claim that unemployed parents on welfare state benefits are encouraged to have more children than families in work and, moreover, are breeding children with damaged personalities. Specifically, Perkins argues that children of welfare-dependent parents breed and inherit a biologically and neurologically programmed 'employment-resistant personality', deficient in the human capital that enables success in the labour market: 'an aggressive, antisocial and rule-breaking personality profile that impairs occupational and social adjustment during adulthood' (2016: 2). Notions of a selective heritable personality trait characterise the welfare-dependent poor as biologically different from other people.[1] Perkins' arguments have been roundly critiqued for poor statistical conclusions,[2] not least by the authors of one of the analyses he cites in evidence.[3] Rather than supporting Perkins' assertions, the data in fact contradict them. They demonstrate that any increases in fertility were to be found among couples receiving tax credits that are conditional on at least one parent being in work. Concerns have also been raised about the author's advocating for 'breeding out' welfare dependency through removal of welfare benefits, and removal of children from poor parents. Perkins' arguments, though, echo those long-standing myths of intergenerational cycles of deprivation (Lambert, 2016), and sustain the neoliberal idea of individual success through positive personal endeavour.

As we have seen throughout this book, biologised intergenerational cycles of disadvantage are a feature of early years policy rhetoric and reports, posing parenting as formative in babies' brain architecture, hard wiring future (anti-)social behaviour and empathetic (in)abilities down through the generations:

> So often, poor attachment is the result of the parents' own unhappy lives. A Mother who was not attached as a baby to her own Mother will struggle to form a bond with her baby. (Andrea Leadsom MP)[4]

> Early Intervention is an approach which offers our country a real opportunity to make lasting improvements in the lives of our children, to forestall many persistent social problems and end their transmission from one generation to the next. (Allen, 2011a: 8)

Also consistent across the centuries is the idea that intervention from experts can promote character reform and interrupt the transmission of a miserable biological and cultural inheritance. Underpinning practitioners' sense of the worthwhile mission they are engaged upon is the belief that their intervention can and will do good. They can save the world (and the public purse) one baby at a time. The practitioners we spoke to often echoed the erroneous but persistent intergenerational theses in their descriptions of their endeavours to make a difference and rescue children from the fate of their parents. Unsurprisingly, they made the same links between brain development, attachment and cycles of deprivation or worklessness that are apparent in the parenting intervention programmes and early intervention policy rhetoric. A theme of many accounts was a strong emphasis around the significance of breaking cycles of insensitive and insufficiently attentive parenting among the poor:

> to think out of the box, where they might have been brought up with a completely different value. So it's putting values that they might not have thought about like education, getting a job, all those things, they might never have had that because their whole family might have always been on income support. (Children's Centre interview 5)

> Obviously a lot of it is around parenting and helping them to explore their own experiences of being parented and maybe see how things could be different for their child. Also helping them to look at their lifecourse development as well, so finding out what their aspirations are. (FNP interview 8)

> The parents didn't have the skills because, again, their upbringing wasn't great in a high deprivation area. They're all stuck in this area so they're all – it's just an ongoing cycle and until we break that cycle the children just constantly are not being fed or not being dressed appropriately, coming in in dirty nappies, haven't slept all night, stayed up until 11 watching TV, lots and lots of issues within the pre-school. (Children's Centre interview 4)

The early years practitioners we interviewed who worked with disadvantaged teenage mothers did so with the key aim of strengthening attachment bonds and increasing maternal sensitivity. At the heart of this intervention is the implicit assumption that poverty and disadvantage are personal failings associated with poor parenting. Indeed teenage pregnancy itself was commonly viewed as evidence of a damaging upbringing:

> Everyone has a history, a pattern of something that's happened before. It's not a surprise that these young girls get pregnant. What would be interesting to see is the baby's outcomes and whether when they're older they make very different choices. (FNP interview 6)

Practitioners often viewed their role as helping to break cycles of deprivation by providing a better start for the new baby:

> A lot of these young people have had complicated young lives and maybe if left just to their own devices just to bring up their new baby they would repeat patterns that they'd had in their young childhood. This programme gives them well-researched advice and an opportunity to discuss a different way of parenting this new baby. So just break cycles of behaviour and patterns of behaviour that have grown up within families through generations.... The more we know, the more we understand, the more appropriate support can be given to perhaps try and break what previous generations have, how they've acted. To help the biological processes play out in the way they're meant to when you're doing everything you should have done. So I think it would have a big impact on a lot of people if they knew as much as perhaps we do. (FNP interview 4)

In fact, it is clear from the evidence that the age at which pregnancy occurs in itself has little effect on future social outcomes, like employment and income, or on current levels of disadvantage for either parents or their children. Rather than their age or their parental upbringing, both young motherhood and social disadvantage are caused by pre-pregnancy exposure to poverty and deprivation, which then continue after birth (Duncan et al, 2010). Easy assertions about intergenerational transmission of low aspirations are challenged by research showing the positive desire to be a good parent and for their children to succeed in education and employment across generational cohorts in families with young mothers. Such research also reveals the importance of support from family and community for young mothers (Duncan et al, 2010). Nonetheless, the idea of detrimental intergenerational transmission seems to be a taken-for-granted assumption in the practitioners' accounts. The cycle-of-deprivation thesis meant that, despite expressing commitments to work with mothers and their family members, practitioners could portray the parents of their clients as a malign influence, undermining their work and modelling how not to care for babies:

> The young mums know what they want, we're just helping them say you can do that. Sadly many a grandparent will

say 'you can't, why do you think you can do that then?', 'she don't need that then'. (FNP interview 4)

The cultural deficit model underpinning early years intervention and the focus on embracing change ensures that disadvantaged families are automatically conceptualised in terms of risk, with little consideration given to wider structural and economic factors.

Implications

There is a long history of pathologising the poor as biologically inferior and evangelising about the need to intervene to save or rescue children from their fate if left only to the inept ministrations of their dysfunctional parents. As Valerie Walkerdine neatly puts it: 'The poor are taken simply to be wanting, rather than to have suffered, experienced, or endured the effects of exploitation and oppression' (2015: 175). This directs attention onto parenting as causal, as the means of alleviating social inequalities, rather than focusing on the damaging social and material structural foundations of poverty and adversity, and alleviation of their effects on how families may cope with deprived life circumstances. Poverty is recast as the social and biological outcome of maternal behaviour.

While the practitioners we spoke to would not understand their early intervention practices as having any link to eugenics, there are concerns that ideas about intergenerational cultures linked to biological difference point us in this direction. For example, the political blogger Kitty S. Jones decries the notion of the made-up category of 'employment-resistant personality' and its easy elision with notions of improving the qualities of particular populations and concerns about the reproduction of people with 'undesirable' qualities.[5] She points to the recent limiting of tax credit support for children in poor families to two children only, with the intent to discourage them from having 'too many' children. Jones warns against the eugenicist consequences of 'neuro-liberalism'. Its focus on individuals as biologised neoliberal commodities obscures wider social issues of neglect, poverty, inequality, power relationships, oppression and abuse. Sue White and David Wastell (2016) raise the question of how it changes social work practitioners' understandings of parenting if the children of poor parents are seen as genetically compromised by similarly biologically broken mothers. They point to the moral project that becomes manifest. In the next chapter, we turn to the positioning of mothers as cause and solution at one and the same time, and the resulting gendered, classed and raced inequalities embedded in early years intervention informed by brain science.

Notes

[1] www.taxresearch.org.uk/Blog/2016/02/28/the-adam-smith-institute-is-now-willing-to-argue-that-those-on-benefits-are-genetically-different-to-the-rest-of-us/

[2] https://johnnyvoid.wordpress.com/2016/03/10/what-an-embarrassment-basic-errors-exposed-in-adam-perkins-benefits-bashing-book

[3] www.iser.essex.ac.uk/blog/2016/03/10/a-comment-on-the-use-of-results-from-does-welfare-reform-affect-fertility-evidence-from-the-uk

[4] www.andrealeadsom.com/downloads/Oxford-parent-infant-project-oxpip.pdf

[5] https://kittysjones.wordpress.com/2016/02/28/adam-perkins-conservative-narratives-and-neuro-liberalism/

SEVEN

Reproducing inequalities

Introduction

The ideas about brain science and early intervention put forward by its proponents in government policy reports, lobbyist websites and professional materials, give off an aura of optimism – what has been referred to as a 'hopeful ethos' (Rose and Abi-Rached, 2013). The hopeful ethos captures the idea that our fate is not pre-determined by our biology or social position, but is shaped by early social processes that mould the brain. It leads to the idea that, as individuals and as a nation, we have the opportunity to do something about that: 'we are now acquiring the obligation to take care of our brain – and the brains of our families and children – for the good of each and all' (Rose and Abi-Rached, 2013: 223). The notion of being able to invest and intervene in parenting so as to shape a baby's brain development to ensure better life chances for the young child and for the future of the nation feels constructive and positive. All that is required in this view is for experts to explain and demonstrate to mothers how to bring their children up for best effect, and for mothers to listen, learn and step up to fulfil the responsibility to take good care of their children's brain development. The complex web of relationships between adults and children in families and communities, and the accompanying array of childhood interactions, are scaled down to the level of the relationship between a baby and what is referred to as their 'primary caregiver'. It is mothers who are positioned as, and overwhelmingly are, 'primary carers'. This is a point with major implications for mothers that we explore in this chapter. We need to pay attention to the way that the early intervention doctrine invigorates a 'neurosexism' (Fine, 2010) that chimes with innately gendered ideas about women and their place. Traditional stereotypes of women as biological nurturers and notions of maternal responsibility lead to mothers becoming de facto sites for early intervention (Kenney and Müller, 2016), ultimately holding women accountable for the wellbeing of the nation and for poverty, crime and other social ills that may threaten this.

Left aside in the seemingly common-sense and straightforward scenario of early intervention to save young children's brains is the unequal gendered, classed and raced environment in which 'parents' and children live out their lives. Ideas about the brain engage with these unequal contexts. Rather than transcending ingrained inequalities, discriminatory social divisions are reinforced by the process of early intervention informed by brain science, and by gendered, classed and racialised accounts of family competence. Indeed, rather than a 'hopeful ethos', the attachment of brain science to early intervention is far more of a 'cruel optimism'. This is a term that Lauren Berlant (2011) uses when she argues that promises of political and social equality and upward mobility that are prevalent in liberal-capitalist societies such as the USA and UK are unachievable and psychically damaging fantasies. With a socioeconomic system that is characterised by a growing gulf between the rich and poor within countries as well as between them globally, advancement up the ladder for the marginalised and disadvantaged is against the odds. The cruel optimism is the propagation of the unrealistic possibility that opportunities to make good from inauspicious beginnings become attainable through the way mothers bring up their children. This is more oppressive than liberating. Mothers are positioned as what the Harvard Center on the Developing Child enthusiastically refers to as 'buffers' between their children and a deeply unequal society.[1] As buffers, they are held personally responsible for inculcating what the Harvard Center terms 'a biological resistance to adversity' and for outcomes over which they have limited control. Yet the hopeful discourse of brain science in early years policy sidesteps this reality in favour of instilling optimal parenting practices and holding out the promise of upward social mobility; and in the process it silently reinforces the very social divisions that it asserts it can overcome.

Social divisions and inequalities concern regular patterns of advantages and disadvantages, affluence and deprivation, privilege and oppression, and norms and pathologies, associated with membership of particular social categories and groups. In the version of brain science that has gained such a strong hold in early years intervention discussions, these social inequalities are attributable to stunted brain development, which is in turn a product of dysfunctional parenting. Divisions and inequalities crosscut each other at various levels, from the way people are categorised through to everyday social relations (Anthias, 2013), with gender, class and race articulating in the way that particular mothers are positioned and treated. As we will discuss, working-class and minority ethnic mothers are far more likely to find themselves, and their mothering values and practices, marginalised and pathologised in the face of policy rhetoric, professional benchmarks and practice interventions. Within a systematic view that deficient mothering/parenting is the greatest threat to children's wellbeing, the economic, environmental and cultural barriers that parents face in bringing up their children become ignored and obscured (Featherstone et al, 2016).

This notion of deficiency can often be implicit in models rather than a deliberate and intentional message from practitioners. The child development theories that underpin professional practice, for example, depend on ideas of development towards a version of adulthood rooted in Western values of liberal democracy. They are built around what Heidi Keller (2014) refers to as 'psychological autonomy', concerned with the inner world of the individual and defining attachment as mother–infant emotional bonds, regulation and expressiveness. This is in distinction to other models and understandings of development that put more of an emphasis on social community and caregiving environments. But it is a particular version of children's needs and expectations of appropriate 'outcomes', the psychological autonomy model, produced within a specific cultural paradigm, that is presented as a scientifically and biologically based universal. The power of the classic focus on the 'needs' of the individual but universal child in the dominant theories of child development can impose Western, middle-class, white cultural understandings and values – a form of imperialism that fails to take account of diversity and divisions across global contexts and within societies (Ottoman and Keller, 2014), and which leads to any differences being seen as aberrations and deficiencies in bringing up children and how they turn out.

In this chapter, we show how the use of brain science in early years intervention ideas and practices reproduces inequalities through two main processes: (i) it positions mothers as buffers who can militate against and overcome the effects of a harsh wider environment for their children; and (ii) it asserts the effacement of social divisions at the same time as it embeds a range of inequalities. We look in particular here at the ways that inequalities of gender are reproduced through the use of a particular version of attachment theory that keys into an 'intensive parenting' culture and is coupled with brain development. We show how these gendered inequalities link into the further engraining of social class distinctions through early intervention and brain science ideas that position deprived mothers and children as biologically and culturally different. Finally, we consider how race and ethnicity oppressions are carried through the imposition of Eurocentric notions of optimal childrearing roles and practices in early intervention initiatives.

Intensive attachment

In the same way that babies are encouraged to 'latch' on to their mother's breast as part of the mantra of providing the best for your baby to set them up for the future, early years intervention doctrines have latched onto brain science. We discussed how this happened initially through a public relations exercise in the USA in Chapter Three, from where it has taken on a life of its own. It has been melded with already well-embedded psychological ideas about socio-emotional child development, notably particular versions of attachment theory that chime very neatly with a social investment model (as discussed in Chapter Four). The model of parenting and its implications in early years intervention rhetoric and programmes thus represent a confluence of cultural ideas about intensive mothering, a rendering of attachment theory and a depiction of neuroscience. Together, they form a rather moralistic practice that positions women as the 'natural' and most important environment for their children, and draws on stereotypical notions of maternal agency and responsibility.

Contemporary ideas about good parenting are shaped by a powerful set of cultural features that have been termed 'intensive mothering'. Sharon Hays (1998), who introduced the term, has identified these elements as: mothers are the best possible people to care for their children, mothering should centre around the child's needs (as interpreted by experts), and that children should be considered emotionally rewarding and fulfilling for mothers. The significance attached to mothering as shaping the next generation is achieved through the separation out of children and their parents from acknowledgement of the wider economic and community life in which they are located. Further, Ellie Lee and colleagues (2014) argue that this intensive parenting culture is built on a portrayal of bringing up children as fundamentally important and far more risky than recognised previously. It presumes that there is a deficit in parental practice that requires remedying through training and regulation from experts as to the correct way to parent a child. This broad social notion of a child-centred and labour-intensive parenting practice sits well with a specific version of attachment theory that has annexed brain science (Thornton, 2011a, 2011b).

In previous chapters we looked at the way that attachment theorising has ebbed and flowed and been reanimated over the years. Davi Johnson Thornton (2011a, 2011b) argues that dominant versions of attachment theory have shifted over the past half century as they have keyed into ideas about increasing babies' brain capacity. What began as a focus on babies' reflexive biological need to attach themselves to their mothers during a formative period following birth, and notions of the deprivation of a maternal presence (physical or mental) leading to dysfunctional physical and emotional outcomes for children, latterly has shifted in emphasis. It is now firmly fixed not merely on mothers' presence but on a certain type of attentive, attuned, responsive and focused presence that is necessary to build babies' brains. While Bowlby asserted that what was required was for a mother to be present and act instinctively with her infant, the current emphasis is on a deliberated form of intensive mothering. An example of the stress on a sustained attachment presence can be found on the Harvard Center for Developing Child website, where at the end of a page devoted to the importance of 'adult caregivers'[2] responses to young children, the concocted question, 'Will occasional lapses in attention from adults harm a child's development?' meets with the somewhat grudging, equivocal answer 'Probably not.'[3]

The contemporary mix of intensive mothering, attachment theory and brain science requires mothers – or certainly particular groups of classed and raced mothers – to be informed and advised about how to interact purposively and in the best, prescribed way with their babies. The focus has developed into a stress on mothers needing to invest time and positive emotional connection in their children as an intense self-managed project – the success of which can be captured in baby brain scan images (Wall, 2010; Macvarish, 2014). It is this particular combination of attachment theory and neuroscience that underpins the assertion in a Sutton Trust report that research shows that 40% of British babies are not attached securely to their 'parents' (Sutton Trust, 2014) and which led the founder of PIPUK (see Chapter Five), Andrea Leadsom MP, to refer to a 'pandemic' that is the cause of 'our broken society' (2008). This is an assertion that has been challenged as full of misunderstandings and misinterpretations of the attachment tests and evidence, as we noted in Chapter Three (Horsley, 2014; Keller, 2014; LeVine, 2014; Meins, 2014).

Nonetheless, devoting time to enacting intensive maternal attunement is promoted as absolutely fundamental if babies' brains are to develop optimally. The argument goes that if the mother does not model emotional attachment to the baby, then for the rest of the child's life, into adulthood, the relevant connections in their brain will not have developed and so they will not know how to enter into and deal with relationships (Schore, 2000). There is no questioning of the underlying system of cultural assumptions about what constitutes a 'good' relationship (Keller, 2014; LeVine, 2014). Rather, attachment is promoted as an observable biological process that is engraved in the architecture of babies' brains, for which mothers bear moral responsibility. The neuromyth about the brain-damaging consequences of poor maternal 'responsiveness' is, as we discussed previously, highly speculative with little established basis in neuroscience, and as we have also pointed out in Chapter Three, the original Bowlby version of attachment theory has been criticised as flawed methodologically, as essentialising and as ethnocentric (Keller, 2014; LeVine, 2014; see also Rose and Rose, 2013: 93–9).

Nonetheless, it is an intoxicating combination of these two unsupported ideas that propels early years intervention policy, investment and practice, with the aim of preventing damage and maximising children's development. The 'Five to Thrive' campaign is a good example of the way that elements of brain science and attachment theory are woven together (Macvarish, 2014) by advocates of a social investment model. The campaign is produced and promoted by the Kate Cairns Associates training and consultancy business. It builds on the *Parenting matters* report addressing social mobility – written by a corporate lawyer (Paterson, 2011), and seeks to support professionals working in the early years field. The campaign provides resources and training in the 'science behind the messages' to make brain-based and attachment ideas accessible to parents and to educate them as to what they need to do to optimise their children's life chances. It echoes the public health 'Five a Day' nutrition campaign, in identifying a set of five key activities as the 'Building blocks for a healthy brain': 'Respond, Cuddle, Relax, Play, Talk'. The campaign is also an example of the way that brain science ideas are mixed with intensive attachment assertions and most zealously promoted by proponents who are not neuroscientists themselves (Bruer, 1999). Another example is the author of the bestselling book *Why love matters: How affection shapes a baby's brain*, Sue Gerhardt (2004). Her book warns that if mothers do not love their babies in the prescribed way and demonstrate this through the prescribed activities, then the damage will be inscribed on their baby's brain. Gerhardt is not a neuroscientist and it is clear that if she had asked one to fact check her assertions that we dissected in Chapter Two, the book might have read quite differently. Gerhardt's book, though, is regarded as a 'must read' by many professionals working in the early intervention field. As one of the Family Nurse Partnership practitioners we interviewed (FNP interview 3) told us:

> When we started we were all given the *Why love matters* book to go away and read, by Sue Gerhardt. All the research that she's pulled together about all the research

that's happened over the last few years about the developing brain really.... That really feeds into this programme, why the FNP programme is from early pregnancy until the child is 2, because of the research has shown that those two and a half years or whatever are crucial for brain development and attachment for children.

Yet neuroscientific knowledge about the brain identifies its plasticity from childhood through into adulthood, and attachment has also been shown to be a plastic phenomenon in humans (Bruer, 1999). The early intervention advocates roll on and over such challenges to their declarations however.

'Parenting' as gendered, biologised and learnt

Early intervention policies and services are often couched in the gender-neutral terminology of 'parenting', or even 'primary caregiver', a term that works to detach bringing up babies from the family and community relationships in which they are embedded. This may be driven by the intention to move away from sexist assumptions and to be inclusive of fathers. What it does, however, is to efface gender at the same time as it embeds gendered inequalities and renders mothers morally to blame. The link made between attachment theory and brain science has accompanied an explicit gender encoding of early intervention policy. While the default language of 'parenting' continues to frame much of literature, it is telling that accounts by some of the most influential nodal actors (see Chapter Five) give way to female pronouns and references to mothers. For example, the first Allen report (2011a) discusses 'the emotions in the exchanges between mother and baby' (2011a: 13), 'the mother's mental state' (2011a: 15), 'maternal responsiveness' (2011a: 16) and 'the bonding of an infant to their mother' (2011a: 73); and George Hosking's 'Nursery crimes' piece reviews the emotional deficit 'crimes' committed by immature, unresponsive mothers with the 'wrong style' of interaction.[4] Similarly, while the early years practitioners who we talked to mentioned fathers, it was mothers who were the main focus of their attention.

Early intervention largely is directed at mothers as the core mediators of their children's development. Pregnant women and new mothers are targeted. The core significance of mother–child relationships in the early years is underlined through reference to the developing brain and the child's need for an available and responsive primary caregiver. The quality of care is claimed to be reflected in the anatomical structure of the child's neural circuits, with sensitive mothers producing 'more richly networked brains'. Such a biological emphasis embeds and justifies the gendered focus on mothers as naturally better attuned to their infant's needs. The potent brew of brain science ideas, attachment theorising and early intervention mantras smuggles in two contradictory ideas – that mothers are biologically primed to be attuned to their children's needs at the same time as asserting that they need to be taught how to be responsive.

In the early years intervention documents, the foundations for secure attachment and optimal brain development are traced back to pregnancy, with the pre-natal period identified as physiologically and psychologically vital – both in terms of neural growth of the foetus and the establishment of a healthy attachment bond between mother and child. This neuroscientised theme is also played out through a focus on the mother's as well as the child's brain, reflecting an essentialist turn towards viewing sensitive motherhood as both biologically determined and in need of regulation (Lowe et al, 2015). Some scientists claim that mothers' brains are re-programmed during pregnancy to increase their emotional sensitivity (Pearson and Lightman, 2009; Sandman and Glynn, 2009), with this article in *Scientific American* (19 January 2010) being just one example:

> The bodily changes of childbearing are obvious, but as we are discovering, the changes in the brain are no less dramatic.... The maternal brain is a formidable object, a singular entity forged by hormones, neurochemicals, and exposure to the ravening demands and irresistible cuteness of offspring. During pregnancy, the female brain is effectively revving up for the difficult tasks that await.... Among its remarkable changes are those that allow the mother to focus on her infant in the persistent attempt to puzzle out the child's needs and wants. (Kinsley and Franssen, 2010: n.p.)

We have already critically appraised concerns around the mother's brain as potentially producing too much of the stress hormone cortisol and adversely affecting the neural development of the foetus in Chapter Three, and revealed the overblown, and even dangerous, nature of the claims about its toxicity in the early intervention material. Yet over-extended claims are made, such as that exposure to 'excessive' stress hormones in the womb is linked to mood disorders like depression in adult life, based on a study of genetically modified mice (quite what indicates a depressed mouse is not stated).[5] Maternal bodies become positioned as an 'environment' that poses a risk before and during pregnancy (Lappé, 2016; Lupton, 2012). There are major implications for women's control over their own bodies in this portrayal of mothers as a biological and emotional risk to their babies during the '1001 critical days' from conception to age 2 (Leadsom et al, 2013). One is that portraying a foetus as a 'baby' with whom the mother has a 'relationship' and whose brain can be damaged from the point of conception has implications for women's rights to abortion. Another is the way that pregnant women are opened up to public scrutiny and surveillance, and even punishment for the 'crimes' they commit against the 'precious cargo' of their foetus (Lupton, 2012). There are many reports that pregnant women in the USA can be routinely tested for drug use and, however legal or casual that use, their baby may be taken into state care at birth and the mother can be charged with assault, with Black women more likely to be reported and prosecuted than white women.[6] And even though the UK Court of Appeal ruled that a mother drinking alcohol while pregnant could not be construed as a criminal offence against a foetus, this was in response to a case where a mother was prosecuted for criminal injuries compensation by a local authority.[7]

Such ideas about the risks that mothers pose to the foetus find their way into professional practice. They extend through into concerns not just about the chemicals that mothers may put into their bodies, but also the chemicals that they produce through emotional response to their environment. The interviews with early years practitioners for our study show that there is a strong emphasis on the significance of the mother's brain as potentially producing too much of the stress hormone cortisol. Some had been trained to regard maternal stress as a biological risk factor:

> I knew physical violence was dangerous, but I hadn't thought of stress as being dangerous prior to that training. And when I realised what cortisol, the mother's cortisol levels would do to the baby, specifically the baby's brain, made me think no actually it's not about keeping a baby once they're born safe, it's how do we antenatally keep this baby safe. (FNP interview 6)

This concern about cortisol levels positions mothers as in control of their stress reactions, and was expressed through appeals to consider what getting stressed might do to the little baby inside them. Practitioners seemed to be encouraged to conceptualise stress primarily in terms of relationships rather than pressures associated with disadvantage or lack of resources:

> They often have very stressful lives so there's a lot of arguing and tension, so it's a way of talking about the relationships they already have. Relationships where they argue a lot with parents, boyfriends and just thinking about what's happening to your little baby, you know, when you're getting really stressed and 'you're feeling stressed, do you think maybe baby is?' And just having those sort of conversations, not in any kind of accusatory way, just having those conversations. (FNP interview 8)

Consequently, the advice to mothers from practitioners was to control their anxiety in the context of coping with poverty and housing insecurity, and to avoid arguments, implicitly advocating a submissive position where young pregnant women may be at risk of domestic violence (Wiggins et al, 2005). And once babies are born, post-natally in relation to domestic violence, mothers experiencing domestic abuse from their (usually male) partner becomes redefined as mothers posing a risk to their children by undergoing this harm. Rather than receiving any support from what remains of a domestic abuse services sector decimated by austerity cuts, they are threatened with having their children taken into care because they are not protecting their children from risk and damage (Featherstone et al, 2016).

The mantra 'breast is best' is a strong message from professionals to mothers, such that it has become a requirement rather than a choice,[8] linked to the intensive attachment type of 'total motherhood' and concerns with eliminating risks that mothers' behaviour may pose to children (Wolf, 2013). Early years practitioners we spoke to mentioned how they emphasised the link between breastfeeding and brain development, for example IQ scores, to the mothers that they worked with. This is despite the inconsistent evidence as to whether or not breastfeeding is always 'best' and in relation to which outcomes (for example, Evenhouse and Reilly, 2005; Kramer et al, 2009). As Joan Wolf (2013) points out, mothers who breastfeed are a self-selecting group. This means that breastfeeding can be what researchers call a 'chaotic concept' in relation to better outcomes for children, where it is actually social class that is the issue: for example, middle-class mothers are more likely to 'self-select' into breastfeeding than are deprived mothers (Oakley et al, 2013). This chaotic concept is also evident in the neuro workover given to the 'breast is best' mantra. For example, a study comparing images of the brain growth of babies who had been breastfed exclusively for three months or more with those who had not, argued that the breastfed babies showed more pronounced development in parts of the brain associated with language, emotions and cognition (Deoni et al, 2013). Infants breastfed for more than a year had even greater growth of 'white matter', they report. Apart from the issue that this study cannot say anything about long-term implications, and leaving aside the nonetheless crucial point of inconsistent evidence about outcomes, the ability to breastfeed your baby's brain growth for extended periods of time is a luxury that resource-poor mothers may not have. Indeed, in the USA where the study originates, some states require single mothers to find a job within three months or even less of the birth of their child, before their temporary assistance benefits are cut off (Hill, 2012), and generally one in four mothers had to skimp or skip maternity leave, returning to work within two weeks, because the USA does not have a paid maternity leave policy.[9]

The primacy and quality of mother–child relationships is presented as a decisive lever in building children's brains, and is a core principle structuring the everyday work of many early years intervention programmes. The early years practitioners we interviewed were enthusiastic about neuroscience and its application to practice, feeling that it provided strong proof of attachment theory to policy makers, funders and mothers themselves. The FNP programme requires practitioners to raise the subject of brain development in the first visit to the pregnant mother as a way of underlining the crucial significance of participation in the programme and the associated imparted advice: 'We start very early on about your baby's developing brain. That's one of the first things we do' (FNP interview 8). Mothers are provided with a photocopied sheet titled 'How to build your baby's brain' featuring a list of activities claimed to enrich neural connectivity. These include reading books to their babies, singing nursery rhymes and playing on the floor with them (we return to the selection of activities that are pointed to as neurally enriching below). Practitioners can draw on a variety of creative methods to convey this information. For example, one explained that she gave mothers a dot-to-dot puzzle and called out random numbers to demonstrate the importance of correct brain wiring, while another spoke of dropping Alka-Seltzer tablets into a glass of water to illustrate how activities fired up new synapses in infant brains.

In the febrile climate where mothers are rendered fundamentally responsible for the brain development and outcomes of their children, at the same time as day care can be posed as bad for babies' developing brains because it stimulates the production of cortisol in response to stress (for example, Gunnar et al, 2010), it can be promoted for some groups of mothers who are judged not to be able to stimulate their children for optimal development and school readiness, with arguments that it can reduce inequalities (for example, Hansen and Hawkes, 2009). On the one hand, assertions that day care is damaging to young children's brains play to an agenda that pushes mothers back into their traditional role as homemakers. On the other hand, the responsibility loaded onto mothers is especially pronounced in relation to low-income, working-class mothers (Singh, 2012; Kenney and Müller, 2016), and Black and minority ethnic mothers (Mansfield, 2012), reflecting long-standing assumptions about good and bad mothers and mothering practices. We turn to these issues now.

Biologising, buffering and effacing social class

Maija Holmer Nadeson (2002) has described the way that ideas about brain science are used to legitimise interventions in the childrearing habits of working-class families that seek to prevent infants from developing into young people who potentially are a risk and threat to society. Instead their character and attainment will be transformed so they become the type of entrepreneurial workers required for neoliberal corporate capitalism. She argues that brain science is used as 'a tool of social engineering for the poor' (2002: 424), a means of eliminating barriers to upward social mobility. As we will show here, the deprivation facing poor working-class families is presented as a result of a lack of intensive attachment mothering, and consequently the stunted brains of their offspring – brains that are biologically different from those of the middle classes. And again, mothers are positioned as buffers. The rationale of early intervention is that intensive attached mothering will protect children being brought up in poverty from any effects of their disadvantage, and send them soaring up the social mobility ladder. It will also protect society from the risks posed by their children.

The depiction of poor working-class families as not quite civilised, indeed not quite human, runs through the appropriation of brain science in early intervention rhetoric. The *Early intervention: Good parents, great kids, better citizens* report (Allen and Duncan Smith, 2008) blamed 'a marked expansion of the "dysfunctional base" of our society' on children growing up in homes where they receive inadequate mothering and consequently their brain does not develop 'properly'

(2008: 10, 12). Left unchecked, the authors argue, 'we face a feral future on our streets' (2008: 22). A vision of the poor being wild and biologically different to the rest of us is captured in newspaper headlines such as: 'How being poor can change your brain: children from deprived families have minds that are six per cent smaller, claims study' and 'Poor and uneducated are biologically different to affluent, UCL finds'.[10] And, as we identified in Chapter Three, much early intervention and brain science material erroneously claims an evolutionary and hierarchical account of brain development, from primitive reptilian, through emotional mammalian to the rational human (for example, Allen, 2011a; Brown and Ward, 2013; Gerhardt, 2004; Solihull Approach, 2004). Babies who are inadequately parented are purported to rely on their primitive instinctive amygdala and mammalian emotionally volatile limbic system because their social and rational pre-frontal cortex has been damaged. This is claimed to leave them unable to regulate their emotions and exercise self-control. These biologically maimed children are the feral working class of the future: 'Children who experience hostility from their parents, in particular, and whose parents who, during their babyhood, do not model how to resolve conflicts or how to maintain self-control often become the offenders of tomorrow' (Gerhard, 2004: 90).

Such developmental separations of the social classes mean that the failure of social class mobility or the demographics of prison populations are no longer linked to marginalisation and excluding structures in society, but can now be explained by biological difference (Kenney and Müller, 2016: n.p.). This explanation leads into class-based assessments of the type of problems mothers may face and their capacities for improvement. In an interview for our research project, Andrea Leadsom MP made a clear distinction between mothers struggling to bond with their babies because of post-natal depression and those suffering 'psycho-deprivation'. According to Leadsom, the former are often high-flying, high-earning professionals struck down with a biological illness, whereas the latter lack attunement with their babies because they had no experience of bonding with their own mothers and may have got pregnant just to get a council house. Practitioners may also pick up the class-based assessments that can infuse their training, regarding educated middle-class mothers as more able to respond rationally to good advice while uneducated working-class mothers pose more of a challenge:

> A while ago I went to a family who had a baby and mum
> just had no attachment to the baby whatsoever and we

sort of dissected that a bit and talked about it, and I mean they were both very well-educated people. But for her, the whole attachment thing, to know what actually happens to the child and why attachment is important.... It really helped her to know that something actually happens in the brain when you do all the emotional things and social things, you know.... Part of my job is to try and improve the home environment to create a more stimulating healthy home environment ... [but] very often, I get parents who say, 'Oh, he doesn't like books.' Well, at the end of six sessions he likes books. He's just never been, you know, introduced to it in an interesting way maybe. But the parent, that's where I find my challenge really. (Children's Centre interview 7)

The stereotype of the risky, irrational, poor working class means that intervention programmes to promote early nurturing and attachment and prevent future dysfunctional behaviour focus on and are delivered through pre- and post-natal provision in poor, working-class communities. Measurement to profile risk is a key element in identifying where to deliver these services, the characteristics of those to whom they are delivered, and assessment as to what progress is being made.[11] For example, the 'A Better Start' programme provides Area Wellbeing Profiles of developmental outcomes for 0–8-year-olds so that intervention programmes can be targeted in areas where children's 'life chances' are at risk,[12] revealing that marginalised, poor and minority ethnic groups are most 'at risk' (Featherstone et al, 2014a). Negative trajectories into the future are projected but it is anticipated that showing mothers in these disadvantaged groups how best to bring up their babies will remedy this and give children the 'best start' on the path to upward social mobility. Social problems can thus be predicted and headed off before they have even manifested themselves (Parton, 2005). The social and structural causes of hardship and need that are being experienced by these families in the present are effectively masked, placing mothers as hidden buffers against the effects of privation on their children.

Mothering practices and behaviour are portrayed as causal in research linking childhood poverty to decreased brain size surface area and reduced cognitive abilities (for example, Reardon, 2015). In this scenario it is deficient mothering that fails to mediate and protect these children's brains from poverty – and good mothering that could act as a buffer between poverty and children's brain development. One of the practitioners we interviewed explained mothers' role as a buffer to us, quoting from a cognitive psychology text book (Eysenck and Keane, 2010):

> I'm reading, it's not me being so clever! ... It says ... 'This research has also shown that more nurturing maternal behaviour can buffer the young animal's hippocampus against the effects of stress. It would appear that children living in a stressful environment of poverty benefit in a similar way from attentive and affectionate parenting.' So I've found that the most challenging part of my job is to get parents not only to ask [their children], 'What colour is this?' and you know, stuff with props, but to try and change the whole atmosphere of the relationship and the nurturing and the positive input and positive expectations and all those things that shape a child's whole – I'm absolutely convinced that has a huge impact on how you view the world, and yourself, and other people as an adult. (Children's Centre interview 7)

As Martha Kenney and Ruth Müller point out generally in relation to the positioning of mothers as the fundamental determining influence on their children's development and outcomes, 'in this narrative being poor becomes almost equivalent to being a bad parent' (2016: n.p.). And any mother who is parenting in poverty thus is doing so because her own brain is stunted as a result of being badly parented herself. This is because good parenting provides the brain power that is the foundation for social mobility. The *Parenting matters: Early years and social mobility* report exemplifies this belief in the goal it sets for itself:

> The paper will outline the key scientific concepts behind the development of early brain architecture and skill formation and identify the crucial challenge these present to the desire to improve social mobility. It will argue that these concepts create the imperative for greater efforts at intervention directed at the family sphere to prevent the squandering of individual potential (particularly among children from lower-income backgrounds). (Paterson, 2011: 5)

The report repeats the mantra that 'what parents do is ultimately more important than who parents are', and thus early intervention is required. In other words, social class does not matter and is redundant. In interviews conducted for our study, an MP and a policy adviser each talked about the way that brain science overcomes old-fashioned ideas about social class as shaping life chances:

> [Brain science] breaks the class spell. 'Oh well, we could have done, you know but it's the wretched class system in our country, it's so tightly drawn, you know, there's not much we can do about it.' And the early years studies seem to show that's not true. (Frank Field MP)

> When sociologists point out that poor kids have worse life chances than rich kids, is there a danger that people on the Left adopt a kind of crude social determinism ... this kind of crude sociological determinism excused, you know, really an abdication of responsibility for the school to do whatever it could to actually change the destiny of those young people whatever their backgrounds. (Matthew Taylor, CEO, Royal Society of Arts)

In their view, and those of others of all political colours, brain science overcomes outmoded ideas about social class as shaping life chances. Brain science 'breaks the class spell' and avoids seeing social forces as deterministic. At the practice level, social class can be overcome through early years intervention. One of the practitioners we interviewed constructed a *Billy Elliot* style story[13] with a subtext of damaging working-class culture and masculinity, and low aspirations, holding back the development of working-class infants whose brains would be stimulated if exposed to high culture:

> The two young people I saw yesterday. He'd never told anyone but he'd wanted to be a ballet dancer. He didn't dare tell anyone because he would be laughed at, so he took up skateboarding. Which was a sort of halfway house sort of thing. They both love classical music but they'd never dare tell anyone because they'd be laughed at. But actually when they told me I was so excited for them and I said 'you know this is going to help your baby'. They were scared to almost say it even to me who's a lot older, it wasn't someone from their own generation, but it was refreshing to hear it, that they didn't dare tell anyone else about. Quite cool really isn't it. He's damaged his knees too much though to

be a ballet dancer with his skateboarding so that's a shame. But he's artistic, he's learning to be a tattooist. So he's got art, you know, you can see it in him. But his father didn't want to hear about it, any dancing, wanted football, rugby, that was fine, but any of that other stuff, no don't mention it again. Because he probably did mention it when he was 10, 11, quite bravely. But if his children were allowed to say it in the future aged 10, that would be great wouldn't it? (FNP interview 4)

This *Billy Elliot* type story hints at the way that, viewed through the cloudy lens of brain science, ideas about what counts as suitable development and as demonstrating the right sort of brain, are not straightforward but in fact reproduce gendered and classed value judgements. In a view that presents parenting as determining, then it must be good parenting that has provided the middle classes with their merited social and economic position. In this logic, the parental behaviour that builds the brain architecture that promotes or maintains social mobility for middle-class children must also result in social mobility for working-class children. Deeper consideration of this logic, however, provides a clearer view. Not only is it impossible for everyone to move up the social scale (there have to be losers as well as winners), but the social mobility of a few individuals in an age of austerity cannot dismantle the entrenched position of the most advantaged and compensate for large structural inequalities (Payne, 2012; Reay, 2013). Diane Reay (2013) captures the fairytale of social mobility in her notion that echoes the Hans Christen Andersen story of the emperor with no clothes:

> [social mobility is] a mirage, a source of immense collective hopes and desires for those in the bottom two-thirds of society but in reality it is largely a figment of imagination brought to life in policy and political rhetoric … social mobility operates as a very inadequate sticking plaster over the gaping wound social inequalities have become. (2013: 662–3)

It is a widely promulgated fairytale nonetheless, that is raced as well as classed.

Neoliberalised race and biolologised brains

The construction of individualised risk and responsibility that presents mothers both as threats to their infants' developing brain and as buffers who are able to inculcate a neural resistance to adversity in their children through their behaviour, is raced as well as classed. In the process, the social division of race becomes neoliberalised and biologised. The term 'racial neoliberalism' has been coined to capture the way that race has been silenced as an institutional and structural inequality in assertions about the primacy of individualised choice and personal responsibility (Goldberg, 2009; Wade, 2010). Racism is made irrelevant through 'relocating racially coded economic disadvantage and reassigning identity-based biases to the private and personal sphere' (Davis, 2007: 349), and racial disparity is rationalised away with reference to the cultural or biological flaws of those at the bottom of the racial hierarchy (Wise, 2010). In the process, ethnic practices and racialised difference can become reified as biological difference rather than a socially designated and produced category (Duster, 2005; Mansfield and Guthman forthcoming) – it is not just the poor working class who have biologically different brains but also minority ethnic families in the UK and globally, and it is mothers who are placed at the epicentre of its culturally created parenting cause and cure.

The message about brain science in early intervention rhetoric is that it provides indisputable facts as a basis for practice. Practitioners saw neuroscience knowledge as undermining any objections made on the grounds of cultural relativity, and some reflected on how their sensitivities to difference in the past had prevented them from intervening in a way they now know is right:

> I think [brain science] really gives me that oomph to stick by it, rather than just give in to what society might think is okay. So we'll stand by it and give more definite 'this is the right thing to be doing' ... The [minority ethnic] community[14] are a particular concern for us, because in [country] there's a long tradition of girls rarely leaving the house. They certainly don't have education, and that's continued to fairly recent times. Therefore we deal with the issues of lots of young mums out there, who have missed schooling, don't necessarily agree with girls going to school, and we're basically trying to get those children into school. (Children's Centre interview 2)

Through a neoliberalised early intervention lens, minority ethnic mothers are viewed as simply able to overturn collective cultural practice through their individual choices about bringing up their individual children, in a similar way as social mobility is individualised in relation to social class. The need to address household gender relations and the broader gendered inequalities of a patriarchal culture is left aside.

The neoliberalisation and biologisation of race and of minority ethnic cultures in early years intervention endeavours is bolstered by the intensive version of attachment we explored above. The normative promotion of intensive mothering engrains Eurocentric assumptions, delegitimising alternative values and ways of life. The version of attachment theory underpinning intervention models relies on a white, Western conception of ideal family life. In many communities across the world childrearing is shared among wide social networks. Kinship care and interdependent households are the norm and exclusive parental care is rare (Ottoman and Keller, 2014). But rather than a cultural and context-appropriate assessment of caregiving arrangements, secure attachment and risk, a specific model and set of measures is imposed based on a middle-class Western model of interactional style with a small number of offspring (Keller, 2014). Applying a scientised logic of early intervention positions some cultures at greater risk of genetic impairment and brain damage simply because of their childrearing practices. The implications of this reasoning range from a sanctioning of culturally insensitive professional practice to a potential resurgence of biologised racism.

The ideas that the poor have caused their own poverty through the way that they bring up their children, that mothers can act as buffers for their children against adverse and oppressive circumstances, and that early years intervention to promote brain development is required to deal with this, have spread internationally. The United Nations Children's Fund report, *The state of world's children 2001*, exemplifies such assertions, with its repetition of neuromyths:

> Most brain development happens before a child reaches three years old. Long before many adults even realise what is happening, the brain cells of a new infant proliferate, synapses crackle and the patterns of a lifetime are established.... Choices made and actions taken on behalf of children during this critical period affect not only how a child develops but also how a country progresses.... The time of early childhood should merit the highest priority

attention when responsible governments are making decisions about laws, policies, programmes and money. Yet, tragically both for children and for nations, these are the years that receive the least. (UNICEF, 2001: 9)

Thus, just as we noted in Chapter Two, in particular in relation to the UK, the nation's future and how mothers bring up their children become hooked together. In this construction, mothers in developing and war-torn countries are culprits in having created their own poverty and the nation's lack of progress through deficient childrearing practices. But with early intervention to rectify those practices they will be able to protect children from the onslaughts of deprivation and conflict and save the nation state. Recent UNICEF material brings together early years development and parenting to offset children's experiences of war and hunger on the basis of the speed of new neural connections formed in the brain in the early years. For example, a 2014 UNICEF Connect blog on how 'neuroscience is redefining early childhood development' opines:

in early childhood neurons form new connections at a rate of 700 to 1000 a second. At this point in a child's life, nutrition and good health are most critical. But so too is caring, stimulation and good parenting – especially for children faced with multiple adversities of violence, disaster and poverty.[15]

The jaw-dropping notion of countering global traumas and inequalities through parenting is echoed in a 2016 blog for a health and development US media newsletter, titled 'Why countries need to make sure their kids learn to play nice'. In the blog, Harvard associate professor of education, Dana McCoy, explains that that mothering practices to inculcate good child behaviour will help reduce poverty in conflict-ridden countries like Afghanistan because 'the first 1000 days of life are key':

What does helping a 3-year-old control her temper tantrums have to do with reducing global poverty? Quite a lot, says Dana McCoy ... children's early cognitive and social development [in low- and middle-income countries] has largely been an 'overlooked' issue in global poverty fighting circles, says McCoy.... In Afghanistan, 47 percent of children are in trouble [developmentally]. In 11 countries in Africa the share tops 50 percent.[16]

As an example of what can be done, McCoy points to evidence of the long-term beneficial effects of early intervention supposedly demonstrated in a Jamaican experimental study – the same study that we discussed in Chapter One as roundly criticised for its statistical flaws.

Despite the overall paucity of evidence that early years intervention works (see Chapter One), initiatives are being rolled out by Western philanthropic foundations across the developing world, in the belief that improved mothering will surely benefit the state of the nation. 'Saving Brains' is a partnership of Western philanthropic initiatives such as the Bill and Melinda Gates Foundation and the Bernard van Leer Foundation, and the philanthropic entrepreneurial arm of the wealth management firm UBS Optimus Foundation. It seeks to 'save' both brains and nations through funding early intervention to promote children's brain development in sub-Saharan Africa and generally in developing countries. For example, the 'Fine Brains' (Family-Inclusive Early Brain Stimulation) programme seeks to promote parental stimulation and interaction to improve children's brain architecture in sub-Saharan countries. According to the Fine Brains web page, mothers in these countries are 'ill-equipped to maximise the benefits' of interaction, need to be trained, and then to train their husbands to parent properly:

> Poor stimulation and poor social interaction can affect brain structure and function ... parents in sub-Saharan countries are ill-equipped to maximise the benefits from [child–parent] interaction ... it is expected that [trained] mothers will in turn train their male partners and other caregivers on these skills, within the context of the home setting.... The intervention will be a randomized control trial.... The effectiveness of the intervention will be evaluated by quantifying the effects on early brain development of children.[17]

At a stroke the complex and diverse historical, economic, political, social and religious contexts of sub-Saharan Africa are obscured in favour of a focus on individual mothers as able to overcome poverty, conflict and post-conflict problems, engrained gendered inequalities and so on, through improving their knowledge of child development and home engagement practices. This smacks of imperialism, and displays little sense of gender and intergenerational relations. And, of course, intervention is to be evidenced through randomized controlled trials, with little sense of the problematic issues of context and statistical practice that we looked at in Chapter One.

Conclusion

In this chapter we have seen the way that ideas about brain science and early intervention animate a 'neurosexism' that assumes mothers as the 'natural' environment for early intervention, and ultimately holds them to be both cause of and solution for the wellbeing of the nation. This gendered focus is interlaced with inequalities of class and race. The policy and practice preoccupation with how poor mothers and deprived families bring up and nurture their children relies on a meritocratic construction of the wealthy and privileged as having better developed brains. This is a statement that many of us might find offensive. But within the confluence of brain science and early years intervention, success is naturalised and unproblematically correlated with brain structure and intelligence. From this perspective, the solution to poverty is to make people smarter. Working-class mothers, Black and minority ethnic mothers, and mothers in the global South can enable their children to think their way out of their predicament. The idea that real hardship and discrimination is to do with how much attention of the right sort mothers give to their children, and is nothing to do with systematically and structurally engrained local, national and global inequalities, is a cruel optimism.

So what should be done then? In the final chapter of this book we turn to some alternative visions of interventions. Some of them go further along the route we have charted so far in this book, intervening even further in the micro-details of how children are parented, and by whom. Others provide a challenge to the whole idea.

Notes
1   http://developingchild.harvard.edu/science/key-concepts/toxic-stress/; http://developingchild.harvard.edu/science/key-concepts/resilience/
2   Note the use of 'adult'. Beneficial interactions with other young children, or even young people as caregivers, are erased.
3   http://developingchild.harvard.edu/science/key-concepts/serve-and-return/
4   www.wavetrust.org/our-work/publications/articles/nursery-crimes-2001
5   'Fetal exposure to excessive stress hormones in the womb linked to adult mood disorders', *Science Daily*, 7 April 2013: www.sciencedaily.com/releases/2013/04/130407090835.htm

[6] http://reason.com/archives/2014/05/16/prosecuting-pregnant-women-for-drug-use; www.theguardian.com/commentisfree/cifamerica/2012/apr/26/flaws-prosecuting-mothers-drug-addiction

[7] www.independent.co.uk/life-style/health-and-families/health-news/drinking-alcohol-while-pregnant-is-not-criminal-court-of-appeal-rules-9904053.html

[8] For example, see: www.theatlantic.com/magazine/archive/2009/04/the-case-against-breast-feeding/307311/ and www.spectator.co.uk/2015/08/the-biggest-heretic-in-baby-feeding-and-why-i-like-her/

[9] For an analysis based on US Department of Labour data see http://inthesetimes.com/article/18151/the-real-war-on-families

[10] www.dailymail.co.uk/sciencetech/article-3044384/Being-poor-change-brain-Children-deprived-families-minds-six-cent-smaller-claims-study.html and www.telegraph.co.uk/news/health/news/12064058/Poor-and-uneducated-are-biologically-different-to-affluent-UCL-finds.html

[11] The UK's PREVENT agenda has now been extended to early years provision, where all registered childcare providers are subject to the duty under section 26 of the Counter-Terrorism and Security Act 2015, to protect children from the risk of radicalisation. This places Muslim mothers and their children under particular scrutiny. See www.foundationyears.org.uk/files/2015/06/prevent-duty-departmental-advice.pdf

[12] http://betterstart.dartington.org.uk/

[13] *Billy Elliot* was a film and then a musical telling the story of a young boy growing up in a mining village during the 1984–5 miners' strike who aspires to be a ballet dancer. Billy's father initially forbids this fearing his son will be considered a 'poof' (gay) but eventually comes around and is supportive, overcoming the dominant narrow version of working class masculinity.

[14] The practitioner was referring to a particular minority group who are concentrated in a particular area. Reference to the ethnicity may identify that area and thus the Children's Centre, so we have not identified it.

[15] https://blogs.unicef.org/blog/neuroscience-is-redefining-early-childhood-development/

[16] www.npr.org/sections/goatsandsoda/2016/06/09/481399255/kids-development

[17] www.savingbrainsinnovation.net/projects/0581-03/

EIGHT

Reclaiming the future: alternative visions

In this book we have aimed to trouble current policy and practice orthodoxies through an interrogation of the evidence and the politics of early years intervention. We have highlighted how misrepresentation and misinterpretation of neuroscience, along with political expediency and vested interests, drive a contemporary fixation with parenting and child development. In particular we have shown how 'evidence-based' rhetoric has been used to conceal the deeply political nature of decisions about what is best for children and families. In this concluding chapter we change tack to explore potential future policy directions, contrasting the dystopian vision that flows from current interventionist logics with more collectivist ideals of family support, social harm reduction and the immediate, humane social good.

The brave new world of prevention science

The attraction of early intervention, as we have shown, lies in its promise to optimise and regulate human behaviour. Replete with optimistic interventionist logic, the aim is to protect and enhance infant brain development, transforming the world through improved parenting. Soft hereditary principles of neurogenesis (the generation of neurons in the brain) and epigenetics (modifications to gene expression) have captivated the imaginations of policy makers to the extent that the complexities, contradictions and uncertainties characterising scientific progress are erased to accommodate simple narratives of cause and effect. The ends are viewed as justifying the means. Targeting pre- and post-natal development, we are told by early intervention proponents, is the progressive way to minimise individual and societal risk while enhancing equality of opportunity and social mobility. Far from pioneering new ground though, contemporary efforts to harness and manipulate biological traits tread worryingly familiar territory. The same ambitions propelled the British establishment, from Victorian-era social Darwinism to the 20th-century biological determinism of the Eugenics Society.

An historically grounded perspective demonstrates how a broad and deep consensus on what the problem is and how to deal with it, can obscure fundamental moral and ethical questions. In the last century state-sanctioned eugenic programmes were embraced widely as a benevolent method of augmenting biological development for the sake of the national good. While eugenics broadly is rejected today as unprincipled, the same objectives and justifications now circulate in different guises. And, more significantly, contemporary technocratic visions of a biologically optimised world invoke remarkably similar configurations of domination and oppression. Social policy returns to a long-standing preoccupation with the behaviour, lifestyle and reproductive choices of women, with epigenetics in particular extending the responsibility of mothers backwards in time and forwards through the generations, potentially rendering them forever 'pre-pregnant' (Meloni, 2016). The biologised focus on marking out socially divided cultural practices through patterns in brain structure and gene expression revives a centuries-old preoccupation with sorting and ranking populations according to their deviation from white, privileged norms. And, as we have shown, the consequences of this approach are similarly brutal, with babies removed from poor families on the premise that to allow them to remain will damage their brains. It is also worth noting that, in November 2016, the Department for Education awarded £6.8 million in funding to Pause, an organisation that seeks to support mothers of children taken into care through prescribing long-acting, reversible contraception.[1] From here it is only a small leap to imagine a future in which biological forecasts are drawn on to determine reproductive rights, suggesting that we are considerably closer to the eugenic past than many realise.

Technocratic utopias offer the promise of solutions for every ill but their repertoires operate outside human dimensions of social justice and ethical practice. David Wastell and Sue White (2016) point to current directions of travel when they highlight an experimental study into the effects of early-life adversity on epigenetic mechanisms. This experiment involved stressing mothers of newly born rats in a laboratory by depriving them of adequate nesting material and placing them in an unfamiliar environment. Observations showed the mother rats subsequently displayed abusive behaviour towards their own offspring. This was correlated with high levels of methylation (a process of epigenetic pattern modification) in the pups' DNA. The authors of the experiment found that administering a particular chemical into the rat pup's pre-frontal cortex reduced mythylation, leading them to propose drug treatment as a potential therapeutic strategy for reversing the effects of early-life adversity on children. As Wastell and White pertinently remark:

> is a relevant solution to (inflicted) poor housing really the drug treatment of one's offspring? It would seem that current epigenetic forms of reasoning suggest greater opportunities for big pharma and possibly fewer for social housing projects and food cooperatives which have little currency at the molecular level and often struggle to demonstrate the sort of outcomes economists prefer to plug into their models aimed at the optimisation of 'human capital'. It is easier in the short term to show the effects of a pill on a biomarker than of access to decent food and some human company on the wellbeing of a community. (2016: 16–17)

This example shows how a logic of prevention science recalibrates accepted moral and ethical sensibilities through a focus on the apparently objective realm of the molecular. Critical consideration of the values driving interventions are rendered redundant in an age where biological truth is seen to speak for itself. Particular kinds of values are then reified and redeployed as rhetorical mechanisms of persuasion, precluding discussion, delegitimising alternative beliefs and stifling dissent.

Values beyond value

Organisations that promote and/or deliver early intervention programmes tend to trade heavily on values. For example, the Early Intervention Foundation (EIF) proclaims its 'mission' and 'vision' for 'every baby, child and young person to realise their potential'.[2] The Family Nurse Partnership (FNP) has a similar 'mission and 'vision' 'that every baby, child and young parent can thrive, fulfil their aspirations and contribute to society'.[3] These kinds of value statements have spread from the private sector, where they are used strategically to position corporations as socially responsible and working in the public interest. In the context of early intervention, 'missions' and 'visions' operate to place social investment beyond question as an obvious social good. Wrapped in a 'motherhood and apple-pie' language of inclusion, prosperity and human potential, a logic of intervention becomes difficult to criticise without appearing to oppose children's wellbeing. Yet it is through this appeal to common values that a narrow and particular set of meanings monopolise policy and practice debates, silencing and delegitimising alternative values and aspirations.

The sociologist Beverley Skeggs (2011) notes how, in public discourse, a monetised conception of value has come to eclipse an appreciation of values. It hampers our ability to see beyond an economic logic of capital, and to recognise alternative and more meaningful modes of existence. More specifically, a preoccupation with human capital acquisition has reduced objectives of social transformation to matters of individualised venture, speculation and investment. Yet so much of what matters the most to people: love, care, kindness, generosity, loyalty, dignity and so on, largely operates outside of this dominant framework of capital. In the rest of this chapter we want to consider what it would mean to locate policy and practice within this alternative domain; to prioritise human relations, social justice and ethical practice above economic rationales of childhood investment and return. What if we direct policy making to a goal of promoting social good rather than optimising individual strengths and capacities?

In Britain a utilitarian philosophy has traditionally informed approaches to public policy and welfare services. This moral reasoning seeks to maximise wellbeing and bring about the most effective balance of good over harm: 'the greatest happiness for the greatest number' as the 18th-century classical utilitarian, Jeremy Bentham put it. But such assessments depend heavily on the standards of valuation applied. How should wellbeing calculated? What counts as good or harm? Moreover, any promotion of the greater good surely must accommodate broad principles of social justice, given that morally reprehensible practices like slavery or forced euthanasia potentially could be, and indeed have been, legitimated on the basis that they benefit a majority. While governments of the last 40 years have relied on research and cost–benefit analyses to guide their expenditure, implementation of policies has always been (and always will be) guided by political and ethical contingencies and sensibilities. The contemporary turn towards 'evidence-based' policy and practice was an attempt to transcend this deeply political decision-making domain through an appeal to scientific objectivity. Highly selective use of randomised controlled trials (RCTs) and fMRI scans has worked to regulate and silence debates about how policy should promote the social good.

Increasingly though, there are now demands for a radically different relationship between citizens and the state, challenging prevailing top-down, mechanical approaches to policy. Alternative models have been drawn up by variety of actors and interest groups covering a wide range of issues and concerns. For example, at the overarching societal level, the social policy analyst Anna Coote (2015) advocates a 'new social settlement' that prioritises wellbeing and equality, works within environmental limits, decentres economic growth and shifts power towards ordinary citizens, while fostering solidarity and reciprocity. Echoing this call for greater participatory democracy, academic and activist Peter Beresford (2016) has set out an alternative vision of a collaborative, person-centred welfare state that is structured on the ideas and experiences of service users. Other expert analysts are pushing for a fundamental restructuring of particular areas of state provision. For example, academic and social work adviser Brid Featherstone and colleagues (2014b) have called for a more humane, relational approach to social work that is marked by a shift away from risk-dominated conceptualisations of early intervention. Writing from the perspective of early years education, Peter Moss (2014, 2015) is similarly keen to emphasise interdependence in his challenge to the instrumental, economistic and technical fixation on 'quality' and high returns that shapes pre-school provision. Identifying specific international examples in Italy, Sweden and New Zealand, Moss highlights how principles of democracy, experimentation and potentiality might be centred, in place of human capital production and market compliance.

Key fundamentals of this thinking are not new. Feminists have long theorised relational approaches to social policy, drawing on an 'ethic of care' to challenge assumptions of an 'autonomous ego' underpinning prevailing models (Tronto, 1993; Sevenhuijsen, 1998, 2002; Noddings, 2002; Barnes, 2012). An ethic of care reformulates liberal, contract-based interpretations of subjectivity, morality and justice. It embraces an alternative conception of autonomy that emphasises mutuality, relatedness and recognition of the needs of the other. From this perspective, individuals exist because of, and through their relationships with others. Personal development is achieved within a framework of obligation and relational morality. Many ethics-of-care analysts, such as the feminist philosopher Nel Noddings (2002), take this reasoning further, arguing that care as an elementary human need should be positioned at the centre of all public policy.

Critically engaged academics, practitioners and service users are rejecting the contemporary quest for technocratic fixes; instead they are revisiting fundamental political questions. Their realignment of values and priorities reveals very different possibilities and solutions to long-standing social problems that pose a challenge to the heavily ingrained economism that rules out progressive alternatives to social investment. New ideas and designs for service reform are each motivated by the same deep dissatisfaction with alienating and dysfunctional neoliberal ideologies. At the same time, there is little desire for a return to the top-down bureaucratic approach that characterised the post-war Keynesian welfare state, with its emphasis on economic growth through government spending to stimulate private sector activity and increase employment. As Anna Coote (2015) suggests, a new social settlement is required, that extends beyond economic productivity to encompass the 'non-productive' realm of creativity, care and participation, while promoting a longer term approach to securing the health and wellbeing of future generations.

Meanwhile, within austerity-hit communities, many ordinary families themselves have become involved directly in political activism to secure vital services, decent, safe housing and reasonable income levels. Among the most prominent of these grassroots movements is 'Focus E15'.[4] The campaign was set up by 29 young mothers from Newham, London, to resist their eviction from a hostel and relocation away from their friends and family on the grounds of council spending cuts. The mothers fought back hard, occupying council offices and empty flats on a nearby council estate awaiting demolition. In a partial victory, eventually they were rehoused locally, but in high-rent, badly maintained accommodation. Focus E15 continues to campaign vigorously on housing issues, opposing evictions, homelessness and social injustice in their own community and beyond. They have also inspired and supported a range of other campaigns such as Boundary House Residents Fight Back, which seeks to challenge the dangerous and unsanitary conditions in which families (many with babies) are being forced to live in London and the rest of the UK.[5]

Material matters

The grassroots struggles mentioned above, as well as a host of other similar campaigns,[6] expose the gaping holes in the logic of contemporary social investment approaches. The deprivation and desperate need characterising the lives of so many poor families in austerity-riven Britain is barely acknowledged in early years and early intervention policy strategies. Emphasis is placed on improving mother–infant bonds and parenting skills while children living on the Boundary House estate endure black mould, cockroach infestations, severe overcrowding and dangerous electrics. As the Focus E15 campaigners have chronicled, there are no special cases made for the 'critical first 1001 days' when it comes to the harmful material conditions in which they reside:

One resident, pregnant and living with her young daughter, had to survive the winter with no heating. Still today, their heating has not been fixed. On the third floor of Boundary House there is a young mother living with her now four month old baby, who was delivered by C-section. As there are no lifts in the block of flats, and the block is not safe or secure enough to leave the pushchair down stairs, every time this mother wants to go out she must carry her baby in the pushchair up and down three flights of stairs. The strain of this has meant that she has not been able to fully heal from the operation.[7]

The mothers' protests highlight the extent to which early years policies in the UK have become detached from basic considerations of human needs and social justice. Behind narrow preoccupations with infant brain development and children's future outcomes lie much broader moral and political questions which are routinely silenced. Figures from the Office of National Statistics reveal that one in three people have experienced an episode of poverty in recent years.[8] A staggering 1.25 million people, including over 300,000 children, were destitute at some point in 2015, meaning they lacked access to the basic essentials they needed to eat, keep clean and stay warm and dry.[9] The number of households relying on food banks has risen sharply (Loopstra et al, 2016), as has family homelessness (DCLG, 2016). Few would attempt to justify the extent of this deprivation in the world's fifth richest country, but mechanisms of redistribution and social protection have been supplanted by hollow promises to future-proof subsequent generations.

A recentring to a social justice lens would see emphasis placed on increasing access to material and economic resources. It would mean greater recognition of the harm, distress and disadvantage poverty inflicts on children and families in the here and now. Rather than constructing policy and practice around individualised models that personalise and normalise inequality, initiatives would start from a framework of civil rights, to housing, income thresholds, education and health care services. More specifically, poverty and all its cumulative impacts would need to be acknowledged and addressed in terms of financial deprivation, as opposed to cultural or psychological deficits. The will to portray the poor as authors of their own misfortune runs deep in the face of overwhelming evidence to the contrary. As we outlined in Chapter Two, the notion that poverty is culturally transmitted through the generations extends back in time, reflecting long-held convictions among the wealthy and privileged that deprivation is distinct, self-perpetuating and disconnected from mainstream society. Yet as Professor David Gordon, an adviser on official multidimensional poverty measures and head of an extensive and rigorous study of poverty in the UK (see poverty.ac.uk), points out:

> The idea that poverty is 'transmitted' between generations is an old libel which is entirely without foundation or supporting evidence. Poverty is not like syphilis or a biblical curse across the generations – poverty is not a disease and it cannot be caught and all creditable evidence shows that it is not 'transmitted' to children by their parents' genes or culture.... Despite almost 150 years of scientific investigation, often by extremely partisan investigators, not a single study has ever found any large group of people/ households with any behaviours that could be ascribed to a culture or genetics of poverty. (2011: 5)

Gordon is also very clear that increasing family income and reducing material deprivation is the fastest and most effective way to generate measurable improvements in children's lives. As he and his team demonstrated, child poverty has a devastating impact on health, educational attainment and wellbeing, blighting future life chances in the process:

> Children who grow up living in poverty are unsurprisingly more likely to suffer from poverty during their adult lives than their non-poor peers. There are also of course many families which have problems (sometimes multiple problems) who could benefit from additional help and services. However, any policy based on the idea that there are a group of 'Problem Families' who 'Transmit' their 'Poverty/Deprivation' to their children will inevitably fail, as this idea is a prejudice, unsupported by scientific evidence. (Gordon, 2011: 6)

There is then a clear and compelling moral case to be made for ensuring children and their families have sufficient resources to thrive and participate in the everyday activities that others take for granted. But even from a more traditional utilitarian perspective, evidence is stacking up that material support in the form of money can be transformative. The beneficial impacts of providing cash handouts to struggling families across the developing world is among the best evidenced of all anti-poverty strategies, with countless studies (many of them RCTs) demonstrating positive effects on health, nutrition, school attendance and cognitive development (Hagen-Zanker et al, 2016). There is also substantial evidence from Save the Children (2012) that cash transfers to families protect children in developing countries from abuse, neglect, exploitation and violence. In contrast with early childhood intervention, the simple practice of giving money to poor families 'works' regardless of what measure is applied. Moreover, providing financial support is substantially cheaper than sustaining the early years intervention industry we described in Chapter Four.

Evidence of the positive effects of cash transfers on children's outcomes is not confined to developing countries. Studies of initiatives based in Canada and the USA have demonstrated similarly impressive impacts. For example, in Canada the introduction of two cash benefit systems for families, the Canada Child Tax Benefit in 1993 and the National Child Benefit in 1998, has significantly reduced poverty, raised children's educational test scores (particularly boys), reduced stress in low-income households, and improved maternal and child mental health (particularly among girls), as well as increasing employment in lone-parent households (Milligan and Stabile, 2009).

Evidence supporting the effectiveness of unconditional cash supports for struggling families in Canada is surprisingly long-standing. The province of Manitoba first experimented with a Guaranteed Annual Income programme in 1974. For four years monthly cheques (calculated at 60% of a low-income cut-off figure) were delivered to the province's poorest residents effectively eliminating poverty, until an incoming Conservative government called a halt to the project. Researchers conducting an RCT were forced to pack away their material into storage at this point, and there the data languished until an academic from the University of Manitoba came across it some 30 years later. Dr Evelyn Forget (2011) constructed a quasi-experimental design drawing on routinely collected health administration data. She found that during period in which the programme operated, hospital visits were significantly reduced with fewer incidents of work-related injuries, and fewer emergency room visits from accidents and injuries. In addition, rates of psychiatric hospitalisation and mental illness-related consultations with health professionals were also considerably reduced. Forget was also able to determine that high school students participating in the programme were more likely to stay on in education.

The aborted Manitoba project was in fact based on an even older set of experiments initiated in the USA to test the effects of a negative income tax scheme. In the late 1960s there was growing dissatisfaction with American public welfare, and many were advocating a guaranteed income as an alternative to administering the complex and inefficient system of variable benefits in place. This alternative was politically controversial and widely opposed on the basis that a guaranteed income for the poor would reduce their incentive to work and place a heavy burden on the taxpayer. In the context of this debate, the US federal government funded four large-scale RCTs between 1968 and 1990 with the explicit aim of investigating how supplementing the incomes of the poor might affect their working practices and the labour supply. Robert Levine and colleagues (2005) have documented the changing political winds that buffeted the project during this period, eventually running it aground. The experiment was initially introduced under President Lyndon Johnson's administration, and many expected it to be discontinued when Richard Nixon came to power in 1969. Instead, Nixon appointed new project leaders (Donald Rumsfeld and his assistant Dick Cheney) and pressurised researchers for early indications that there were no work disincentives. These premature findings were used to launch Nixon's Family Assistance Plan, which directed welfare payments at working, two-parent, male-breadwinner families, rather than the politically unpopular working poor and (largely black) lone-parent households (see O'Connor in Levine et al, 2005).

In the late 1970s the Carter administration began to look again at designing a guaranteed income system. By this time the long-term findings from the experiments indicated a small but measurable reduction in employment, mainly among dual-earner families and individuals working very long hours. This was seized on by the media as evidence of a dangerous disincentive to work. The final nail in the programme's coffin was an analysis of data from one of the experiments appearing to suggest that families receiving guaranteed income were more likely to break up (Groeneveld et al, 1983). While this finding was widely criticised and disputed by social scientists, it chimed with an emerging New Right political agenda that was opposing welfare dependency and its impact on families. The US historian of poverty, Alice O'Connor, remarks that:

> looking at the [Negative Income Tax] experiments as a political undertaking shows us how politics can confound efforts to inform policy with scientific knowledge. Even as social scientists were sorting through and debating the meaning of the experimental findings, political opponents were using those findings to tell a simple story of lazy poor people and family decline. (in Levine et al, 2005: 105)

Yet today there is broad agreement that the experiments established a strong case for income guarantees. Work disincentives are now acknowledged to be minimal while numerous health and education benefits of receiving a basic income have been documented. Those participating in the US negative income tax studies saw a range of significant life improvements, including higher quality nutritional intake, few low-weight babies, higher levels of school attendance and increased educational attainment (Salkind and Haskins, 1982). Even a leading proponent of the US New Right and critic of welfare payments, Charles Murray, is now a strong supporter of the guaranteed basic income (see Murray, 2016).

Supporting families

Material and financial resources are vital to the health and wellbeing of families but needs can and do extend far beyond a basic standard of living to encompass broader social support and services. The prevailing model of a self-contained parent entirely responsible for all current and future aspects of their own and their children's lives and wellbeing belies the socially grounded nature of raising a child and a necessary reliance on other individuals, agencies and professionals. For example, widely available and affordable child care is a necessity where parents want to work or pursue their education. Child care is even more fundamental in the context of family illness, disability or other special needs, as are a range of services and provisions. Many parents rely on the social and emotional support they access through voluntary agencies or children's services, while many others encounter particular difficulties and depend on the advice and help of specific health or education professionals.

All families from time to time experience disruption, challenges and troubles that, depending on the context and the actors involved, may be interpreted and addressed in very different ways (Ribbens McCarthy et al, 2013). Yet existing support for disadvantaged and struggling families operates largely through top-down diagnosis and the imposition of an 'evidence-based' response. In the rush to apply a technical fix that 'works', parents and children themselves rarely are consulted on what would make their lives better. Instead their needs are viewed through a risk lens that prioritises the protection and outcomes of children in isolation from their broader family relations, culture and values (Featherstone et al, 2016). This characteristically neoliberal individualisation and dismemberment of family as an inherently collective endeavour positions children as distinct, separately conceived beings who are attached to families primarily through contingent (state-regulated) relationships with their parents (Gillies, 2014). The result is an increasingly paternalistic, child-centric interventionism that disparages and devalues the parenting practices and choices of disadvantaged families. As Brid Featherstone and colleagues argue, there is an urgent need to challenge this relentlessly child-focused orthodoxy in children's services:

> Children are not simply 'individuals' in a neoliberal fantasy of unfettered market actors. Across a range of disciplines from psychology to philosophy to the sciences, the recognition has emerged of our profound interdependence as human beings. To think of a child as a free floating individual denies elemental ties: to the body that gave birth to her, the breast that fed her, the aunt who sneaked her sweets, the streets where she played, the friends she played with. Interdependence is the basis of human interaction and autonomy and independence are about the capacity for self-determination rather than self-sufficiency. (2014b: 32)

Recognising interdependence as the core of human flourishing would require greater understanding and acknowledgement of the way family and community ties generate crucial resources for children and adults. Rather than promoting parent education and family intervention, efforts would focus on strengthening and supporting the capacity for such relationships to thrive. This means listening to and advocating for families. As Featherstone and colleagues suggest, practitioners 'should engage with the complexities of relationships, to have the kinds of conversations they might themselves wish to have if they were in desperate circumstances' (2014b: 128). Moreover, such engagement involves accepting and meeting the needs that mothers themselves identify. These may revolve around addressing seemingly mundane issues that politicians rarely concern themselves with, such as broken lifts in tower blocks, lack of safe play spaces and facilities for children, isolation from shops and amenities, and other quality-of-life factors that impact heavily on the wellbeing of parents and children.

Research points to the high value mothers attached to the local Sure Start Children's Centres, launched and expanded under the New Labour government. Sure Start provision was controlled by local authorities and the services provided at each centre were able to develop in response to the expressed needs of parents themselves as well as other local organisations. Parents were found to value particularly those centres offering a range of practical and emotional support facilities, such as childcare, playgroups, toy libraries, cafes, educational and training opportunities, access to information and advice, as well as the sensitive, non-judgemental relationships with early years workers (Williams, 2008; Churchill and Clarke, 2009). Ironically, the closure of Children's Centres has accelerated in line with the ramping up of early intervention rhetoric. Thus, while programmes that proselytise and demand personal change have expanded, the flexible, community-based model of family support associated with the early Sure Start initiative is being wound down and discontinued. At the same time, more urgent needs for family support and specialist services frequently go unmet. When specific problems are encountered with a child's health or education, mothers often find appropriate help very difficult to obtain (Gillies, 2007). Long waiting lists for speech therapists, developmental and educational psychologists, occupational therapists, child and adolescent mental health support, and a range of other specialist services have been exacerbated by austerity-led cuts, escalating families' difficulties and compounding disadvantage.

In emphasising the financial, material and emotional support needs of parents we are not denying that some children may be at risk of harm within their own families. Research by Paul Bywaters and colleagues, however, have established that there is a clear link between poverty and the incidence of child abuse and neglect. This association is evident across developed countries and spans different types of abuse and operational definitions of poverty. In the UK, a child living in the deprived Lancashire district of Blackpool is 12 times more likely to be subject to child protection measures than a child living in the wealthy London borough of Richmond (Bywaters et al, 2014; Bywaters, 2015). The very real risk that poverty and deprivation poses to children is almost completely occluded by a contemporary fixation on the individual actions and intentions of parents. There are no simple causal determinants driving the complex and multifaceted problem of child abuse and neglect (most poor children are not at risk from their parents while some from privileged backgrounds are) but the effect of family hardship on the distribution and incidence of child harm is seriously under acknowledged at present.

Featherstone and colleagues (2016) argue that preoccupations with early intervention have been characterised by a toxic shift towards risk aversion in the field of social work and child protection. They describe a statutory system that is both punitive and neglectful. It threatens families with the removal of children while at the same time leaving them without the resources or support to meet the 'child-centred' demands of professionals. They cite figures from the NSPCC (National

Society for the Prevention of Cruelty to Children) to show how more than three-quarters of child protection plans now relate specifically to neglect or emotional abuse, in a context where rising numbers of families are forced to cope with hunger, homelessness and the stress and shame of poverty. It is also sobering to note that approximately one in five children in England are now referred to social services for child protection investigation (Bilson and Martin, 2016).

Featherstone and colleagues (2014b) advocate a very different approach to understanding and dealing with suffering, harm and complex needs within families. They argue for a foregrounding of moral issues around ethics and justice, recognition of the centrality of relationships and relational practice, and for replacement of an actuarial concept of risk with care. More specifically, they have also set out an alternative that builds on a social model of child protection (Featherstone et al, 2016). Drawing on a philosophy and framework that originated from disability studies, Featherstone and colleagues challenge prevailing biomedical models and their narrow preoccupation with individual impairments, disease and risk. Applied to the area of child protection, this social model centres the child's relational identity by positioning family relationships as fundamental to children's wellbeing and identity, while recognising the social and structural sources of families' troubles.

From individual risk to social harm

A redirection of attention to the social and structural factors framing conceptualisations of individual troubles also opens up new strategies for reducing personal and social injury. Early intervention is rooted in the uncontroversial axiom that prevention is better than cure. It extends this common-sense reasoning to the belief that social problems can be nipped in the bud by cultivating strengths and virtues in childhood. The broader social, structural and cultural context shaping children's outcomes and difficulties are excluded from this dominant prevention narrative. Rather, a prevailing liberal orthodoxy foregrounds personal agency. This convention sustains the notion that individual actions, intentions, behaviours and biological traits are at the root of all social ills. Formative issues that relate to social status, distribution of resources and environment are viewed neither as part of the problem, nor of the solution. It is such a denial of collective responsibility for human travails and wellbeing that drives futile attempts to manage risk at the level of the individual through expensive and often ineffectual intervention programmes.

An alternative to the actuarial preoccupation, with its obsessive assessment and management of personal risk, is to adopt a much broader concept of social harm as a framework for understanding and tackling social ills. This is a perspective that has been developed by criminologists and embraced by those keen to escape the restrictive judicial orthodoxies informing understandings of crime and criminals (Hillyard and Tombs, 2007; Dorling et al, 2008; Pemberton, 2016). Social harm theorists seek a more inclusive understanding of human suffering, extending the lens of responsibility to corporations, states and those wielding financial and or political power:

> The approach that we have sought may encompass the detrimental activities of local and national states and of corporations upon the welfare of individuals, whether this be lack of wholesome food, inadequate housing or heating, low income, exposure to various forms of danger, violations of basic human rights, and victimisation to various forms of crime. Of course, when we speak of people's welfare, we refer not (simply) to an atomised individual, or to men and women and their families, the social units who often experience harm. For it is clear that various forms of harms are not distributed randomly, but fall upon people of different social classes, genders, degrees of physical ability, racial and ethnic groups, different ages, sexual preferences, and so on. (Dorling et al, 2008: 14)

Rather than attempting to calculate individual risk, social harm theorists identify collective responses to personal injuries, avoiding individualistic concepts of blame and responsibility. This approach enables a much wider investigation of precipitating factors and accountability, as well as an appreciation of the consequences of governments failing to act to address deprivation or corporate exploitation. Indeed, a key advantage of this perspective is its capacity to highlight injuries that are otherwise naturalised and placed beyond societal accountability. A social harm lens reveals that the most pervasive and intractable social injuries derive from the pursuit of particular political and policy directions rather than intentional actions or personal deficits. Infant mortality provides a good example of how harms commonly represented as personal misfortunes may instead be viewed as mediated through particular governmental regimes. As Simon Pemberton (2016) shows, there are clear disparities in rates of infant mortality between nation states accompanied by a patterning of socio-demographic factors suggesting that many of these deaths are preventable. A similar conclusion could be drawn from the research by Paul Bywaters and colleagues discussed above in relation to child abuse and neglect (Bywaters et al, 2014).

Pemberton takes his analysis further to argue that the social organisation pursued within particular countries determines the forms and distributions of particular kinds of social harm. He examines comparative rates of homicide, suicide, obesity, road traffic injuries, poverty, financial insecurity, long working hours, youth unemployment, social isolation, as well as infant mortality, across 31 OECD (Organisation for Economic and Co-operation and Development) countries. This analysis demonstrates how different policy regimes mitigate or intensify these particular social ills. Starting from the premise that harm is integral to all forms of capitalist societies, Pemberton outlines how nation states can be categorised in relation to the harm reduction strategies they pursue. He then assessed the variance of statistical indicators of these harms across the different regimes.

Pemberton's analysis demonstrates that neoliberal regimes that are characterised by highly individualised societies with weak collective responsibility for others, a minimal welfare safety net, and heavily privatised and means-tested social services, are associated with the highest levels of social harm. In contrast, social democratic regimes were found to be the least harmful. More specifically, Pemberton identified three facets of social democracies that appear to reduce the incidence of social harm. First, social solidarity is evident, in the form of low levels of inequality and high levels of empathy towards others. Second, the predominant sensibilities work to decommodify people, that is, to separate the worth of human beings from their ability to accumulate wealth. Rather, the regime operates through more generous universal welfare provision. And, third, there is an application of fetters on the production of capital. The exploitation of workers is reduced through enforcing employment rights and supporting union membership.

In producing this statistically grounded analysis Pemberton is not advocating a particular version of social democracy. Rather he is seeking to highlight how negative impacts of capitalist production are effectively diminished in some societies and exacerbated in others. This lesson echoes many of the conclusions drawn by the epidemiologists, Richard Wilkinson and Kate Pickett (2011) in their meticulous research on the demographics of inequality and its pernicious consequences. Wilkinson and Pickett analysed indices from 23 of the world's richest nations for a range of different health and social issues, including child wellbeing, education, physical and mental health, imprisonment, trust, and community life. They found that outcomes for adults and children are significantly worse in unequal rich countries such as Britain, while they do better in more equal societies with the narrowest income differentials. This is a powerful insight: that social injuries are produced by, and can therefore be reduced by, political organisation. It strongly suggests that governments should turn their attention away from the brains and morals of poor families and focus instead on the negative impacts of their own technocratic regimes. Social harm analyses make the human cost of prioritising value over values increasingly clear, paving the way for an alternative, humane politicisation of the social good.

While futile and damaging early intervention programmes are being pursued, austerity bites ever deeper for poor families, underscoring the urgent need for political and policy reform. Policy makers are inflicting the harm that they claim to be addressing. Their initiatives are perpetuating a social investment myth and indulging the whims, imaginaries and interests of wealthy philanthrocapitalists. But this status quo is sustained through false hope and complicity. There is space here for academics, practitioners and families to exercise the power to disrupt and unsettle. Stephen Ball describes this in terms of a 'politics of refusal' and 'a struggle over and against what it is we have become, what it is that we do not want to be' (2015: 15). Others have been more explicit in recommending 'guerrilla warfare' and 'small-scale resistance' against institutional strictures that might further disadvantage the poorest in society (Ferguson, 2009).

We can engage critically with professional knowledge and expectations. We can question orthodoxies. And we can challenge the routine pathologisation of individuals to help to make a better world possible. That is what we have attempted to do in this book. At the very least, we hope that contesting manufactured truths about biological cycles of deprivation helps to fracture a dangerous consensus. Alternative ways of practising, caring and valuing can then come into view. We have opened up to question and criticism the social investment, outcomes-based notion of the social good embedded in early years intervention policies and programmes, and their annexation of the molecular focus of brain science. Rather than a reductionist, instrumental set of mantras about saving the nation and the world that reifies both the self-responsibility of suffering individuals and anticipated returns on strategic investment, we can work with a notion of social good that could be worked on for its own sake. Such an intrinsically, humane approach is founded on social interdependence, and wider social justice and equality as an end in themselves in the present moment. From this grounding, we can envisage providing support to families on their own terms, meeting their expressed needs to enhance parents' and children's lives in the here and now, simply because that is a good thing to do.

Notes

[1] www.pause.org.uk/dfe-announcement
[2] www.eif.org.uk/about-us/
[3] http://fnp.nhs.uk/about-us
[4] focuse15.org/
[5] www.facebook.com/boundaryhouseresidents/
[6] See *Rise of the housing activists*, www.oceanmediagroup.co.uk/features/housingprotests/
[7] https://focuse15.org/2016/06/29/children-forced-to-live-in-appalling-conditions/
[8] www.ons.gov.uk/peoplepopulationandcommunity/personalandhouseholdfinances/incomeandwealth/articles/persistentpovertyintheukandeu/2014
[9] www.jrf.org.uk/press/destitute-uk

References

All Party Parliamentary Group for Conception to Age Two (2015) *Building great Britons*, www.wavetrust.org/sites/default/files/reports/Building_Great_Britons_Report-APPG_Conception_to_Age_2-Wednesday_25th_February_2015.pdf

Allen, G. (2011a) *Early intervention: The next steps.* An independent report to Her Majesty's Government, London: Cabinet Office.

Allen, G. (2011b) *Early intervention: Smart investment, massive savings.* Second Independent Report to Her Majesty's Government, London: Cabinet Office.

Allen, G. and Duncan Smith, I. (2008) *Early intervention: Good parents, great kids, better citizens,* London: Centre for Social Justice and the Adam Smith Institute.

Anthias, F. (2013) 'Intersectional what? Social divisions, intersectionality and levels of analysis', *Ethnicities*, 13: 3–19.

Back, L. (2015) 'On the side of the powerful: The "impact agenda" and sociology in public', Sociological Review Blog, www.thesociologicalreview.com/blog/on-the-side-of-the-powerful-the-impact-agenda-sociology-in-public.html

Ball, S. (2010) 'New voices, new knowledges and the new politics of education research: The gathering of a perfect storm?', *European Educational Research Journal*, 9(2): 124–37.

Ball, S.J. (2015) 'Subjectivity as a site of struggle: Refusing neoliberalism?', *British Journal of Sociology of Education*, 37(8): 1129–1146. DOI: 10.1080/01425692.2015.1044072

Ball, S.J. and Junemann, C. (2012) *Networks, new governance and education,* Bristol: Policy Press.

Barn, R. (2013) '"Race" and adoption crusades in 21st-century Britain', *Huffington Post*, www.huffingtonpost.co.uk/professor-ravinder-barn/race-and-adoption-michael-gove_b_2657383.html

Barnardo, T. (1885) *Worse than orphans: How I stole two girls and fought for a boy*, London: J.F. Shaw & Co.

Barnes, J., Ball, M., Meadows, P., McLeish, J., Belsky, J. and the FNP Implementation Research Team (2008) *Nurse–Family Partnership programme: First year pilot sites implementation in England: Pregnancy and the post-partum period*, London: Birkbeck College, http://dera.ioe.ac.uk/8581/1/dcsf-rw051%20v2.pdf.

Barnes, M. *(2012) Care in everyday life: An ethic of care in practice*, Bristol: Policy Press.

Bate, A. (2016) *The Troubled Families programme (England)*, Briefing Paper CBP 07585, 9 August, London: House of Commons Library.

BBC News (2015) 'Invest in the first 1001 days say experts', 25 February, www.bbc.co.uk/news/education-31607711

Becker, G. (1981) *Treatise on the family*, Cambridge, MA: Harvard University Press.

Behlmer, G.K. (1998) *Friends of the family: The English home and its guardians, 1850–1940*, Stanford, CA: Stanford University Press.

Belfiore, E. (2009) 'On bullshit in cultural policy practice and research: Notes from the British case', *International Journal of Cultural Policy*, 15(3): 343–59.

Bellamy, C. (2000) *The state of the world's children 2001: Early childhood*, UNICEF, www.unicef.org/sowc/archive/ENGLISH/The%20State%20of%20the%20World's%20Children%202001.pdf

Bennett, C.M., Baird, A.A., Miller, M.B. and Wolford, G.L. (2009) 'Neural correlates of interspecies perspective taking in the post-mortem Atlantic salmon: An argument for multiple comparisons correction', *Neuroimage*, 47: S125, http://prefrontal.org/files/posters/Bennett-Salmon-2009.pdf

Beresford, P. (2016) *All our welfare: Towards participatory social policy*, Bristol: Policy Press.

Berlant, L. (2011) *Cruel optimism*, Durham NC: Duke University Press.

Bernier, A. and Meins, E. (2008) 'A threshold approach to understanding the origins of attachment disorganization', *Developmental Psychology*, 44(4): 969–82.

Bilson, A. and Martin, E.C. (2016) 'Referrals and child protection in England: One in five children referred to children's services and one in nineteen investigated before the age of five', *British Journal of Social Work*. DOI: 10.1093/bjsw/bcw054

Bishop, M. and Green, M. (2008) *Philanthrocapitalism: How the rich can save the world*, London: Bloomsbury.

Blair, T. (2006) 'Our nation's future – social exclusion', Speech, York, 5 September, http://webarchive.nationalarchives.gov.uk/20040105034004/http:/number10.gov.uk/page10037

Boddy, J., Smith, M. and Statham, J. (2011) 'Understandings of efficacy: Cross-national perspectives on "what works" in supporting parents and families', *Ethics and Education*, 6: 181–96.

Boucher, E. (2014) *Empire's children: Child emigration, welfare, and the decline of the British world, 1869–1967*, Cambridge: Cambridge University Press.

Broad, W.J. (2014) 'Billionaires with big ideas are privatizing American science', *New York Times*, 16 March, www.nytimes.com/2014/03/16/science/billionaires-with-big-ideas-are-privatizing-american-science.html?_r=0

Brown, R. and Ward, H. (2013) *Decision-making within a child's timeframe: An overview of current research evidence for family justice professionals concerning child development and the impact of maltreatment*, Working Paper 16, London: Childhood Wellbeing Research Centre.

Bruer, J.T. (1999) *The myth of the first three years: A new understanding of early brain development and lifelong learning*, New York: Simon and Schuster.

Button, K.S., Ioannidis, J.P.A., Mokrysz, C., Nosek, B.A., Flint, J., Robinson, E.S.J. and Munafo, M.R. (2013) 'Power failure: Why small sample size undermines the reliability of neuroscience', *Nature Reviews Neuroscience*, 14: 365–76.

Bywaters, P. (2015) 'Inequalities in child welfare: Towards a new policy, research and action agenda', *British Journal of Social Work*, 45(1): 6–23.

Bywaters, P., Brady, G., Sparks, T. and Bos, E. (2014) 'Inequalities in child welfare intervention rates: The intersection of deprivation and identity', *Child and Family Social Work*, 21(4): 452–463.

Bywaters, P., Bunting, L., Davidson, G., Hanratty, J., Mason, W. McCartan, C. and Stelis, N. (2016) *The relationship between poverty, child abuse and neglect: An evidence review*, JRF Report, York: Joseph Rowntree Foundation.

Cabinet Office (2006) *Reaching out: An action plan on social exclusion*, London: HM Government.

Cabinet Office (2014) *What works? Evidence for decision makers*, www.gov.uk/government/uploads/system/uploads/attachment_data/file/378038/What_works_evidence_for_decision_makers.pdf

Cartwright, N. (2007) 'Are RCTs the gold standard?', *BioSocieties*, 2(1): 11–20.

Chugani, H., Behen, M.E., Muzik, O., Juha, C., Nagy, F. and Chugani D. (2001) 'Local brain functional activity following early deprivation: A study of postinstitutionalized Romanian orphans', *Neuroimage*,14: 1290–301.

Chugani, H., Phelps, M.E. and Mazziota, J.C. (1987) 'Positron emission tomography study of human brain function development', *Annals of Neurology*, 22: 487–97.

Churchill, H. and Clarke, K. (2009) 'Investing in parenting education: A critical review of policy and provision in England', *Social Policy and Society*, 9(1): 39–53.

CIPD (Chartered Institute of Personnel and Development) (2015) 'Over-qualification and skills mismatch in the graduate labour market', www.cipd.co.uk/publicpolicy/policy-reports/overqualification-skills-mismatch-graduate-labour-market.aspx

Clark, C.L., St John, N., Pascam, A.M., Hyde, S.A., Hornbeak, K., Abramova, M., Feldman, H., Parker, K.J., Penn, A.A. (2013) 'Neonatal CSF oxytocin levels are associated with parent report of infant soothability and sociability', *Psychoneuroendocrinology*, 38(7): 1208–12.

Clayton, J. (2015) *Breaking the cycle of deprivation*, NCT Service Development and Policy, www.nct.org.uk/sites/default/files/related_documents/Clayton%20J%20Breaking%20the%20cycle%20of%20disadvantage.pdf

Coote, A. (2015) 'People, planet, power: Towards a new social settlement', The New Economics Foundation blog, http://neweconomics.org/people-planet-power/?lost=true&_sf_s=+publications+++++planet+power+towards+a+new+social+settlement?source=new+social+settlement

Cottam H. (2011) 'Relational welfare', *Soundings*, https://www.lwbooks.co.uk/soundings/48/relational-welfare

Crone, E.A. and Ridderinkhof, K.R. (2011) 'The developing brain: From theory to neuroimaging and back', *Developmental Cognitive Neuroscience*, 1: 101–9.

Crossley, S. (2015) 'The Troubled Families programme: The perfect social policy?', Centre for Crime and Justice Studies Briefing Paper 13, www.crimeandjustice.org.uk/sites/crimeandjustice.org.uk/files/The%20Troubled%20Families%20Programme%2C%20Nov%202015.pdf

CSJ (Centre for Social Justice) (2014) 'Fully committed? How a government could reverse family breakdown', http://www.centreforsocialjustice.org.uk/core/wp-content/uploads/2016/08/CSJJ2072_Family_Breakdown.pdf

Cunha, F. and Heckman, J. (2007) 'The technology of skill formation', *American Economic Review*, 97(2): 31–47.

Daly, M. (2013) 'Parenting support policies in Europe', *Families, Relationships and Societies*, 2(2): 159–74.

Daly, M. and Bray, R. (2015) 'Parenting support in England: The bedding down of a new policy', *Social Policy and Society*, 14(4): 633–44.

Dartington Social Research Unit, University of Warwick and Coventry University (2015) *The best start at home*, Early Intervention Foundation, www.eif.org.uk/publication/the-best-start-at-home/

Davies, B. (2003) 'Death to critique and dissent? The policies and practices of New Managerialism and of "evidence-based practice"', *Gender and Education*, 15(1): 91–103.

Davies, W. (2012) 'The emerging neocommunitarianism', *Political Quarterly*, 83(4): 767–76.

Davis, D.A. (2007) 'Narrating the mute: Racialising and racism in a neo-liberal moment', *Souls*, 9(4): 346–60.

DCLG (Department for Communities and Local Government) (2016) 'Statutory homeslessness, January to March 2016, and homelessness prevention and relief 2015/16', England, Housing Statistical Release, 30 June, www.gov.uk/government/uploads/system/uploads/attachment_data/file/533099/Statutory_Homelessness_and_Prevention_and_Relief_Statistical_Release_January_to_March_2016.pdf

Deoni. S.C., Dean, D.C., Piryatinsky, I., O'Muircheartaigh, J., Waskiewicz, N., Lehman, K., Hands, M. and Dirks, H. (2013) 'Breastfeeding and early white matter development: A cross-sectional study', *Neuroimage*, 82: 77–86.

DfE (Department for Education) (2014) 'Measures to help schools instil character in pupils announced', Press release, 8 December, www.gov.uk/government/news/measures-to-help-schools-instil-character-in-pupils-announced

DfE (2015) 'Children looked after in England (including adoption and care leavers) year ending 31 March 2015', www.gov.uk/government/uploads/system/uploads/attachment_data/file/464756/SFR34_2015_Text.pdf

DWP and DfE (Department for Work and Pensions and Department for Education) (2011) *A new approach to child poverty: Tackling the causes of disadvantage and transforming families' lives*, Cmnd 8061, London: HM Stationery Office.

Diamond, P. (2013) *Governing Britain: Power, politics and the prime minister*, London: I.B. Tauris.

Dikötter, F. (1998) 'Race culture: Recent perspectives on the history of eugenics', *American Historical Review*, 103(2): 467–78.

Dodds, A. (2009) 'Families "at risk" and the Family Nurse Partnership: The intrusion of risk into social exclusion policy', *Journal of Social Policy*, 38(3): 499–514.

Dorling, D., Gordon, D., Hillyard, P., Pantazis, C., Pemberton, S.A. and Tombs, S. (2008) *Criminal obsessions: Why harm matters more than crime*, London: Centre for Crime and Justice Studies, Kings College.

Duncan, S., Edwards, R. and Alexander, C. (eds) (2010) *Teenage parenthood: What's the problem?*, London: Tufnell Press.

Duster, T. (2005) 'Race and reification in science', *Science*, 307: 1050–1.

Earp, B. (2016) 'The unbearable asymmetry of bullshit', *Health Watch*, 101, www.healthwatch-uk.org/images/Newsletters/Number_101_BE.pdf

Ecclestone, K. (2012) 'From emotional and psychological well-being to character education: Challenging policy discourses of behavioural science and "vulnerability"', *Research Papers in Education*, 27(4): 463–80.

Edwards, M. (2008) *Just another emperor? The myths and realities of philanthrocapitalism*, London: The Young Foundation.

Edwards, R. and Gillies, V. (2004) 'Support in parenting: Values and consensus concerning who to turn to', *Journal of Social Policy*, 33(4): 627–47.

Edwards, R. and Gillies, V. (2016) 'Family policy: the Mods and Rockers', in H. Bochel and M. Powell (eds) *The Coalition government and social policy*, Bristol: Policy Press.

Edwards, R., Gillies, V. and Horsley, N. (2015a) 'Brain science and early years policy: Hopeful ethos or "cruel optimism"?', *Critical Social Policy*, 35(2): 167–87.

Edwards, R., Gillies, V. and Horsley, N. (2015b) 'Early intervention and evidence-based policy and practice: Framing and taming', *Social Policy and Society*, 15(1): 1–10.

Eikhoff, S.B., Laird, A.R., Fox, P.M., Lancaster, J.L. and Fox, P.T. (2016) 'Implementation errors in the GingerALE software: Description and recommendations', *Human Brain Mapping* PMID: 27511454.

Eklund, A., Nichols, T.E. and Knutsson, H. (2016) 'Cluster failure: Why fMRI inferences for spatial extent have inflated false-positive rates', *Proceedings of the National Academy of Sciences of the United States of America*, 113(28): 7900–5, http://www.pnas.org/content/113/28/7900.full

Equality and Human Rights Commission (2015) *Is Britain fairer?* https://www.equalityhumanrights.com/en/britain-fairer [accessed online 19.4.17]

Evans, B., Rahman, S. and Jones, E. (2008) 'Managing the "unmanageable": Interwar child psychiatry at the Maudsley Hospital', www.historyandpolicy.org/policy-papers/papers/the-dangerous-age-of-childhood-child-guidance-in-britain-c.1918-1955

Evenhouse, E. and Reilly, S. (2005) 'Improved estimates of the benefits of breastfeeding using sibling comparisons to reduce selection bias', *Health Services Research*, 40(6:1): 1781–802.

Eysenck, M.W. and Keane, M.T. (2010) *Cognitive psychology: A student's handbook*, Hove and New York: Psychology Press.

Family Law Week (2013) 'Court of Appeal gives important guidance on adoption applications', 22 September, http://familylawweek.co.uk/site.aspz?i=ed117222

Farah, M.J. and Hook, C.J. (2013) 'The seductive allure of "seductive allure"', *Perspectives on Psychological Science*, 8(1): 88–90.

Featherstone, B. and Bywaters, P. (2014) 'An ideological approach to adoption figures means we are missing important trends', *Community Care*, www.communitycare.co.uk/2014/10/07/ideological-approach-adoption-figures-means-missing-important-trends/

Featherstone, B., Morris, K. and White, S. (2014a) 'A marriage made in hell: Early intervention meets child protection', *British Journal of Social Work*, 44(7): 1735–49.

Featherstone, B., White, S. and Morris, K. (2014b) *Re-imagining child protection: Towards humane social work with families*, Bristol: Policy Press.

Featherstone, B., Gupta, A., Morris, K. and Warner, J. (2016) 'Let's stop feeding the risk monster: Towards a model of "child protection"', *Families, Relationships and Societies*, http://dx.doi.org/10.1332/2046 74316X14552878034622

Ferguson, I. (2009) '"Another social work is possible!" Reclaiming the radical tradition', in V. Leskošek (ed.) *Theories and methods of social work: Exploring different perspectives*, Ljubljana: University of Ljubljana, pp. 81–98.

Fernald, L.C.H., Gertler, P.J. and Neufeld L.M (2008) 'The importance of cash in conditional cash transfer programs for child health, growth and development', *The Lancet*, 371(9615): 828–37.

Field, F. (2010) *The foundation years: Preventing poor children becoming poor adults*. Report of the Independent Review on Poverty and Life Chances, London: Cabinet Office, http://webarchive.nationalarchives.gov.uk/20110120090128/http:/povertyreview.independent.gov.uk/media/20254/poverty-report.pdf

Fine, C. (2010) *Delusions of gender: How our minds, society and neurosexism create difference*, New York: W.W. Norton.

Foresight Report (2008) *Mental capital and wellbeing: Making the most of ourselves in the 21st century*, London: Government Office for Science.

Forget, E. (2011) 'The town with no poverty: The health effects of a Canadian guaranteed annual income field experiment', *Canadian Public Policy*, 37(3): 283–305.

FrameWorks Institute (2009) *Summary research memo: FrameWorks' analysis of frame effects on PCAA policies and implications for messaging*, www.frameworksinstitute.org/assets/files/child_abuse_neglect/child_abuse_neglect_prevention_summary_research_memo.pdf

Gaffney, D. (2010) 'The myth of the intergenerational workless household', Left Foot Forward, www.leftfotfoward.org/2010/09/the-myth-of-the-intergenerational-workless-household/

Gee, J.P. (2012) *An introduction to discourse analysis: Theory and method*, 3rd edn, London: Routledge.

Gelman, A. (2013) 'Childhood intervention and earnings', *Symposium Magazine*, www.symposium-magazine.com/childhood-intervention-and-earnings/

Gelman, A. (2014) 'Estimated effect of early childhood intervention downgraded from 42% to 25%', Statistical Modeling, Causal Interference, and Social Science blog, 6 August, http://andrewgelman.com/2014/08/08/estimated-effect-early-childhood-intervention-downgraded-42-25/

Gerhardt, S. (2004) *Why love matters: How affection shapes a baby's brain*, Hove: Brunner-Routledge.

Gertler, P., Heckman, J., Pinto, R., Zanolini, A., Vermeersch, C., Walker, S., Chang, S.M. and Grantham-McGregor, S. (2013) *Labor market returns to early childhood stimulation: A 20 year follow-up to an experimental intervention in Jamaica*, National Bureau of Economic Research Working Paper 19185, www.nber.org/papers/w19185

Gertler, P., Heckman, J., Pinto, R., Zanolini, A., Vermeersch, C., Walker, S., Chang, S.M. and Grantham-McGregor, S. (2014) 'Labor market returns to an early childhood stimulation in Jamaica', *Science*, 344(6187): 998–1001.

Gillies, V. (2007) *Marginalised mothers: Exploring working class experiences of parenting*, Abingdon: Routledge.

Gillies, V. (2011) 'From function to competence: Engaging with the new politics of family', *Sociological Research Online*, 16 (4), www.socresonline.org.uk/16/4/11.html

Gillies, V. (2014) 'Troubling families: Parenting and the politics of early intervention', in S. Wragg and J. Pilcher (eds) *Thatcher's grandchildren*, London: Palgrave Macmillan.

Gogtay, N., Giedd, J.N., Lusk, L., Hayashi, K.M., Greenstein, D., Vaituzis, A.C. and Thompson, P.M. (2004) 'Dynamic mapping of human cortical development during childhood through early adulthood', *Proceedings of the National Academy of Sciences of the United States of America*, 101: 8174–9.

Goldberg, D.T. (2009) *The threat of race: Reflections on racial neoliberalism*, Oxford: Wiley Blackwell.

Goodman, A. (2006) *The story of David Olds and the Nurse Home Visiting Program*, Special Report, Robert Wood Johnson Foundation, www.socialimpactexchange.org/sites/www.socialimpactexchange.org/files/RWJ%20DavidOldsSpecialReport0606.pdf

Gordon, D. (2011) 'Consultation response; Social Mobility & Child Poverty Review', Policy Response Series No.2, www.poverty.ac.uk/sites/default/files/attachments/WP%20Policy%20Response%20No.%202%20Consultation%20Resp%20Social%20Mobility%20%26%20Child%20Poverty%20%28Gordon%20Oct%202011%29.pdf

Gove, M. (2012) Speech given at the Isaac Newton Centre for Continuing Professional Development, 23 February, www.gov.uk/government/speeches/michael-gove-speech-on-adoption

Gregg, D. (2010) *Family intervention projects: A classic case of policy-based evidence*, London: Centre for Crime and Justice Studies.

Groeneveld, L.P., Hannan, M.P. and Tuma, N.P. (1983) 'Marital stability', in *Final Report of the Seattle–Denver Income Maintenance Experiment, vol. 1: Design and results*, Washington, DC: U.S. Government Printing Office.

Guardian, The (2012) 'Apparent consensus on social mobility masks fundamental split', 29 May, www.theguardian.com/society/2012/may/29/consensus-social-mobility-fundamental-split

Guardian, The (2015) 'David Cameron urges faster adoptions doubling number of early placements', 2 November, www.theguardian.com/society/2015/nov/02/david-cameron-urges-faster-adoptions-doubling-number-of-early-placements?CMP=share_btn_tw

Gunnar, M.R., Kryzer, E., Van Ryzin, J.M. and Phillips, D.A. (2010) 'The rise in cortisol in family daycare: Associations with aspects of care quality, child behaviour and child sex, *Child Development*, 81(3): 851–69.

Hagen-Zanker, J., Bastagli, F., Harman, L. Barca, V., Stugre, G. and Schmidt, T. (2016) *Understanding the impact of cash transfers: The evidence*, Overseas Development Institute, www.odi.org/sites/odi.org.uk/files/resource-documents/10748.pdf

Hallsworth, S. (2011) 'Gangland Britain? Realities, fantasies and industry', in B. Gouldson (ed.) *Youth in crisis? 'Gangs', territoriality and violence*, Abingdon: Routledge, pp. 183–98.

Hammersley, M. (2007) *Educational research and evidence-based practice*, London: Sage.

Hansen, K. and Hawkes, D. (2009) 'Early childcare and child development', *Journal of Social Policy*, 38(2): 211–39.

Hartas, D. (2011) 'Families' social backgrounds matter: Socio-economic factors, home learning and young children's language, literacy and social outcomes', *British Educational Research Journal*, 37(6): 893–914.

Hartas, D. (2012) 'Inequality and the home learning environment: Predictions about seven-year-olds' language and literacy', *British Educational Research Journal*, 38(5): 859–79.

Hays, S. (1998) *The cultural contradictions of motherhood*, New York: Yale University Press.

Hemerijck, A. (2015) 'The quiet paradigm revolution of social investment', *Social Politics: International Studies in Gender, State and Society*, 22(2): 242–56.

Hill, H.D. (2012) 'Welfare as maternity leave? Exemptions from welfare work requirements and maternal employment', *Social Services Review*, 86(1): 37–67.

Hillyard, P. and Tombs, S. (2007) 'From "crime" to social harm?', *Crime, Law and Social Change*, 48(1): 9–25.

HM Government (2016) *Social investment: A force for social change. 2016 strategy*, www.gov.uk/government/uploads/system/uploads/attachment_data/file/507215/6.1804_SIFT_Strategy_260216_FINAL_web.pdf

Horsley, N. (2014) 'Are we the 60 percent? Claims about attachment as an evidence base for family policy', Weeks Centre for Social and Policy Research Blog, 10 April, http://weekscentreforsocialandpolicyresearch.wordpress.com/2014/04/10/are-we-the-60-percent-claims-about-attachment-as-an-evidence-base-for-family-policy/

Horsley, N., Gillies, V. and Edwards, R. (2016) 'Researchers' reflections on interviewing policy makers and practitioners: feeling conflicted in critical research', Women's Studies International Forum, www.sciencedirect.com/science/article/pii/S0277539515301990

House of Commons Public Administration and Constitutional Affairs Committee (2016) *The collapse of Kids Company: Lessons for charity trustees, professional firms, the Charity Commission, and Whitehall*, London: The Stationery Office, www.publications.parliament.uk/pa/cm201516/cmselect/cmpubadm/433/433.pdf

Howard-Jones, P.A., Washbrooke, E.V. and Meadows, S. (2012) 'The timing of educational investment: A neuroscientific perspective', *Developmental Cognitive Neuroscience*, Suppl. 1: S18–29.

Hubel, D.H. and Wiesel, T.N. (2004) *Brain and visual perception: The story of a 25-year collaboration*, Oxford: Oxford University Press.

Huckfield, L. (2014a) *The rise and influence of social enterprise, social investment and public service mutuals*, National Coalition for Independent Action, www.independentaction.net/wp-content/uploads/2011/03/Social-enterprise-final.pdf

Huckfield, L. (2014b) 'Social enterprise – a mouthpiece for Britain's New Colonialism', www.huckfield.com/blog/social-enterprise-a-mouthpiece-for-britains-new-colonialiasm/

Huttenlocher, P.R. (1979) 'Synaptic density in human frontal cortex: Developmental changes of aging', *Brain Research*, 163: 195–205.

Irwin, L.G., Siddiqi, A. and Hertzman, C. (2007) *Early child development: Powerful equalizer*, Final report for the World Health Organization's Commission on the Social Determinants of Health.

ISG (2014) 'UK public sector outsourcing market outstrips commercial sector', www.isg-one.com/web/media-center/press/140707-UK.asp

Jenson, J. (2004) 'Changing the paradigm: Family responsibility or investing in children', *Canadian Journal of Sociology*, 29(2): 169–92.

Jenson, J. (2010) 'The social investment perspective in Europe and Latin America', *Global Social Policy*, 10 (1): 59–84.

Jessop, B. (1997) 'Capitalism and its future: remarks on regulation, government and governance', *Review of International Political Economy*, 4: 561–81.

Jessop B. (1998) 'The rise of governance and the risks of failure', *International Social Science Journal*, 155(1): 29–45.

Johnson, M. and Mansell W. (2014) *Education not for sale*, TUC Research Report, www.tuc.org.uk/sites/default/files/Education_Not_For_Sale_Repor_Report.pdf

Jones, R (2015a) 'The stealth privatisation of children's services', *Community Care*, http://www.communitycare.co.uk/2015/01/07/stealth-privatisation-childrens-services/

Jones, R. (2015b) 'Hedge funds have no place in children's services', *The Guardian*, 17 September, www.theguardian.com/social-care-network/2015/sep/17/hedge-funds-no-place-childrens-services-market

Jones, R., Pykett, J. and Whitehead, M. (2013) *Changing behaviours: On the rise of the psychological state*, Cheltenham: Edward Elgar.

Juengstemail, E., Fishman, J. R., McGowan, M. L, and Settersten Jr R. A. (2014) 'Serving epigenetics before its time', *Trends in Genetics*, 30 (10): 427–429.

Kagan, J. (1998) *Three seductive ideas*, Cambridge, MA: Harvard University Press.

Kagan, J. (2011) 'Bringing up baby: Are we too attached?', *Psychotherapy Networker*, 35(2), www.questia.com/library/p61464/psychotherapy-networker/i2475050/vol-35-no-2-march-april

Keller, H. (2014) 'Introduction: Understanding relationships – what we would need to know to conceptualise attachment as the cultural solution to a universal human need', in H. Ottoman and H. Keller (eds) *Different faces of attachment: Cultural variation on a universal human need*, Cambridge: Cambridge University Press.

Kenney, M. and Müller, R. (2016) 'Of rats and women: Narratives of motherhood in environmental epigenetics', *BioSocieties*. DOI 10.1057/s41292-016-0002-7

Kent, K.S. (2002) *Gender and power in Britain 1640–1990*, London: Routledge.

Kinsley, C. and Franssen, A. (2010) 'The pregnant brain as a revving race car', *Scientific American*, www.scientificamerican.com/article/pregnant-brain-as-racecar/

Kramer, M.S., Matush, L., Vanilovich, I., Platt, R.W., Bogdanovich, N., Sevkovskaya, Z., Dzikovic, I, Shishko, G., Collet, J-P., Martin, R.M., Smith, G.D., Gillman, M.W., Chalmers, B., Hodnett, E. and Shapiro, S. (2009) 'A randomized breast-feeding promotion intervention did not reduce child obesity in Belarus', *Journal of Nutrition*, 139(2): 4175–215.

Kuchta, T. (2010) *Semi-detached empire. Suburbia and the colonization of Britain 1880 to today*, Charlottesville: Virginia University Press.

Lake, A. and Chan, M. (2014) 'Putting science into practice for early child development', *The Lancet*, 385(9980): 1816–17.

Lambert, M. (2016) 'In pursuit of "the welfare trait": Recycling deprivation and reproducing depravation in historical context', *People, Place and Policy*, 10(3): 225–38.

Lappé, M. (2016) 'The maternal body as environment in autism science', *Social Studies of Science*, 46(5): 675–700.

Leadsom, A. (2008) 'Support for early attachment is the single greatest thing we can do to men our broken society', Conservative Home, 15 September, www.conservativehome.com/platform/2008/09/andrea-leadsom.html

Leadsom, A. (2012) 'Better early years intervention can help create a generation of emotionally secure children', Conservative Home, www.conservativehome.com/platform/2012/10/from-andrealeadsom-mp-better-early-years-intervention-can-create-a-generation-of-emotionally-secure.html

Leadsom, A., Field, F., Burstow, P. and Lucas, C. (2013) *The 1001 critical days: The importance of the conception to age two period*. An All-Party Manifesto, www.1001criticaldays.co.uk/

Lee, E., Bristow, J., Faircloth, C. and Macvarish, J. (2014) *Parenting culture studies*, Basingstoke: Palgrave Macmillan.

Levine, R.A., Watts, H., Hollister, R., Williams, W., O'Connor, A. and Widerquist, K. (2005) 'A retrospective on the negative income tax experiments: Looking back at the most innovate field studies in social policy', in K. Widerquist, M.A. Lewis and S. Pressman (eds) *The ethics and economics of the basic income guarantee*, Aldershot: Ashgate, pp. 95–106.

LeVine, R.A. (2014) 'Attachment theory as cultural ideology', in H. Ottoman and H. Keller (eds) *Different faces of attachment: Cultural variation on a universal human need*, Cambridge: Cambridge University Press.

Lewis, J. (1995) *The voluntary sector, the state and social work in Britain*, Aldershot: Edward Elgar.

Lewis, J. (2011) 'Parenting programmes in England: Policy development and implementation issues, 2005–2010', *Journal of Social Welfare and Family Law*, 33(2): 107–21.

Lister, R. (2003) *Citizenship: Feminist perspectives*, Basingstoke: Palgrave Macmillan.

Lister, R. (2006) 'Children (but not women) first: New Labour, child welfare and gender', *Critical Social Policy*, 26(2): 315–335.

Liverpool Maritime Archive and Library (2014) *Information sheet 10: Child emigration*, www.liverpoolmuseums.org.uk/maritime/archive/sheet/10

Loopstra, R., Fledderjohann, J., Reeves, A. and Stuckler, D. (2016) 'The impact of benefit sanctioning on food insecurity: A dynamic cross-area study of food bank usage in the UK, online publication', www.sociology.ox.ac.uk/working-papers/the-impact-of-benefit-sanctioning-on-food-insecurity-a-dynamic-cross-area-study-of-food-bank-usage-in-the-uk.html

Lowe, P., Lee, E. and Macvarish, J. (2015) 'Growing better brains? Pregnancy and neuroscience discourses in English social and welfare policies', *Health, Risk and Society*, 17(1): 15–29.

Lupton, D. (2012) '"Precious cargo": Foetal subjects, risk and reproductive citizenship', *Critical Public Health*, 22(3): 329–40.

Lyons, D.M. and Parker, K.J. (2007) 'Stress inoculation-induced indications of resilience in monkeys', *Journal of Traumatic Stress*, 20: 423–33.

MacDonald, R., Shildrick, T. and Furlong, A. (2013) 'In search of "intergenerational cultures of worklessness": Hunting the Yeti and shooting zombies', *Critical Social Policy*, 34(2): 199–220.

Macmillan, L. (2011) *Measuring the intergenerational correlation of worklessness*, Working Paper 11/278, Centre for Market and Public Organisation, University of Bristol.

Macnicol, J. (1987) 'In pursuit of the underclass', *Journal of Social Policy*, 16(3): 293–318.

Macvarish, J. (2014) 'Babies' brains and parenting policy: The insensitive mother', in E. Lee, J. Bristow, C. Faircloth and J. Macvarish (eds) *Parenting culture studies*, Basingstoke: Palgrave Macmillan.

Macvarish, J. (2016) *Neuroparenting: The expert invasion of family life*, London: Palgrave Macmillan.

Macvarish, J., Lee, E.J. and Lowe, P.K. (2014) 'The "first three years" movement and the infant brain: A review of critiques', *Sociology Compass*, 8(6): 792–804.

Macvarish, J., Lee, E. and Lowe, P. (2015) 'Neuroscience and family policy: What becomes of the parent?', *Critical Social Policy*, 35(2): 248–69.

McBurnett, K., Lahey, B.B., Rathouz, P.J. and Loeber, R. (2000) 'Low salivary cortisol and persistent aggression in boys referred for disruptive behavior', *Archives of General Psychiatry*, 57: 38–43

McCabe, D.P. and Castel, A.D. (2007) 'Seeing is believing: The effect of brain images on judgements of scientific reasoning', *Cognition*, 107(1): 343–52.

McDonald, C. (2003) 'Forward via the past? Evidence-based practice as strategy in social work', *The Drawing Board: An Australian Review of Public Affairs*, 3(3): 123–42.

McGoey, L. (2014) 'The philanthropic state: Market–state hybrids in the philanthrocapitalist turn', *Third World Quarterly*, 35(1): 109–25.

McGoey, L. (2015) *No such thing as a free gift: The Gates Foundation and the price of philanthropy*, London: Verso.

Manchester Institute of Education (2015) Promoting Alternative Thinking Strategies (PATHS): Evaluation report and executive summary, https://v1.educationendowmentfoundation.org.uk/uploads/pdf/PATHS.pdf

Mansfield, B. (2012) 'Race and the new epigenetic biopolitics of environmental health', *BioSocieties*, 7(4): 352–72.

Mansfield, B. and Guthman, J. (forthcoming) 'Epigenetic life: Biological plasticity, abnormality and new configurations of race and reproduction', *Cultural Geographies*.

Marcus, G. (2012) 'Neuroscience fiction', *The New Yorker*, 30 November, www.newyorker.com/news/news-desk/neuroscience-fiction?currentPage=all

Mead, M. (1962) 'A cultural anthropologists approach to maternal deprivation', *Public Health Papers*, 14: 45–62.

Meaney, M. (2014) 'Epigenetics offer hope for disadvantaged children', Child and Family Blog, http://childandfamilyblog.com/epigenetics-offer-hope-disadvantaged-children/

Meins, E. (2014) 'Focus on attachment in parenting policy is misplaced', *The Conversation*, 16 April, http://theconversation.com/focus-on-attachment-in-parenting-policy-is-misplaced-25461

Meloni, M. (2016) *Political biology: Science and social values from eugenics to epigenetics*, London: Palgrave.

Miller, G. (2010) 'The seductive allure of behavioural epigenetics', *Science*, 329, 2 July.

Milligan, K. and Stabile, M. (2009) 'Do child tax benefits affect the well-being of children? Evidence from Canadian child benefit expansion', *American Economic Journal Economic Policy*, 3(3): 175–205.

Ministerial Group on the Family (1998) *Supporting families: A consultative document*, London: The Stationery Office.

Mitchell, K. (2014) 'The trouble with epigenetics, Part 3 – Over-fitting the noise', Wiring the Brain, www.wiringthebrain.com/2014/04/the-trouble-with-epigenetics-part-3.html

Moore, K. (2001) *Frameworks for understanding the intergenerational transmission of poverty and well-being in developing countries*, CPRC Working Paper 8, Manchester: Chronic Poverty Research Centre.

Moss, P. (2014) *Transformative change and real utopias in early childhood education: A story of democracy, experimentation and potentiality*, London: Routledge.

Moss, P. (2015) 'There are alternatives! Contestation and hope in early childhood education', *Global Studies of Childhood*, 5(3): 226–38.

Munro, E. (2011) *Munro Review of Child Protection: Final report – a child-centred system*, London: Department for Education.

Murdoch, L. (2006) *Imagined orphans: Poor families, child welfare, and contested citizenship in London*, New Brunswick, NJ: Rutgers.

Murray, C. (1994) *Underclass: The crisis deepens*, London: Institute of Economic Affairs.

Murray, C. (2016) 'A guaranteed income for every American', *Wall Street Journal*, www.wsj.com/articles/a-guaranteed-income-for-every-american-1464969586

Nadeson, M.H. (2002) 'Engineering the entrepreneurial infant: Brain science, infant development toys, and governmentality', *Cultural Studies*, 16(3): 401–32.

Narey, M. (2011) 'The Narey Report: A blueprint for the nation's lost children', *The Times*, 1 November, www.thetimes.co.uk/article/the-narey-report-a-blueprint-for-the-nations-lost-children-7b2ktmcrf0w

National Audit Office (2015) 'Investigation: The government's funding of Kids Company', www.nao.org.uk/report/investigation-the-governments-funding-of-kids-company/

Noble, K. G., Houston, S.M., Brito, M.H, Bartshc, H., Kan, E., Kuperman, J.M., Askscoomoff, N., Amaral, D. G., Bloss, C.S., Libiger, O., Schork, N.J., Murray, S.S., Casey, BJ., Chang, L., Ernst, T.M., Frazier, J.A., Gruen, J.R., Kennedy, D.N., Van Zijl, P., Mostofsky, S., Kaufmann, W.E., Kenet, T., Dale, A.M., Jernigan, T.L., Sowell, E.R. (2015) 'Family income, parental education and brain structure in children and adolescents', *Nature Neuroscience*, 18 (5): 773–778.

Noddings, N. (2002) *Starting at home: Caring and social policy*, Berkeley: University of California Press.

O'Mara, S., Rose, S. and Foster, R.G. (2016) 'When will neuroscience blow our minds?', *Times Higher Education*, 4 August, www.timeshighereducation.com/features/when-will-neuroscience-blow-our-minds

Oakley, L.L., Renfrew, M.J., Kurinczuk, J.J. and Quigley, M.A. (2013) 'Factors associated with breastfeeding in England: An analysis by primary care trust', *British Medical Journal Open*. DOI: 10.1136/bmjopen-2013-002765

Olds, D., Henderson, C.R. Jr, Cole, R., Eckenrode, J., Kitzman, H., Luckey, D., Pettitt, L., Sidora, K., Morris, P. and Powers J. (1998) 'Long-term effects of nurse home visitation on children's criminal and antisocial behaviour: 15-year follow-up of a randomized control trial', *JAMA Network*, 280(14): 1238–44.

Olds, D.L., Arcoleo, K.J. and Henderson, C.R. (2010) 'Enduring effects of prenatal and infancy home visiting by nurses on maternal life course and government spending', *Archives of Paediatric Medicine*, 164(5): 419–24.

Open Science Collaboration (2015) 'Estimating the reproducibility of psychological science', *Science*, 349(6251), http://science.sciencemag.org/content/349/6251/aac4716

Ottoman, H. and Keller, H. (eds) (2014) *Different faces of attachment: Cultural variation on a universal human need*, Cambridge: Cambridge University Press.

Parton, N. (2005) *Safeguarding childhood: Early intervention and surveillance in late modern society*, Basingstoke: Palgrave.

Paterson, C. (2011) *Parenting matters: Early years and social mobility*, London: CentreForum.

Payne, G. (2012) 'A new social mobility? The political redefinition of a sociological problem', *Contemporary Social Science*, 7(1): 55–71.

Pearce, W., Ramen S. and Turner, A. (2015) 'Randomised trials in context: Practical problems and social aspects of evidence-based medicine and policy', *Trials*, DOI: 10.1186/s13063-015-0917-516:394

Pearson, R.M. and Lightman, S.L. (2009) 'Emotional sensitivity for motherhood: Late pregnancy is associated with enhanced accuracy to encode emotional faces', *Hormonal Behaviour*, 56(5): 557–63.

Peck, J. and Tickell, A. (2002) 'Neoliberalizing space', *Antipode*, 34(3): 380–404.

Pemberton, S. (2016) *Harmful societies: Understanding social harm*, Bristol: Policy Press.

Perkins, A. (2016) *The welfare trait: How state benefits affect personality*, London: Palgrave Macmillan.

Perry, B., Pollard, R., Blakely, T., Baker, W. and Vigilante, D. (1995) 'Childhood trauma, the neurobiology of adaptation, and "use-dependent" development of the brain', *Infant Mental Health Journal*, 16 (4): 271–291.

Perry, B.D. (2002) 'Childhood experience and the expression of generic potential: What childhood neglect tells us about nature and nurture', *Brain and Mind*, 3: 79–100.

Pickersgill, M. (2016) 'Epistemoic modesty, ostentatiousness and the uncertainties of epigenetics: On the knowledge machinery of (social) science', *Sociological Review*, 64(1): 186–202.

Pickersgill, M., Niewohnerl, J., Muller, R., Martin, P and Cunningham-Burley, S. (2013) 'Mapping the new molecular landscape: social dimensions of epigenetics', *New Genetics and Society*, 32 (4): 429–447.

Pimmer, G. (2015) 'Public service outsourcing jumps under coalition', *Financial Times*, www.ft.com/cms/s/0/244f0bd8-eccb-11e4-a81a-00144feab7de.html#axzz495pF1iTj

Pipkin, J. (2013) 'There is no "primitive" part of the brain', *Empirical Planet*, http://empiricalplanet.blogspot.co.uk/2013/07/there-is-no-primitive-part-of-brain.html

Poldrack, R., Baker, C.I., Durnez, J., Gorgolewski, K., Matthews, P.M., Munafo, M., Nicohols, T., Poline, J-B., Vul, E. and Yarkoni, T. (2016) 'Scanning the horizon: Future challenges for neuroimaging research', *bioRxiv* preprint first posted online 16 June, http://biorxiv.org/content/early/2016/06/16/059188

Puttick, R. (2012) 'Why we need to create a NICE for social policy', Nesta, www.nesta.org.uk/sites/default/files/why_we_need_to_create_a_nice_for_social_policy.pdf

Ramaekers, S. and Suissa, J. (2012) *The claims of parenting: Reasons, responsibility and society*, Dordrecht: Springer.

Ramus, F. (2013) 'What's the point of neuropsychoanalysis?', *British Journal of Psychiatry*, 203: 170–71.

Reardon, S. (2015) 'Poverty shrinks brains from birth', *Nature News*, 30 March. DOI: 10.1038/hature.2015.17227

Reay, D. (2013) 'Social mobility, a panacea for austere times: Tales of emperors, frogs, and tadpoles', *British Journal of Sociology of Education*, 34(5–6): 6609–77.

Rhodes, R. A. W. (2007) 'Understanding governance: ten years on', *Organization Studies*, 28 (8): 1243–1264.

Ribbens McCarthy, J., Hooper, C.-A. and Gillies, V. (eds) (2013) *Family troubles? Exploring changes and challenges in the family lives of children and young people*, Bristol: Policy Press.

Robinson, D. and Miller, L. (2013) 'The family nurse workforce study: assessment of the FNP programme', *Journal of Health Visiting*, 1(5): 290–6.

Rohling, M., Bekkers, M-J., Bell, K., Butler, C., Cannings-John, R., Chanon, S., Martin, B.C., Gregory, J.W., Hood, K., Kemp, A., Kenkre, J., Montgomery, A.A., Moody, G., Owen-Jones, E., Pickett, K., Richardson, G., Roberts, Z.E.S., Ronaldson, S., Sanders, J., Stamuli, E. and Togerson, D. (2016) 'Effectiveness of a nurse-led intensive home-visitation programme for first-time teenage mothers (Building Blocks): A pragmatic randomised controlled trial', *The Lancet*, www.thelancet.com/pdfs/journals/lancet/PIIS0140-6736(15)00392-X.pdf

Rooff, M. (1972) *A hundred years of family welfare*, London: Michael Joseph.

Rose, H. and Rose, S. (2016) *Can neuroscience change our minds?* Cambridge: Polity Press.

Rose, N. (1987) 'Beyond the public/private division: Law, power and the family', *Journal of Law and Society*, 14(1): 61–76.

Rose, N. (1999) *Governing the soul: The shaping of the private self*, London: Routledge.

Rose, N. and Abi-Rached, J.M. (2013) *Neuro: The new brain sciences and the management of the mind*, Princeton, NJ: Princeton University Press.

Rosenberg, E. (2002) 'Missions to the world: Philanthropy abroad', in L.J. Friedman and M.D. McGarvie (eds) *Charity, philanthropy, and civility in American history*, Cambridge: Cambridge University Press.

Rossi, P.H. (1987) 'The iron law of evaluation and other metallic rules', *Research in Social Problems and Public Policy*, 4: 3–20.

Rutter, M. (1972) *Maternal deprivation reassessed*, Harmondsworth: Penguin.

Rutter, M. (1999) 'Autism: Two-way interplay between research and clinical work', *Psychology and Psychiatry*, 40(2): 169–88.

Rutter, M. (2002) 'Nature, nurture, and development: From evangelism through science toward policy and practice', *Child Development*, 73(1): 1–21.

Rutter, M. (2013) 'The role of science in understanding family troubles', in J. Ribbens McCarthy, C.-A. Hooper and V. Gillies (eds) *Family troubles? Exploring changes and challenges in the family lives of children and young people*, Bristol: Policy Press.

Rutter, M. and Madge, N. (1976) *Cycles of disadvantage: A review of research*, London: Heinemann Educational.

Rutter, M., Sonuga-Barke, E.J., Beckett, C., Castle, J., Kreppner, J., Kumsta, R., Schlotz, W., Stevens, S.E. and Bell, C.A. (2010) *Deprivation-specific psychological patterns: Effects of institutional deprivation*, Monographs of the Society for Research in Child Development, Ann Arbor MI: Society for Research in Child Development, p. 75.

Salkind, N. and Haskins, R. (1982) 'Negative income tax: The impact on children from low-income families', *Journal of Family Issues*, 3(2): 165–80.

Sandman, C.A. and Glynn, L.M. (2009) 'Corticotropin-releasing hormone (CRH) programs the foetal and maternal brain', *Future Neurology*, 4(3): 257–61.

Save the Children (2012) *Cash and child protection: How cash transfer programming can protect children from abuse, neglect, exploitation and violence*, www.savethechildren.org.uk/resources/online-library/cash-and-child-protection

Schaffer, H.R. and Emerson, P.E. (1964) *The development of social attachments in infancy*, Monographs of the Society for Research in Child, Ann Arbor MI: Society for Research in Child Development.

Schmitz, S. and Höppner, G. (2014) 'Neurofeminism and feminist neurosciences: A critical review of contemporary brain research', *Frontiers in Human Neuroscience*, 8, Article 546, journal.frontiersin.org/Journal/10.3389/fnhum.2014.00546/pdf

Schore, A. (2000) 'Attachment and the regulation of the right brain', *Attachment and Human Development*, 2(1): 23–47.

Scott, A., Irwin, R.G. and Greenough, W.T. (2000) 'Dendritic spine structural anomalies in fragile-X mental retardation syndrome', *Cerebral Cortex*, 10(10): 1038–44.

Sevenhuijsen, S. (1998) *Citizenship and the ethics of care: Feminist considerations on justice, morality, and politics*, London: Routledge.

Sevenhuijsen, S. (2002) 'A third way? Moralities, ethics and families: An approach through the ethic of care', in A. Carling, S. Duncan and R. Edwards (eds) *Analysing families: Morality and rationality in policy and practice*, London: Routledge.

Shapira, M. (2015) *The war inside psychoanalysis: Total war, and the making of the democratic self in postwar Britain*, Cambridge: Cambridge University Press.

Shaw, D.S., Owens, E.B., Giovennelli, J. and Winslow, E.B. (2001) 'Infant and toddler pathways leading to early externalizing disorders', *Journal of the American Academy of Child & Adolescent Psychiatry*, 40: 36–43.

Shildrick, T., MacDonald, R., Furlong, A., Roden, J. and Crow, R. (2012) *Are 'cultures of worklessness' passed down the generations?*, Joseph Rowntree Foundation Report, York: JRF.

Shonkoff, J.P. and Bales, S.N. (2011) 'Science does not speak for itself: Translating child development research for the public and its policymakers', *Child Development*, 82(1): 17–32.

Singh, I. (2012) 'Human development, nature and nurture: Working beyond the divide', *BioSocieties*, 7(3): 308–21.

Skeggs, B. (2011) 'Imagining personhood differently: Person value and autonomist working-class value practices', *Sociological Review*, 59(3): 496–513.

Skelcher, C. (2007) 'Democracy in collaborative spaces: Why context matters in researching governance networks', in M. Marcussen and J. Torfing (eds) *Democratic network governance in Europe*, Basingstoke: Palgrave Macmillan, pp. 25–46.

Smuts, A. (2008) *Science in the service of children, 1893–1935*, New Haven, CT: Yale University Press.

Solihull Approach (undated) *Antenatal parenting group facilitators' manual: Understanding pregnancy, labour, birth and your baby*, Solihull: Solihull Approach.

Solihull Approach (2004) *First five years resource pack*, Solihull: Solihull Approach.

Solihull Approach Resource Pack: The school years for care professionals who work with school-aged children, young people and parents (2008), Solihull NHS Care Trust, Cambridge: Jill Rogers Associates Ltd.

Soss, J., Fording, R. and Schram S. (2011) *Disciplining the poor: Neoliberal paternalism and the persistent power of race*, Chicago: University of Chicago Press.

Stedman Jones, G. (2013) *Outcast London: A study in the relationship between classes in Victorian society*, London: Verso.

Stewart, J. (2013) *Child guidance in Britain, 1918–1955: The dangerous age of childhood*, Abingdon: Routledge.

Sullivan, A., Ketende, S. and Joshi, H. (2013) 'Social class and inequalities in early cognitive scores', *Sociology*, 47(6): 1187–206.

Sutton Trust (2014) *Baby bonds: Parenting, attachment and a secure base for children*, www.suttontrust.com/our-work/research/item/baby-bonds/

Swain, S. (2011) 'Failing families: Echoes of nineteenth-century discourse in contemporary debates around child protection', in M.L. Lohlke and C. Gutleben (eds) *Neo-Victorian families: Gender, sexual and cultural politics*, Amsterdam: Rodopi.

Sykes Wylie, M. and Turner, L. (2011) 'The attuned therapist: Does attachment theory really matter?', *Psychotherapy Networker*, 35(2), www.questia.com/library/p61464/psychotherapy-networker/i2475050/vol-35-no-2-march-april

Taylor, M. (2009) 'Left brain, right brain', *Prospect Magazine*, October, www.prospectmagazine.co.uk/issues/163

Thatcher, M. (1988) Speech to the Conservative Women's Conference, 25 May, www.margaretthatcher.org/document/107248

Thompson, R. (2008) 'Early attachment and later development: Familiar questions, new answers', in J. Cassidy and P.R. Shaver (eds) *Handbook of attachment: Theory, research, and clinical applications*, 2nd edn, New York: Guilford Press, pp. 348–65.

Thomson, M. (2013) *Lost freedom: The landscape of the child and the British post-war settlement*, Oxford: Oxford University Press.

Thornton, D.J. (2011a) 'Neuroscience, affect and the entrepreneurialisation of motherhood', *Communication and Critical/Cultural Studies*, 8(4): 399–424.

Thornton, D.J. (2011b) *Brain cultures: Neuroscience and popular media*, New Brunswick NJ: Rutgers University Press.

Tickell, Dame C. (2011) *The Early Years Foundation Stage: Review report on the evidence*, London: Department for Education.

Tomlinson, M., Cooper, P. and Murray, L. (2005) 'The mother–infant relationship and infant attachment in a South African peri-urban settlement', *Child Development*, 76(5): 1044–54.

Toynbee, P. (2014) 'Now troubled children are an investment opportunity', *The Guardian*, 13 May, www.theguardian.com/commentisfree/2014/may/13/troubled-children-investment-extreme-britain-outsourcing-care#comment-35585738

Tronto, J.C. (1993) *Moral boundaries: A political argument for an ethic of care*, New York: Routledge.

True, M.M., Pisani, L. and Oumar, F. (2001) 'Infant–mother attachment among the Dogon of Mali', *Child Development*, 72(5):1451–66.

TUC and NEF (2015) *Outsourcing public services*, www.tuc.org.uk/sites/default/files/TUC%20and%20NEF%20Outsourcing%20Public%20Services.pdf

UNICEF (2001) *The state of the world's children 2001*, New York: UNICEF.

Van Bavel, J. (2016) 'Contextual sensitivity in scientific reproducibility', *Proceedings of the National Academy of Sciences*, 113(2), www.pnas.org/content/113/23/6454

Van IJzendoorn, M.H. and Kroonenberg, P.M. (1988) 'Cross-cultural patterns of attachment: A meta-analysis of the strange situation', *Child Development*, 59(1): 147–56.

Wade, P. (2010) 'The presence and absence of race', *Patterns of Prejudice*, 44(1): 43–60.

Walkerdine, V. (2015) 'Transmitting class across generations', *Theory & Psychology*, 25(2): 167–83.

Wall, G. (2010) 'Mothers' experiences with intensive parenting and brain development discourse', *Women's Studies International Forum*, 33(3): 253–63.

Washbrook, E., Waldfogel, J. and Moulllin, S. (2014) *Baby bonds: Parenting, attachment and a secure base for children*, The Sutton Trust, www.suttontrust.com/researcharchive/baby-bonds/

Wastell, D. and White, S. (2012) 'Blinded by neuroscience: Social policy, the family and the infant brain', *Families, Relationships and Societies*, 1(3): 397–415.

Waters, E. and Valenzuela, M. (1999) 'Explaining disorganized attachment: Clues from research on mildly to moderately undernourished children in Chile', in J. Solomon and C. George (eds) *Attachment disorganization*, New York: Guildford Press.

Wave Trust (2005) *Violence and what to do about it*, Wave Trust Report, www.wavetrust.org/sites/default/files/reports/migrate-wave-report-2005-full-report.pdf

Wave Trust (2013) *Conception to age two: The age of opportunity*, Surrey: Wave Trust.

Webster, A., Webster, V. and Feiler, A. (2002) 'Research evidence, polemic and evangelism: How decisions are made on early intervention in autistic spectrum disorder', *Educational and Child Psychology*, 19(3): 54–67.

Weisberg, D.S., Keil, F.C., Goodstein, J., Rawson, E. and Gray, J.R. (2008) 'The seductive allure of neuroscience explanation', *Journal of Cognitive Neuroscience*, 20(3): 470–7.

Westminster Social Policy Forum (2013) *Early intervention: Joining up services, targeting support and the role of the Foundation*, London: Westminster Forum.

White, A. (2015) 'Questions raised over Kids Company spending and research', Buzzfeed News, 6 July, www.buzzfeed.com/alanwhite/questions-raised-over-kids-company-spending-and-research#.qu3P90Kvv

White, S. and Wastell, D. (2015) 'The rise and rise of prevention science in UK family welfare: Surveillance gets under the skin', *Families, Relationships and Societies*, http://dx.doi.org/10.1332/2046 74315X14479283041843

White, S. and Wastell, D. (2016) 'Epigenetics prematurely born(e): Social work and the malleable gene', *British Journal of Social Work*, http://bjsw.oxfordjournals.org/content/early/2016/11/02/bjsw.bcw157

Whitfield, D. (2014) UK social services: the mutation of privatisation, European Services Strategy Unit, http://www.european-services-strategy.org.uk/publications/books-and-articles-by-dexter-whitfield/uk-social-services-the-mutation-of-privatisati/

Wiggins, M., Oakley, A., Sawtell, M. and Austerberry, H. (2005) *Teenage parenthood and social exclusion: A multi-method study – summary report of findings*, SSRU, Institute of Education, University of London.

Wilkinson, R. and Pickett, K. (2011) *The spirit level: Why greater equality makes societies stronger*, London: Bloomsbury Press.

Williams, F. (2008) 'Empowering parents', in A. Anning and M. Ball (eds) *Learning from Sure Start: Improving services for children and families*, London: Sage.

Williams, M. (2014) 'Child neglect: A change in the law', *Society Central*, 31 March, https://societycentral.ac.uk/2014/03/31/child-neglect-a-change-in-the-law/

Wilson, H. (2002) 'Brain science, early intervention and "at risk" families: Implications for parents, professionals and social policy', *Social Policy and Society*, 1(3): 191–202.

Wise, T. (2010) *Colorblind: The rise of post-racial politics and the retreat from racial equity*, San Francisco: City Lights.

Wolf, J.B. (2013) *Is breast best? Taking on the breastfeeding experts and the new high stakes of motherhood*, New York: New York University Press.

Wolff, N. (2000) 'Using randomized controlled trials to evaluate socially complex services: Problems, challenges and recommendations', *Journal of Mental Health Policy and Economics*, 3: 97–109

Wootton, B. (assisted by V.G. Seal and R. Chambers) (1959) *Social science and social pathology*, London: George Allen and Unwin.

Zevalkink, J., Riksen-Walraven, J.M. and Van Lieshout, CFM. (1999) 'Attachment in the Indonesian caregiving context', *Social Development*, 8(1): 21–40.

Zilberstein, K. (2014) 'The use and limitations of attachment theory in child psychotherapy', *Psychotherapy*, 51(1): 93–103.

Index

Note: Page numbers in *italics* indicate figures. Page numbers followed by an 'n' refer to footnotes.